What Your Colleagues Are Saying ...

"This is a powerful and readable guide to shifting our high school mathematics instruction toward maximizing our students' learning. But it's the clarity and familiarity of the challenges we all face when trying to implement these five practices—and the practicality and detail of the guidance provided in each chapter to address these challenges—that set this book apart and make it so useful for professional growth."

Steve Leinwand
Researcher/Change Agent
American Institutes for Research
Washington, DC

"This book takes *5 Practices for Orchestrating Productive Mathematics Discussions* to the next level as readers experience what these practices look like in real mathematics classrooms in high school. Readers will engage in analysis of videos and student work as they deepen their understanding of the five practices. The authors specifically address the challenges one might face in implementing the five practices in classrooms by providing recommendations and concrete examples to avoid these challenges."

Cathy Martin
Executive Director, Curriculum and Instruction
Denver Public Schools
Denver, CO

"Peg Smith has done it again. Building on her previous work with Mary Kay Stein (2018), Smith and coauthors Miriam Sherin and Michael Steele have taken the next step in supporting teachers to engage students in rich mathematics discussions. Filled with examples and insights, both in print and on video, this book allows teachers to 'see it in action,' make sense, and reflect on the challenges, and it provides support and guidance to implement the five practices in their own instruction. Perfect for teachers, teacher leaders, coaches, or others who support teachers in their instructional practices, this book literally connects theory to practice and provides honest and thoughtful reflections and guidance to work towards our ultimate goals—students' mathematics learning and agency."

Cynthia H. Callard
Professor and Executive Director
Center for Professional Development and Education Reform
Warner Graduate School of Education and Human Development
University of Rochester
Rochester, NY

"The authors insightfully anticipate teachers' challenges and have designed a creative tool to support teacher learning. Their book is filled with highly practical reflective questions all tied to the five practices, enabling teachers to think for themselves. The result is a book that empowers high school teachers to determine the best ways to advance their own professional development to improve students' mathematical lives."

Ruth M. Heaton
Chief Executive Officer
Teachers Development Group
West Linn, OR

"This book is packed with practical guidance, support, and actual footage of what it looks like to enact ambitious teaching through these practices. If there's a teacher or leader out there wondering how to ensure their classroom embraces ambitious teaching that is empowering and equitable, this is your guide. Read it. Practice it. Make it yours. There just isn't anything else out there pushing us to think and act as strategically in our math classrooms like this does."

Levi J. Patrick
Assistant Executive Director of Curriculum and Instruction
Oklahoma State Department of Education

"At Illustrative Mathematics we were looking for a framework that would enable us to embed in our curriculum ambitious but achievable goals for teacher practice. The five practices was the perfect fit: a memorable, learnable set of principles that could be used by novice and veteran teachers alike to get their students thinking and sharing their reasoning."

Bill McCallum
President, Illustrative Mathematics
University Distinguished Professor of Mathematics
University of Arizona

"One of the biggest struggles I faced when teaching high school mathematics was finding a way to teach students through problem solving. After multiple lesson flops, I was beginning to think that teaching through task was just not something that was possible for me and my students. When I first read *The 5 Practices For Orchestrating Productive Mathematics Discussions*, I now knew *what* specifically I had been overlooking and *why* I was struggling, but it took me years of practice to start to understand *how* to implement these practices effectively and consistently. Now, high school math teachers have the benefit of being able to unpack the *what, why,* AND the *how* with *The 5 Practices In Practice: Successfully Orchestrating Mathematics Discussions in Your High School Classroom* book and multimedia resources to begin transforming how you do business in your math class right now."

Kyle Pearse
K-12 Mathematics Consultant
Belle River, Ontario

"Insightful, go-to handbook for high school math class. This book addresses many questions and challenges I had while implementing the 5 practices into my high school classroom. The insightful examples give me a window into learning how to effectively apply the 5 practices so I can teach ambitiously so that my students deepen their understanding and enjoyment of mathematics."

Jon Orr
High School Math Teacher
John McGregor Secondary School
Chatham, Ontario

"The Five Practices in Practice: Successfully Orchestrating Mathematics Discussion in Your High School Classroom makes the five practices accessible for high school mathematics teachers. Teachers will see themselves and their classrooms throughout the book. High school mathematics departments and teams can use this book as a framework for engaging professional collaboration. I am particularly excited that this book situates the five practices as ambitious and equitable practices."

Robert Q. Berry, III
NCTM President 2018–2020
Samuel Braley Gray Professor of Mathematics Education
University of Virgina

"The five practices can help high school students express their thinking, make connections, and form deep mathematical connections. In the *Five Practices in Practice: High School*, the authors bring the practices to life, including video clips showing how teachers respond to student thinking in real time."

Carl Oliver
Assistant Principal
City-As-School High School
New York, NY

"The Five Practices in Practice is a valuable tool for teacher teams who are ready to dig into the challenging work of collaboratively planning lessons that engage all students in learning rigorous mathematics through high-quality tasks and rich discourse."

Jennifer Lawler
Coordinator of Mathematics
Kenosha Unified School District
Kenosha, WI

"This book is an amazing resource. The five (six) practices are illustrated through classroom-based examples in a way that they come alive. As a reader, I can see the practices, I can make sense of them, and I feel supported to implement them thanks to the different resources provided (e.g., examples of tasks and questions, reflection prompts, teachers' testimonials, video clips). The book is organized in such a way that there is something for everyone, from the single teacher who wants to work on implementing the practices, to a group of teachers in a book study-group, or the teacher educator working with prospective teachers. I can even see using it as part of a professional learning community with college faculty teaching introductory mathematics courses."

Marta Civil
Professor of Mathematics Education
Roy F. Graesser Endowed Chair
University of Arizona

"When coaches, teachers, and supervisors are asked, "What should mathematical discourse look like in my classroom?" they now have a ready answer. *The Five Practices in Practice for Your High School Classroom* not only gives an in depth explanation of what the five practices are and why they are important, but also gives classroom examples, vignettes, and access to videos so practitioners can see exactly what it is they should be doing in classes. This book is an essential resource for all educators – showing the practices in high school classrooms, as well as detailing what educators should know about their efficacy."

Fredrick Dillon
Mathematics Fellow, Institute for Learning, University of Pittsburgh
High School Mathematics Teacher (35 years)
Presidential Awardee for Excellence in Mathematics and Science Teaching

"This book builds a deeper understanding of the *5 Practices for Orchestrating Productive Discussions* in high school classrooms. In addition to an extensive analysis of each practice, the book takes you into the classroom to explore common challenges enacting each one and how to avoid/overcome them through video clips, cases, and teacher commentary. It provides a plethora of examples from actual lessons, accompanied by thought-provoking questions for reflection, analysis, and improved implementation. Whether you are new to or experienced with the 5 practices, this book will give you valuable insights into how to orchestrate productive discussions in you classrooms that advance the mathematics learning of each and every student. A must-read."

Diane Briars
Past President, NCTM (2014–2016)
Pittsburgh, PA

"When I was a preservice teacher, the 5 Practices set the foundation for how I wanted to teach. Years later, the 5 Practices are still the most meaningful tools I use to design and facilitate lessons. I am thrilled that a new book has come out, packed with more vignettes, reflection questions, and lessons learned. I cannot wait to see how this book will help hone my craft as an orchestrator of mathematical discussion."

Chris Nho
Mathematics Teacher
High Tech High
San Diego, CA

The Five Practices in Practice
at a Glance

Candid quotes from been-there teachers illuminate the topic of each chapter.

As I monitor the groups and see where they're at, I'm also thinking about the discussion and what ideas to share and what groups. The key for me is that with selecting and sequencing, I can make sure that the goals are highlighted in a way that helps really create a story for the students.

—CORI MORAN, HIGH SCHOOL MATHEMATICS TEACHER

Pause and Consider moments invite teachers to reflect on and make connections to their own practice.

 PAUSE AND CONSIDER

How could you solve the Cycle Shop task shown in Figure 3.13 using visual, physical, and symbolic representations?

Visual:

Physical:

:tangles, that the base and height of the staircase is *n* for : there are *n* "stair steps" along the diagonal.

dents may be challenged by this task if they do not xperience using geometric approaches to solve visual looking at the staircases, students may recognize that creases by 1 along the height and the width but may use that information to find a generalized solution. In tudents may attempt to use a table to identify a pattern, ey have successfully used this approach to identify linear eriving a quadratic equation from a table is, however, rward (Rhoads & Alvarez, 2017). Instead, what may be ats is the recursive relationship—that is, that the number cessive staircases increases by the stage number.

he task herself and asked two colleagues how they would found a couple of potential solutions online. Through . Moran identified several possible methods for solving that she thought her students might use (see Figure 3.4).

oran thought that students might identify a recursive

Teaching Takeaways provide on-your-feet support for teachers, so they can jump into implementing the strategies discussed.

Video showcase panels highlight the rich film footage available for each topic and include related questions for consideration.

 Analyzing the Work of Teaching 2.1
Launching a Task

Video Clip 2.1
In this activity, you will watch Video Clip 2.1 from Cori Moran's Transition to College Math class. As you watch the clip, consider the following questions:

- What did the teacher do to help her students *get ready* to work on the Staircase task?

- What did the teacher learn about her students that indicated they were ready to engage in the task?

- Do you think the time spent in launching the task was time well spent?

 Videos may also be accessed at
resources.corwin.com/5practices-highschool

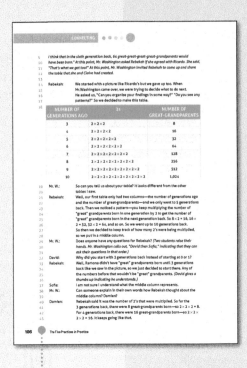

Illustrative vignettes and examples demonstrate real-world applications of the concepts discussed in each chapter.

An in-depth **Linking the Five Practices to Your Own Instruction** feature helps teachers move even deeper into implementation, providing detailed support and additional reflective opportunities.

Linking the Five Practices to Your Own Instruction

SELECTING AND SEQUENCING

It is now time to reflect on the lesson you taught following Chapter 4, but this time through the lens of selecting and sequencing.

1. What solutions did you select for presentation during the whole group discussion?

   - Did the selected solutions help you address the mathematical ideas that you had targeted in the lesson? Are there other solutions that might have been more useful in meeting your goal?

   - How many solutions did you have students present? Did all of these contribute to better understanding of the mathematics to be learned? Did you conclude the discussion in the allotted time?

   - Which students were selected as presenters? Did you include any students who are not frequent presenters? Could you have?

2. How did you sequence the solutions?

   - Did the series of presentations add up to something? Was the storyline coherent?

   - Did you include any incomplete or incorrect solutions? Where in the sequence did they fit?

3. Based on your reading of this chapter and a deeper understanding of the process of selecting and sequencing, would you do anything differently if you were going to teach this lesson again?

4. What lessons have you learned that you will draw on in the next lesson you plan and teach?

Figure 3.8 • The Toothpick Hexagons task

Toothpick Hexagons

A row of hexagons can be made from toothpicks as follows.

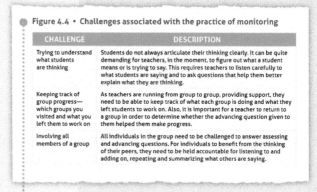

a. How many toothpicks do you need to have a row of 5 hexagons? Explain how you found your answer.

b. How many toothpicks do you need to have a row of 9 hexagons? Explain how you found your answer.

c. How many toothpicks do you need to have a row of 100 hexagons? Explain how you found your answer.

d. Write a generalization that can be used to find the total number of toothpicks when given the number of hexagons. Explain your generalization using the diagram.

e. How long would the row of hexagons be if you had 356 toothpicks to use? Explain how you found your answer.

f. What can you say about the relationship found in this pattern?

g. Create a graph of this pattern. Are there any more observations you can make after viewing the graph?

Source: Developed by the Milwaukee Mathematics Partnership (MMP) with support from the National Science Foundation under Grant No. 0314898.

Clearly designed tasks promote mathematical reasoning and problem solving.

Figure 4.4 • Challenges associated with the practice of monitoring

CHALLENGE	DESCRIPTION
Trying to understand what students are thinking	Students do not always articulate their thinking clearly. It can be quite demanding for teachers, in the moment, to figure out what a student means or is trying to say. This requires teachers to listen carefully to what students are saying and to ask questions that help them better explain what they are thinking.
Keeping track of group progress—which groups you visited and what you left them to work on	As teachers are running from group to group, providing support, they need to be able to keep track of what each group is doing and what they left students to work on. Also, it is important for a teacher to return to a group in order to determine whether the advancing question given to them helped them make progress.
Involving all members of a group	All individuals in the group need to be challenged to answer assessing and advancing questions. For individuals to benefit from the thinking of their peers, they need to be held accountable for listening to and adding on, repeating and summarizing what others are saying.

Challenge and Description charts distill and demystify some of the common issues teachers encounter when teaching the concepts at hand.

What It Takes/Key Questions charts break down the critical components of the practice and explain what it takes to succeed and the questions you need to ask yourself to stay on track.

Figure 4.1 • Key questions that support the practice of monitoring

WHAT IT TAKES	KEY QUESTIONS
Tracking student thinking	How will you keep track of students' responses during the lesson?
	How will you ensure that you check in with all students during the lesson?
Assessing student thinking	Are your assessing questions meeting students where they are?
	Are your assessing questions making student thinking visible?
Advancing student thinking	Are your advancing questions driven by your lesson goals?
	Are students able to pursue advancing questions on their own?
	Are your advancing questions helping students to progress?

In the next sections, we illustrate the practice of monitoring by continuing our investigation of Ms. Moran's implementation of the Staircase task.

THE 5 PRACTICES

in Practice

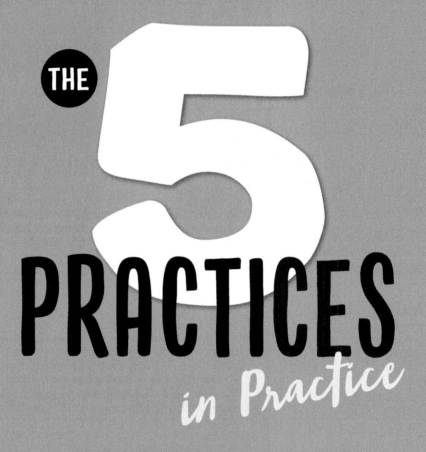

THE 5 PRACTICES
in Practice

Successfully Orchestrating Mathematical Discussions in

Your High School Classroom

Margaret (Peg) Smith • Michael D. Steele
Miriam Gamoran Sherin • Foreword by **Dan Meyer**

A JOINT PUBLICATION

NATIONAL COUNCIL OF
TEACHERS OF MATHEMATICS

For information:

Corwin
A SAGE Company
2455 Teller Road
Thousand Oaks, California 91320
(800) 233-9936
www.corwin.com

SAGE Publications Ltd.
1 Oliver's Yard
55 City Road
London, EC1Y 1SP
United Kingdom

SAGE Publications India Pvt. Ltd.
B 1/I 1 Mohan Cooperative Industrial Area
Mathura Road, New Delhi 110 044
India

SAGE Publications Asia-Pacific Pte. Ltd.
18 Cross Street #10–10/11/12
China Square Central
Singapore 048423

Executive Editor, Mathematics: Erin Null
Associate Content Development Editor:
    Jessica Vidal
Production Editor: Tori Mirsadjadi
Copy Editor: Christina West
Typesetter: Integra
Proofreader: Rae-Ann Goodwin
Indexer: Jeanne R. Busemeyer
Cover and Interior Designer: Gail Buschman
Marketing Manager: Margaret O'Connor

Library of Congress Cataloging-in-Publication Data
Names: Smith, Margaret Schwan, author. | Steele, Michael, author. | Sherin, Miriam Gamoran, author.
Title: The five practices in practice : successfully orchestrating mathematics discussions in your high school classroom / Margaret (Peg) Smith, Michael Steele, and Miriam Gamoran Sherin.
Description: Thousand Oaks : Corwin, [2020] | Includes bibliographical references and index.
Identifiers: LCCN 2019045448 | ISBN 9781544321233 (paperback) | ISBN 9781544321264 (ebook) | ISBN 9781544321257 (ebook) | ISBN 9781544321240 (adobe pdf)
Subjects: LCSH: Mathematics--Study and teaching (Secondary) | Education, Secondary.
Classification: LCC QA11.2 .S59 2020 | DDC 510.71/2—dc23
LC record available at https://lccn.loc.gov/2019045448

Printed in the United States of America.

This book is printed on acid-free paper.

20 21 23 23 24 10 9 8 7 6 5 4 3 2 1

Contents

CHAPTER 1   Introduction

CHAPTER 2   Setting Goals and Selecting Tasks

CHAPTER 3   Anticipating Student Responses

CHAPTER 4   Monitoring Student Work

CHAPTER 5 **Selecting and Sequencing Student Solutions**

CHAPTER 6 — Connecting Student Solutions

CHAPTER 7 — Looking Back and Looking Ahead

Visit the companion website at
http://resources.corwin.com/5practices-highschool
for downloadable resources.

List of Video Clips

Foreword

Why did you become a math teacher?

Perhaps you loved math. Perhaps you were good at math; good, at least, at the thing you called math then. Friends and family would come to you for help with their homework or studying, and you prided yourself not just on explaining the *how* of math's operations but also the *why* and the *when*, helping others see the purpose and application behind the math.

Helping other people understand and love the math *you* understood and loved—perhaps that sounded like a good way to spend a few decades.

Or perhaps you loved kids. Perhaps even at a young age you were an effective caregiver, and you knew how to care for more than just another person's tangible needs. You listened, and you made people feel *listened to*. You had an eye for a person's value and power. You understood where people were in their lives, and you understood how the right kind of question or observation could propel them to where they were going to *be*.

Spending a few decades helping people feel heard, helping them unleash and use their tremendous capacity—perhaps you thought that was a worthwhile way to spend what you thought would be the hours between 7 a.m. and 4 p.m. every day.

Or perhaps you loved both math and kids. It's possible of course that neither of the two previous exemplar teachers will speak fully to the path that brought you to math teaching, although one of them speaks fully to mine. Yet, in my work with math teachers, I find they often draw their professional energy from one source or the other, from math's ideas or its people.

It took me several frustrating years of math teaching—and years of work with other teachers—to realize that each of those energy sources is vital. Neither source is renewable without the other.

If you draw your energy from mathematics, your students can become abstractions and interchangeable. You can convince yourself it's possible to influence *what they know* without care for *who they are*, that it's possible to treat their *knowledge* as deficient and in need of fixing without risking negative consequences for their *identity*. But students know better. Most of them know what it feels like when the adults in the room position themselves as all-knowing and the students in the room as all-unknowing. A teacher's love and understanding of mathematics won't help when students have decided their teacher cares less about them than about numbers and variables, bar models and graphs, precise definitions, and deductive arguments.

If you draw your energy only from students, then the day's mathematics can become interchangeable with any other day's. Some days, it may feel like an act of care to skip students past mathematics they find frustrating or to skip mathematics altogether. But the math you skip one day is foundational for the math of another day or another year. Students will have to pay down their frustration later, only then with compound interest. Your love and care for students cannot protect them from the frustration that is often fundamental to learning.

I could tell you that the only solution to this problem of practice is to develop a love of students *and* a love of mathematics. I could relate any number of maxims and slogans that testify to that truth. I could perhaps convince some of you to believe me.

But the maxim I hold most closely right now is that we act ourselves into belief more often than we believe our way into action. So I encourage you more than anything right now to adopt a series of productive *actions* that can reshape your *beliefs*.

Here are five such actions: anticipate, monitor, select, sequence, and connect.

Those actions, initially proposed by Smith and Stein in 2011, and ably illustrated here with classroom videos, teacher testimony, and student work samples, can convert teachers' love for math into a love for students and vice versa, to act their way into a belief that math and students both matter.

For teachers who are motivated by a love of students, those five practices invite the teacher to learn more mathematics. The more math teachers know, the easier it is for them to find value in the ways their students think. Their mathematical knowledge enables them to monitor that thinking less for *correctness* and more for *interest*. Would presenting this student's thinking provoke an *interesting* conversation with the class, whether the circled answer is correct or not? Teachers' mathematical knowledge enables them to connect one student's interesting idea to another's. Their math knowledge helps them connect student thinking together and illustrate for the students the enormous value in their ideas.

For the teachers like me who are motivated by a love of mathematics, teachers who want students to love mathematics as well, those five practices give them a rationale for understanding their students as people. Students are not a blank screen onto which teachers can project and trace out their own knowledge. Meaning is *made* by the student. It isn't *transferred* by the teacher. The more teachers love and want to protect interesting mathematical ideas, the more they should want to know the meaning students are making of those ideas. Those five practices have helped me connect student ideas to canonical mathematical ideas, helping students see the value of both.

Neither a love of students nor a love of mathematics can sustain the work of math education on its own. We work with *math students*, a composite of their mathematical ideas and their identities as people. The five practices for orchestrating productive mathematical discussions, and these ideas for putting those practices into practice, offer the actions that can develop and sustain the belief that both math and students matter.

You might think your path into teaching emanated from a love of mathematics or from a love of students. But it's the same path. It's a wider path than you might have thought, one that offers passage to more people and more ideas than you originally thought possible. This book will help you and your students learn to walk it.

—Dan Meyer
Chief Academic Officer, Desmos

Preface

In 2001, a group of researchers at the University of Pittsburgh launched the ASTEROID (A Study of Teacher Education: Research on Instructional Design) project funded by the National Science Foundation. The project investigated what mathematics teachers learned from participation in practice-based teacher education courses—courses that used cognitively demanding mathematical tasks, narrative cases, and student work as a focus of critique, inquiry, and investigation (Smith, 2001). Mary Kay Stein and I (Peg) were co-principal investigators of the project and I was the course instructor.

The first course, taught in the summer of 2002, focused on proportional reasoning. The goals of the course were both to enhance teachers' own ability to reason proportionally and enhance their capacity to teach proportional reasoning. The students in the course were 14 elementary and three secondary teachers, some of whom had just completed their Master of Arts in Teaching degree and others who were working on masters of education degrees. In order to investigate what teachers learned and how our instruction supported or inhibited learning, we videotaped each class session. We also gave teachers pre-/post-tests, interviewed them, and kept notebooks of all work produced in the course.

As the research team watched videos of teacher-students solving cognitively challenging (aka high-level) tasks, they noticed a certain pattern in the way I, as the instructor, facilitated work around and discussions of the tasks. I had solved the problems in multiple ways prior to the class, often seeking input from graduate students on alternative approaches. The researchers saw how I interacted with students as they worked and how I made notes of what specific students were doing. They saw how I identified students to present their solutions, how I ordered the solutions in particular ways, and how I helped my students make connections between different strategies, ensuring the mathematical ideas were central. While I was aware of what I was doing, I did not give much thought to why I was doing it, and I did not codify my actions.

The research team noticed the regularity of my teaching pattern and the impact it appeared to have on the quality of the discussions around high-level tasks. They recognized the parallel between a teacher educator teaching teachers and K–12 teachers teaching children. They were excited by the potential this model had to support the work of K–12 classroom teachers. We all knew we were on to something powerful. We gave labels to each of the identified actions so that others could learn them and voila!—

the five practices—anticipating, monitoring, selecting, sequencing, and connecting—were born!

From that moment forward—in collaboration with others—I have written about the five practices in journal articles, and my co-author Mary Kay Stein and I published the book that anchors this new series, which you may know as *5 Practices for Orchestrating Productive Mathematics Discussions* (2011). The book sold over 100,000 copies before we published the second edition in 2018.

What accounts for the surprising success of the five practices? Over the last three decades, there has been a growing consensus that traditional forms of mathematics teaching were not sufficiently preparing students for success in school and beyond. The release of the *Common Core State Standards* (National Governors Association Center for Best Practices & Council of Chief State School Officers, 2010) brought new demands for more ambitious teaching and an increased focus on the importance of engaging students in mathematical discussion. Such discussion gives students the opportunity to share ideas and clarify understandings, develop convincing arguments regarding why and how things work, develop a language for expressing mathematical ideas, and learn to see things from other people's perspective.

So one answer to the question is that the five practices provides a five-step model of what teachers can do before and during instruction that gives them some control in facilitating discussions—an aspect of instruction that has proven to be especially challenging. The five practices are *doable* and something teachers could continue to get better at doing over time.

Despite the uptake of the five practices by teachers and teacher educators, teachers continue to find aspects of the practices challenging. Questions such as "Where do I find good tasks?," "How do I find time to adequately plan?," "What do I do if students all think about a problem the same way?," and "How do I wrap up the conversation at the end of a lesson without taking over?" abound.

In addition, teachers and teacher educators repeatedly ask me, "Do you have any video of teachers doing the five practices?" The need for authentic examples of what these practices look like in real classrooms was clear.

The Five Practices in Practice: Successfully Orchestrating Mathematics Discussions in Your High School Classroom (Smith, Steele, & Sherin, 2020) is the third book in a series that addresses many of the questions that teachers have raised with me over the years, and it provides what teachers and teacher educators have been clamoring for—classroom video of teachers engaged in orchestrating productive discussions. (The middle school book was published in Spring 2019 and the elementary school book was published in Fall 2019.)

This book goes beyond the first and second editions of the original *5 Practices* by providing a detailed unpacking of the practices and by identifying specific challenges teachers face related to each practice. The book includes numerous examples drawn from high school classrooms to illustrate aspects of the five practices and the associated challenges. A central component of these examples is video excerpts from high school classrooms that provide vivid images of real teachers using the five practices in their efforts to orchestrate productive discussions.

We hope this book will be a valuable resource for teachers!

—Peg Smith

Acknowledgments

Since the publication of *5 Practices for Orchestrating Productive Mathematics Discussions* (Smith & Stein, 2011), we have worked with and heard from hundreds of teachers who have reported on their successes and struggles in implementing the five practices in their classrooms. We have taken their feedback to heart. This book is our attempt to provide additional guidance on enacting the five practices in high school classrooms.

While the writing herein is the product of our collaboration, this book would not have been possible without the work, support, and commitment of a number of individuals. Specifically, we acknowledge the contributions of the following:

- Erin Null, Executive Editor for Corwin Mathematics, who encouraged us to write this book and provided thoughtful suggestions and insightful feedback at every step of the process.

- The producer at SAGE, Julie Slattery, and the video crew (Davis Lester, Kurt Denissen, and Ben Nelson) whose expertise is evident in the compelling video clips, which are at the heart of this book.

- Milwaukee Public Schools (MPS) and the School District of South Milwaukee (SDSM) who embraced this project from its inception and provided enthusiastic support throughout the planning, filming, and writing process. In particular,

  - The teachers—Matthew Harmon (Rufus King International High School, MPS), Michael Moore (Ronald Wilson Reagan College Preparatory High School, MPS) and Cori Moran (South Milwaukee High School, SDSM)—who agreed to make their teaching public so that others could learn from their struggles and triumphs.

  - The principals—Tanzanique Carrington (Rufus King International High School, MPS), Mike Roemer (Ronald Wilson Reagan College Preparatory High School, MPS), and Beth Kaminski (South Milwaukee High School, SDSM)—who enthusiastically welcomed us into their schools and accommodated our filming schedule.

  - District Leaders—Keith Posley (Superintendent of Schools, MPS), Rita Olson (Superintendent of Schools, SDSM), Angela Ford (Mathematics Curriculum Specialist, MPS) Joe Giera (Mathematics Coach, SDSM), and Laura Maly (Mathematics Specialist, MPS)—who were instrumental in making the filming for this book possible.

- Martha Mulligan, a mathematics teacher at Northside College Preparatory High School, Chicago, Illinois, for sharing her Sketchy Derivatives lesson (featured in Chapter 5) with us.

- Travis Lemon, a mathematics teacher at American Fork Junior High School, American Fork, Utah, for sharing his Photocopy Faux Pas lesson (featured in Chapter 5) with us.

- Frederick Dillon, former high school mathematics teacher, friend, and colleague, who provided a thoughtful review of the first draft of this book.

- Katherine Linsenmeier, a mathematics teacher at New Trier High School, Winnetka, Illinois, for her feedback in the final stages of preparing the book.

Publisher's Acknowledgments

Corwin gratefully acknowledges the contributions of the following reviewers, who provided input into the creation of this book series:

Cathy Battles
Educational Consultant
University of Missouri–Kansas City Regional Professional
    Development Center
Kansas City, MO

Natalie Crist
Supervisor of Elementary Mathematics
Baltimore County Public Schools
Baltimore, MD

Kevin Dykema
Eighth-Grade Math Teacher
Mattawan Middle School
Mattawan, MI

Cathy Martin
Executive Director, Curriculum and Instruction
Denver Public Schools
Denver, CO

Jennifer Novak
Education Associate, Mathematics
Delaware Department of Education
Elkridge, MD

Lois A. Williams
Adjunct Professor, Mathematics Education Consultant, Author
Mary Baldwin University
Scottsville, VA

Cathy Yenca
Middle School Mathematics Teacher
Eanes Independent School District
Austin, TX

About the Authors

Margaret (Peg) Smith is a Professor Emerita at the University of Pittsburgh. Over the past two decades, she has been developing research-based materials for use in the professional development of mathematics teachers. She has authored or coauthored over 90 books, edited books or monographs, book chapters, and peer-reviewed articles, including the best seller *5 Practices for Orchestrating Productive Mathematics Discussions* (coauthored with Mary Kay Stein). She was a member of the writing team for *Principles to Actions: Ensuring Mathematical Success for All* and she is a co-author of two recent books (*Taking Action: Implementing Effective Mathematics Teaching Practices in Grades 6–8* and *9–12*), which provide further explication of the teaching practices first described in *Principles to Actions*. She was a member of the Board of Directors of the Association of Mathematics Teacher Educators (2001–2003; 2003–2005), of the National Council of Teachers of Mathematics (2006–2009), and of Teachers Development Group (2009–2017).

Photo credit: Nathaniel Edmunds Photography

Michael D. Steele is a Professor of Mathematics Education in the School of Education at the University of Wisconsin-Milwaukee. He is currently the President of the Association of Mathematics Teacher Educators. A former middle and high school mathematics and science teacher, Dr. Steele has worked with preservice secondary mathematics teachers, practicing teachers, administrators, and doctoral students across the country for the past two decades. He has published several books and journal articles focused on supporting mathematics teachers in enacting research-based effective mathematics teaching practices. He is the co-author of NCTM's *Taking Action: Implementing Effective Mathematics Teaching Practices in Grades 6–8* and *Mathematics Discourse in Secondary Classrooms*, two research-based professional development resources for secondary mathematics teachers. He is also the author of *A Quiet Revolution: One District's Story of Radical Curricular Change in Mathematics*, a resource focused on reforming high school mathematics teaching and learning.

Miriam Gamoran Sherin is Associate Provost for Undergraduate Education and the Alice Gabrielle Twight Professor of Learning Sciences at Northwestern University. Her research interests include mathematics teaching and learning, teacher cognition, and the role of video in supporting teacher learning. Sherin investigates the nature and dynamics of teacher noticing, and in particular, the ways in which teachers identify and interpret student thinking during instruction. *Mathematics Teacher Noticing: Seeing Through Teachers' Eyes*, edited by Sherin, V. Jacobs, and R. Philipp, received the AERA Division K 2013 Excellence in Research in Teaching and Teacher Education award. In 2016, Sherin and her colleagues were awarded the National Council of Teachers of Mathematics Linking Research and Practice Outstanding Publication Award.

" We use the five practices as a framework to help teachers see how they can they stop the stand-and-deliver traditional method and really be able to implement a structure in their classes so that the discourse can come out and come alive. "

—LAURA MALY, MATHEMATICS SPECIALIST, MILWAUKEE PUBLIC SCHOOLS

" The five practices is really the centerpiece of our professional development. We frame our discussions around how we can create good conversations so that all kids are advancing in their thinking about a problem. "

—JOE GIERA, MATHEMATICS COACH, SCHOOL DISTRICT OF SOUTH MILWAUKEE

CHAPTER 1

Introduction

At the heart of efforts to help students in Grades 9–12 learn mathematics is the idea of *ambitious teaching*. It's referred to as *ambitious* because of the substantial student learning goals that it encompasses—that all students have opportunities "to understand and use knowledge ... [to] solve authentic problems" (Lampert & Graziani, 2009, p. 492). The Common Core State Standards for Mathematics (National Governors Association Center for Best Practices & Council of Chief State School Officers, 2010) provide a powerful vision of these goals through their description of grade-level, domain-specific content standards and the cross-cutting Standards for Mathematical Practice.

We believe that the phrase *ambitious teaching* is also appropriate because teaching in ways that align with these goals is a formidable task! To help you and other teachers understand what this looks like, *Principles to Actions: Ensuring Mathematical Success for All* (National Council of Teachers of Mathematics, 2014) describes a set of eight teaching practices that serve as a foundation for ambitious teaching (Figure 1.1). These practices are based on what we know from research about how to effectively support students' learning of mathematics.

Figure 1.1 • Eight effective mathematics teaching practices

Establish mathematics goals to focus learning. Effective teaching of mathematics establishes clear goals for the mathematics that students are learning, situates goals within learning progressions, and uses the goals to guide instructional decisions.

Implement tasks that promote reasoning and problem solving. Effective teaching of mathematics engages students in solving and discussing tasks that promote mathematical reasoning and problem solving and allow multiple entry points and varied solution strategies.

Use and connect mathematical representations. Effective teaching of mathematics engages students in making connections among mathematical representations to deepen understanding of mathematics concepts and procedures and as tools for problem solving.

Facilitate meaningful mathematical discourse. Effective teaching of mathematics facilitates discourse among students to build shared understanding of mathematical ideas by analyzing and comparing student approaches and arguments.

Pose purposeful questions. Effective teaching of mathematics uses purposeful questions to assess and advance students' reasoning and sense-making about important mathematical ideas and relationships.

Build procedural fluency from conceptual understanding. Effective teaching of mathematics builds fluency with procedures on a foundation of conceptual understanding so that students, over time, become skillful in using procedures flexibly as they solve contextual and mathematical problems.

Support productive struggle in learning mathematics. Effective teaching of mathematics consistently provides students, individually and collectively, with opportunities and supports to engage in productive struggle as they grapple with mathematical ideas and relationships.

Elicit and use evidence of student thinking. Effective teaching of mathematics uses evidence of student thinking to assess progress toward mathematical understanding and to adjust instruction continually in ways that support and extend learning.

Source: Reprinted with permission from *Principles to Actions: Ensuring Mathematical Success for All,* copyright 2014, by the National Council of Teachers of Mathematics. All rights reserved.

Ambitious teaching also requires attention to equity. Mathematics has long been considered a gatekeeper, limiting opportunities for some students while promoting opportunities for others (Martin, Gholson, & Leonard, 2010). These differences in opportunities are apparent in high schools where students who are Black, Latinx, American Indian, emergent multilingual, or living in poverty are overrepresented in classrooms that focus on learning and practicing procedures (Oakes, 2008), while Asian and White students are more like to be assigned to higher-level classes where they have the opportunity to engage in thinking, reasoning, and problem solving around cognitively challenging tasks (White, Fernandes, & Civil, 2018). Ambitious teaching requires you to challenge these long-standing practices and provide access and opportunity for all students so that they can develop strong positive identities as learners of mathematics (Aguirre, Mayfield-Ingram, & Martin, 2013).

In their most recent policy statement, the National Council of Teachers of Mathematics (NCTM, 2018) stated that the practice of tracking high school students into "qualitatively different or dead-end course pathways" should be discontinued. Eliminating tracking has been successful in strengthening overall mathematics outcomes and providing stronger mathematics pathways for historically underrepresented groups in places such as San Francisco and Escondido, California. Moreover, NCTM states that the practice of teacher tracking—assigning the most experienced teachers primarily to courses with higher-achieving students—should also end. All students should have opportunities to learn high-quality, grade level–appropriate mathematics in classrooms where teachers are enacting research-informed ambitious teaching practices. If your school is engaged in the practice of tracking, now is the time to begin conversations with school and district administrators on how to ensure that each and every student has access to high-quality mathematics instruction. (For information on how to begin such conversations and current efforts to eliminate high school tracking, go to https://www.nctm.org/change/.)

At the center of ambitious teaching is a focus on classroom discourse. As you facilitate meaningful discussions with students, you will typically engage in several of the effective mathematics teaching practices, including asking purposeful questions, eliciting and using evidence of student thinking, connecting to various mathematical representations, and supporting productive struggle among students as they learn mathematics (Figure 1.1). In addition, allowing students to share their thinking with the class can help to position all students as valuable resources for learning and promote an equitable learning environment. In these ways, organizing discussions around students' ideas becomes critical for successfully enacting ambitious instruction.

What does it take then to organize and implement effective discussions? In this book, we present guidelines for using the five practices described by Smith and Stein (2018) in their book *5 Practices for Orchestrating Productive Mathematics Discussions*.

The Five Practices in Practice: An Overview

The five practices are a set of related instructional routines that can help you design and implement lessons that address important mathematical content in ways that build on students' thinking (Figure 1.2). Warning: There is actually a Practice 0, which serves as a foundation for the remaining practices—yup, this means there are six practices in total, but for historical reasons, we will still call the set "the five practices." (In case you are wondering how this could have happened, here is the scoop: After some early articles about the five practices were published, a mathematics coach with whom Peg was working suggested to her that a practice was missing—that before teachers could engage with the five practices, they needed to set goals and select a task. Though this idea was already implied in the five practices, the coach persuaded Peg to make it explicit, and hence Practice 0 was born!)

Figure 1.2 • The five practices in practice

Practices that take place while planning for instruction		**Practice 0: Setting goals and selecting tasks (Chapter 2)** Specifying learning goals and choosing a high-level task that aligns with those goals
		Practice 1: Anticipating student responses (Chapter 3) Exploring how you expect students to solve the task and preparing questions to ask them about their thinking
Practices that take place during instruction but are considered while planning	Students work individually or in small groups	**Practice 2: Monitoring student work (Chapter 4)** Looking closely as students work on the task and asking questions to assess their understanding and move their thinking forward
	As you move from small group work to whole class discussion	**Practice 3: Selecting student solutions (Chapter 5)** Choosing solutions for students to share that highlight key mathematical ideas that will help you achieve lesson goals
		Practice 4: Sequencing student solutions (Chapter 5) Determining the order in which to share solutions to create a coherent storyline for the lesson
	Whole class discussion	**Practice 5: Connecting student solutions (Chapter 6)** Identifying connections among student solutions and to the goals of the lesson that you want to bring out during discussion

Teachers often think that ambitious teaching requires you to make all your instructional decisions during instruction based on what students say and do in class. The five practices, however, help you think through all aspects of the lesson *in advance* of teaching, thus limiting the number of in-the-moment decisions you have to make during a lesson. Careful planning prior to a lesson reduces what you need to think about during instruction, allowing you time to listen more actively, question more thoughtfully, and respond more acutely.

Practice zero, *setting goals and selecting tasks*, lays the groundwork for the remaining five practices. It is essential to be clear on what you want students to learn and to choose a cognitively demanding task that aligns with those goals. Once you have the task in mind, you can move to *anticipating student responses*. Here, the purpose is to think about how students might solve the problem, what challenges they might face, and how you will respond to their thinking. One benefit to doing so is that you can develop—before class—targeted questions you might want to ask students about these different approaches.

Although the next four practices take place during instruction, you will also want to think them through carefully during planning. *Monitoring student work* involves giving students time—usually in groups—to work on the task, while you circulate among them. As you look closely at how students are progressing, you can use the questions you developed earlier to assess what students understand and to try to move their thinking forward. As you prepare to transition students into a whole class discussion, you will engage in *selecting student solutions*—deciding which solutions you want to have shared in the discussion and who should present those solutions—as well as *sequencing student solutions*—deciding how you want to order the presentation of the solutions. Selecting and sequencing require close attention to the mathematical ideas that are highlighted in different solutions and to helping all students have access to the ideas shared in the discussion. As you plan the lesson you will consider what you want to be on the lookout for as you monitor students' work, what solutions will help you surface the mathematical ideas you are targeting, and what order of solutions will provide access to all students.

The final practice, *connecting student solutions*, takes place as the discussion unfolds in your classroom. The purpose is to make explicit the connections between students' solutions and the mathematical goals of the lesson. Drawing out these connections for students is essential to ensure that students take away from the discussion what you intended. This too is something you can consider as you plan the lesson!

Together, the five practices can help you prepare for and carry out meaningful discussions with your students, discussions that revolve around the thinking of your students. And that is the essence of ambitious instruction!

Purpose and Content

The purpose of this book is to deepen your understanding of the five practices as described by Smith and Stein (2018). Toward that end, Chapters 2 to 6 comprise two parts: unpacking the practice (Part One) and challenges teachers face in enacting the practice (Part Two). In Part One, we describe in some detail what is involved in engaging in the practice, provide questions that you should ask yourself as you undertake the practice, and use an example from a high school classroom to illustrate the components of the practice. In Part Two, we highlight aspects of the practice that have proven to be challenging for teachers, suggest ways you can address the challenge, and provide examples of how teachers are overcoming the challenge.

Throughout these chapters, we encourage you to actively engage with the content. Toward this end, we have created three types of opportunities for engagement: *Pause and Consider* questions (reflection), *Analyzing the Work of Teaching* activities (analysis), and *Linking the Five Practices to Your Own Instruction* assignments (implementation). The Pause and Consider questions give you the opportunity to think about an issue, in some cases drawing on your own classroom experience, prior to reading more about it. The Analyzing the Work of Teaching activities engage you in analyzing aspects of teachers' planning for and enacting of grade-level lessons. The Linking the Five Practices to Your Own Instruction assignments provide you with the opportunity to put the ideas discussed in the chapter to work in your own classroom.

Throughout the book we have included a range of different types of examples drawn from high school classrooms to illustrate aspects of the five practices and the associated challenges. The video excerpts and related classroom artifacts—featuring the three teachers who are introduced later in the chapter—provide vivid images of real teachers using the five practices in their efforts to orchestrate productive discussions. These three teachers illustrate the practices and challenges in each of the chapters that follow. In addition, in Chapter 5 we provide authentic descriptions and artifacts from the work of two additional teachers with whom we have worked—Travis Lemon and Martha Mulligan. Other narrative examples that appear in the book are based on our experiences working with high school teachers through professional development initiatives and teacher education courses. These examples are intended to provide insights into specific challenges teachers face when engaging in the five practices and are not exact representations of a specific teacher's practice. Each of these teachers has been given a pseudonym (e.g., Grace Sullivan, George Jacobson, Kendra Nelson, and Denise Hansen featured in Chapter 2). The video and narrative examples are not intended as exemplars to be copied but rather as opportunities for analysis, discussion, and new learning.

If you are coming to the five practices for the first time, you might find it helpful to start with *5 Practices for Orchestrating Productive Mathematics Discussions* by Peg Smith and Mary Kay Stein (2018). Smith and Stein's book offers a wonderful, easy-to-read introduction to and overview of the five practices. The book you are reading now takes a much deeper dive into the five practices, asking you to stop and think, watch videos of the practices in action, and consider what is challenging about each practice. While you can certainly start here, the overview of the five practices provided by Smith and Stein (2018) may help you get the big picture before taking a deeper dive!

This book will be a valuable resource for looking closely at what it takes to be successful with the five practices. For each practice, we offer key questions, which identify the essential components of the practice. We suspect these questions will enhance your understanding of the practices and perhaps provide new information about the goals and expectations for each practice. This book also describes challenges associated with each practice that teachers we have worked with have encountered, as well as specific suggestions for successfully addressing these challenges. If you have already been using the five practices, we suspect that some of these challenges may be familiar to you and that these discussions will be particularly useful.

Classroom Video Context

In identifying teachers to feature on video, we felt that it was important to select teachers who were working hard to improve mathematics teaching and learning in their high school classrooms. We selected teachers who were participating in the Milwaukee Master Teacher Partnership for several reasons. Michael Steele, the second author of this book, is the director and principal investigator of this five-year project funded by the National Science Foundation and works closely with the 24 teacher-participants, all of whom work in urban high schools and are committed to improving learning outcomes for their students.

The greater Milwaukee area has many features of a typical large urban education system but is also unique in a number of ways. From the 1900s through the late 1960s, the City of Milwaukee has geographically shifted from a single municipality to a series of smaller towns surrounding the central city. This factor and others have resulted in Milwaukee being one of the most racially segregated cities in the United States (Brookings Institution, 2018). The region has also been a central focus of the charter and voucher school movements, which have fragmented both the student and teacher populations in significant ways. One of the responses to this privatization has been a push to specialize high schools in Milwaukee as thematic magnet schools with specialized curricular opportunities. Changes to labor and union laws have contributed to more significant teacher mobility between schools and districts. Despite these challenges, the region has a strong legacy in mathematics education. Major research and professional development partnerships have served the region since the early 1990s, including the Quantitative Understanding: Amplifying Student Achievement and Reasoning (QUASAR) project and a two-decade series of teacher professional development projects focused on ambitious teaching through the University of Wisconsin-Milwaukee and their partners. Building on a base of content, pedagogy, and leadership learning related to elementary and middle grades mathematics, recent efforts in the past six years in Milwaukee have bridged into serving high school teachers and their students.

One such project, the Milwaukee Master Teacher Partnership, is a five-year partnership between the University of Wisconsin-Milwaukee, Milwaukee Public Schools, and the School District of South Milwaukee.[1] The goal of the partnership is to enhance teachers' content knowledge, to strengthen their pedagogical skills, and to develop their capacity for leadership. Toward that end, teachers across schools and districts work together to engage in inquiry about their classroom practice. Teachers' work in the partnership is centered on repeated cycles of action research, focusing on some small pieces of their classroom practice such as the tasks they choose to use in the classroom or the questions they decide to ask students. For example, teachers may decide to use different types of tasks or ask different kinds of questions and then investigate the impact the changes they have made had on student learning. Teachers then come

---

[1] The Milwaukee Master Teacher Partnership project is funded by a grant from the National Science Foundation (NSF), awards 1540840 and 1557397, to the University of Wisconsin-Milwaukee. The content of this book does not necessarily reflect the views of the NSF.

together and share what they have tried and what they have learned. According to Steele,

> We equip teachers with the skills to rigorously conduct that inquiry in the classroom—not just say, "Well, you know, I noticed that more kids seem to be paying attention," but to really start to capture some data that they can analyze and say, "Yeah, this is changing the way my students learn."

In the video clip that follows, Dr. Steele discusses how he has woven the five practices into the professional development in which project teachers participate and the impact of this work on student learning and engagement.

A Professional Community Engages in the Five Practices

Video Clip 1.1
In Video Clip 1.1, Michael Steele, director and principal investigator of the Milwaukee Master Teacher Partnership, explains how the five practices align with the work of the project and the impact they are having on teaching and learning.

To read a QR code, you must have a smartphone or tablet with a camera. We recommend that you download a QR code reader app that is made specifically for your phone or tablet brand.

 Videos may also be accessed at
resources.corwin.com/5practices-highschool

Dr. Steele suggests that the five practices can also have an impact more broadly on issues of equity and identity. He explains:

> One of the persistent challenges of high school mathematics has been that we've tended to sort and track kids into the haves and the have-nots. And one of our big initiatives as a profession is to really help teachers and school districts understand that that practice has actually been detrimental in promoting stronger student achievement for all kids. So when we think about putting diverse groups of students together, who have different mathematical identities, who may have or may have not struggled with mathematics in the past, the five practices helps a teacher think about "How do I provide multiple entry points for a student? How do I elevate student voices for all

the students in my classroom? How do I focus less on students' past performance and achievement and more on the mathematical ideas that my students who are in here today are doing and saying, and then how do I make use of those mathematical ideas in advancing the goals of my lesson?" It actually equips the teachers with a broader range of tools because now, as a teacher, I'm not just relying on the good thinking that I know three or four of my kids who are high achievers are walking in with. It opens the door to making use of a broader range of student thinking, of elevating more student voices and positioning each and every student in the classroom as a capable mathematical learner.

Meet the Teachers

The video recordings and related classroom artifacts featured in this book are drawn from the work of three high school teachers who are participating in the Milwaukee Master Teacher Partnership—Matthew Harmon, Michael Moore, and Cori Moran. The lesson taught by Cori Moran will be used in Part One of Chapters 2 to 6 to unpack the focal practice. By focusing on the same teacher across chapters, you will have a coherent picture of instruction in her classroom and a better understanding of how the practices provide synergy. The lessons taught by Matthew Harmon and Michael Moore will be used in Part Two of Chapters 2 to 6 to provide illustrations of how specific challenges can be addressed.

 **Matthew Harmon** has been teaching mathematics at Rufus King International High School in the Milwaukee Public Schools district since he began his career 11 years ago. He has a bachelor's degree in sports management and a master's of education in educational policy and leadership with a focus on curriculum, and he is certified to teach secondary mathematics. He became a teacher because he liked working with kids and he wanted a job that had a meaningful purpose. He has great passion for his job and as he explains, "It makes everything associated with it a little easier."

Matthew wants all of his students to have a positive experience with mathematics education, gaining confidence in their skills and seeing the usefulness of the mathematics they are learning. Toward that end, he has been selecting rich tasks with multiple entry points so that students can access a task and experience success at some level. Then he can move a student forward from wherever they are in their understanding.

Matthew sees the five practices as playing a vital role in preparing for instruction. He explains:

As I incorporate the five practices into my instruction, I've learned that having a clear learning target in mind in the planning process really allows you to come up with questions that drive precisely towards the goal of the lesson. It just really makes a lot of sense to be able to plan for anticipated responses and think about questions that you're going to use to move students towards the goals. And then basically, putting students up there, displaying their work, discussing it, being challenged by other students—that's really when the depth of their understanding is on display. So the five practices gets me to just be much more thoughtful and plan about what I intend to do.

Michael Moore has been teaching at Ronald Wilson Reagan College Preparatory High School in the Milwaukee Public Schools district since he started teaching 11 years ago. He has a bachelor's degree in secondary mathematics education and a master's of education in teaching, learning, and leadership. He became a teacher because he sees it as both rewarding and challenging. He enjoys how quickly each day goes when he is engaged in conversations with students about their ideas.

Michael feels that learning mathematics in his classroom should be fun and engaging for students. He wants students to be challenged to justify their work by sharing their thoughts publicly, which he feels will in turn help other students understand different ways of thinking. Michael explains that task selection is critical in achieving this outcome because it allows students to buy into the idea that mathematics is exciting.

Michael explains how the five practices can make you more aware of your actions as a teacher:

I think every single teacher on the face of the earth struggles with not telling, right? That's really, really, really hard. I think that working with the five practices definitely makes you aware of how often you're leading students, how much you're wanting to control the work, and it really makes you take a step back and value what they have to say and makes you value the fact that they can learn probably more from each other than they can learn from you just talking at the front of the room. If you try to make it a point every day to let the students do the explaining, it becomes routine.

Cori Moran teaches at South Milwaukee High School in the School District of South Milwaukee, a position she has held for the past two years. She previously taught in Milwaukee Public Schools for nine years. She has undergraduate degrees in secondary mathematics education and American sign language and a graduate degree in curriculum and instruction. Cori enjoyed the challenges of mathematics and appreciated the support she received from caring mathematics teachers. Because of her love for learning, her love of helping others, and her connections with her own teachers, she always felt that teaching was her path.

Cori's goal as a teacher is to develop a mathematics community in her classroom where students respect and support each other using Restorative Practice Circles as a framework. She takes her role as a mathematics teacher seriously because mathematics has been shown to be a gatekeeper for student potential and she sees it as a privilege to guide students on their journey in life. She wants to ensure that "the gate is wide open for them and I have added no barriers, and even better, removed some." In her view, the key to accomplishing this is to build trusting relationships with her students.

The five practices have helped Cori feel like a more prepared teacher. As she explains,

> One of the things I have learned is that prior to using the five practices, I did not plan enough. I feel like I'm now a prepared teacher and that my students get a well-prepared lesson. The five practices gave me a tool that helped me direct my planning towards my goals for the lesson. I can now see that I can sequence student solutions in a way that really reaches the goal. And for me, I really enjoy that whole storytelling and connecting the students with the work so that they feel they are part of it. And they also still get to that goal and get to share what they are thinking. I think that the most important part of using the five practices is that you really can see what students can do when they're given that opportunity.

These three teachers are making their teaching practice public so that others can learn from their efforts. Hiebert, Gallimore, and Stigler (2003) argue that we must respect teachers for being "brave enough to open their classroom doors" (p. 56). To honor their courage, as you read about and view excerpts from their classrooms, we encourage you to avoid critiquing what you see or discussing what the teacher "should have done." Instead, our goal is to use the access we have been given as an opportunity for learning—for serious reflection and analysis— in an effort to improve our own teaching in ways that open up new opportunities for our students to learn.

Using This Book

You will likely get the most out of this book if you are committed to ambitious teaching that provides students with increased opportunities to engage in productive discussions in mathematics classrooms. Through engaging with the ideas in the book, you will learn much about how to increase students' engagement in and learning from classroom discussions.

This book can be used in several different ways. You might read through the book on your own, stopping to engage with the questions, activities, and assignments as suggested. Alternatively, and perhaps more powerfully, you can work through the book with colleagues in professional learning communities, department meetings, or when time permits. The book would also be a good choice for a book study with a group of peers interested in improving the quality of their classroom discussions. You might also encounter this book in college or university education courses for practicing or preservice teachers or in professional development workshops during the summer or school year. We will explore more ideas about ways to make the five practices central to your instruction in Chapter 7.

Norms for Video Viewing

The video excerpts that accompany this book are intended to provide authentic examples from high school classrooms on which to base discussions of the five practices. To take full advantage of these examples, we encourage you to consider the following three norms for video viewing. These norms are based on recent research that documents how video can support teacher learning and reflection (Sherin & Dyer, 2017; Sherin & van Es, 2009).

Focus on student sense-making. The majority of the video clips that you will watch in this book focus on students. That is intentional. While the five practices describe actions that you as the teacher will take, this work involves looking closely at what students do and say. The videos thus provide an opportunity for you to do just that outside of the immediate demands of teaching.

As you explore students' actions in the videos, we encourage you to look beyond simply whether a student's idea is correct or incorrect. Instead, examine what it is that the student understands. What is the student's idea? Where does it come from? Why is it sensible, given what the student understands? Focus on what it is that makes sense about the students' thinking.

Be specific about what you notice. Much of the value of video viewing is the sense that you can slow down classroom interactions and have the time to notice what is taking place in a detailed way. In addition, with video you can often focus on just a subset of events and look closely, for example, at what a particular student is saying and to whom, what gestures or drawings the student is making, and more.

As you view the video excerpts, we encourage you to be specific about what you notice. Provide detailed evidence to support your claims about what is happening. Explain what it is you see in the video that leads you to a particular interpretation.

Consider alternative interpretations. As you watch the video, you may find yourself quickly making assumptions about what is taking place and why. As teachers, we must often respond quickly, diagnosing student confusions, responding to student questions, and making changes in the direction of a lesson. Video, however, provides the luxury of time. Use this to your advantage!

Once you have an idea of what you think is taking place in the video, look for alternatives. How else might you understand what is happening? This is particularly important when examining students' ideas. Rather than assume you know the reason behind a student's strategy or statement, look for alternatives. Considering alternate interpretations is important because when we assume we understand what a student means, we often limit ourselves to what we have heard from students previously.

Getting Started!

You are now ready to begin a deep dive into the five practices. In the next five chapters, you will learn more about the practices. We encourage you to keep a journal or notebook in which you can respond to questions that are posed and make note of questions you have. Such a journal can be helpful in conversations with other teachers or in reflecting from time to time about how your thinking is evolving and changing.

"One benefit of stating a clear math learning goal is just that it permeates the conversations that you're having and the questions that you're asking. It's just giving a focus to all your intentional movements within the class. "

—MATTHEW HARMON, HIGH SCHOOL MATHEMATICS TEACHER

CHAPTER 2

Setting Goals and Selecting Tasks

Before you can begin to work on the five practices, you must first set a goal for student learning and select a task that aligns with your goal. Smith and Stein (2018) have described this as *Practice 0*—a necessary step in which teachers must engage as they begin to plan a lesson that will feature a whole class discussion. As they explain,

> To have a productive mathematical discussion, teachers must first establish a clear and specific goal with respect to the mathematics to be learned and then select a high-level mathematical task. This is not to say that all tasks that are selected and used in the classroom must be high level, but rather that productive discussions that highlight key mathematical ideas are unlikely to occur if the task on which students are working requires limited thinking and reasoning. (Smith & Stein, 2018, p. 27)

In this chapter, we first unpack what is involved in setting goals and selecting tasks and illustrate what this practice looks like in an authentic high school classroom. We then explore challenges that teachers face in engaging in this practice and provide an opportunity for you to explore setting a goal and selecting a task in your own teaching practice.

Part One: Unpacking the Practice: Setting Goals and Selecting Tasks

What does it take to engage in this practice? This practice requires first specifying the learning goal for the lesson and then identifying a high-level task that aligns with the learning goal. Figure 2.1 highlights the components of this practice along with key questions to guide the process of setting goals and selecting a task.

Figure 2.1 • Key questions that support the practice of setting a goal and selecting a task

WHAT IT TAKES	KEY QUESTIONS
Specifying the learning goal	Does the goal focus on what students will learn about mathematics (as opposed to what they will do)?
Identifying a high-level task that aligns with the goal	Does your task provide students with the opportunity to think, reason, and problem solve?
	What resources will you provide students to ensure that all students can access the task?
	What will you take as evidence that students have met the goal through their work on this task?

In the sections that follow, we provide an illustration of this practice drawing on a lesson taught by Cori Moran in her Transition to College Math class, a course that prepares eleventh- and twelfth-grade students for college and career pathways that are not STEM intensive. As you read the description of what Ms. Moran thinks about and articulates while planning her lesson, consider how her attention to the key questions influences her planning.

Specifying the Learning Goal

Your first step in planning a lesson is specifying the goal(s). Consider Goals A and B for each of the mathematical ideas targeted in Figure 2.2. How are the goals the same and how are they different? Do you think the differences matter?

For each of the mathematical ideas targeted in Figure 2.2, the goal listed in Column A is considered a *performance goal*. Performance goals indicate what students will be able to do as a result of engaging in a lesson. By contrast, each of the goals listed in Column B is a *learning goal*. The learning goals explicitly state what students will understand about mathematics as a result of engaging in a particular lesson. The learning goal needs to be stated with sufficient specificity such that it can guide your decision making during the lesson (e.g., what task to select

Figure 2.2 • Different goals for learning specific mathematical ideas

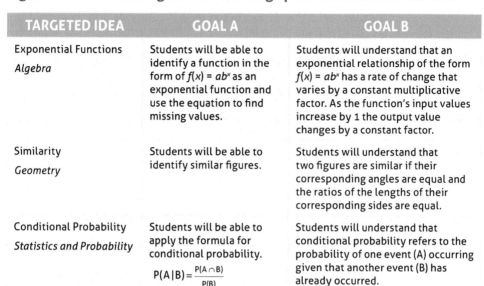

TARGETED IDEA	GOAL A	GOAL B
Exponential Functions *Algebra*	Students will be able to identify a function in the form of $f(x) = ab^x$ as an exponential function and use the equation to find missing values.	Students will understand that an exponential relationship of the form $f(x) = ab^x$ has a rate of change that varies by a constant multiplicative factor. As the function's input values increase by 1 the output value changes by a constant factor.
Similarity *Geometry*	Students will be able to identify similar figures.	Students will understand that two figures are similar if their corresponding angles are equal and the ratios of the lengths of their corresponding sides are equal.
Conditional Probability *Statistics and Probability*	Students will be able to apply the formula for conditional probability. $P(A \mid B) = \frac{P(A \cap B)}{P(B)}$	Students will understand that conditional probability refers to the probability of one event (A) occurring given that another event (B) has already occurred.

for students to work on, what questions to ask students as they work on the task, which solutions to have presented during the whole class discussion). According to Hiebert and his colleagues (2007),

> *Without explicit learning goals, it is difficult to know what counts as evidence of students' learning, how students' learning can be linked to particular instructional activities, and how to revise instruction to facilitate students' learning more effectively. Formulating clear, explicit learning goals sets the stage for everything else.* (p. 51)

In general, "the better the goals, the better our instructional decisions can be, and the greater the opportunity for improved student learning" (Mills, 2014, p. 2).

According to Hunt and Stein (in press), "too often, we define what mathematics we wish students to come to 'know' as performance, or what students will 'do,' absent the understandings that underlay their behaviors." If we want students to learn mathematics with understanding, we need to specify what exactly it is we expect them to understand about mathematics as a result of engaging in a lesson. Hence, goals you set for a lesson should focus on what is to be learned, not solely on performance.

Ms. Moran and her eleventh- and twelfth-grade students were working on a unit on polynomial functions. They had previously discussed what constitutes a term and defined a polynomial function as a mathematical function that is the sum of a number of terms. Since students had previously worked with linear functions, they had established that a linear function was a polynomial function of degree 1. In this lesson, students would be exploring quadratic functions, a specific type of polynomial function of degree 2. As a result of the lesson, Ms. Moran wanted her students to understand that

1. Quadratic functions may be characterized by two-dimensional growth.

2. Quadratic functions, unlike linear functions, do not have a constant rate of change.

3. Quadratic growth can be expressed in both recursive and explicit forms.

4. Quadratic growth can be modeled in a variety of ways—with a diagram in which width and height increase linearly, with a table where the second difference is constant, with a graph where the shape of a function is a parabola, and with an equation of degree 2.

The level of specificity at which Ms. Moran articulated the learning goals for the lessons will help her in identifying an appropriate task for her students, and subsequently, it will help her in asking questions that will move students toward the goal and in determining the extent to which students have learned what was intended. As Ms. Moran commented,

One of the benefits of setting clear goals is everything you do is a jumping point off from there. Once I set the goal, I knew what task I wanted to use, what questions I might ask, what solutions I might anticipate, and how I wanted to sequence solutions. I even could get some connecting questions ready. I was able to connect everything to those goals.

TEACHING TAKEAWAY

Specificity is one of the keys to setting learning goals and finding appropriately aligned tasks.

Identifying a High-Level Task That Aligns With the Goal

Your next step in planning a lesson is to select a high-level task that aligns with the learning goal. High-level or cognitively challenging mathematical tasks engage students in reasoning and problem solving and are essential in supporting students' learning mathematics with understanding. By contrast, low-level tasks—tasks that can be solved by applying rules and procedures—require limited thinking or understanding of the underlying mathematical concepts. According to Boston and Wilhelm (2015), "if opportunities for high-level thinking and reasoning are not embedded in instructional tasks, these opportunities rarely materialize during mathematics lessons" (p. 24). In addition, research provides evidence that students who have the opportunity to engage in high-level tasks on a regular basis show greater learning gains than students who engage primarily in low-level tasks during instruction (e.g., Boaler & Staples, 2008; Stein & Lane, 1996; Stigler & Hiebert, 2004).

Tasks that provide the richest basis for productive discussions have been referred to as *doing-mathematics* tasks. Such tasks are nonalgorithmic—no solution path is suggested or implied by the task and students cannot solve them by the simple application of a known rule. Hence students must explore the task to determine what it is asking them to do and develop and implement a plan drawing on prior knowledge and experience in order to solve the task (Smith & Stein, 1998). These tasks provide students with the opportunity to engage in the problem-solving process—understand the problem, devise a plan, carry out the plan, and look back (Polya, 2014). Central to this process is the opportunity for students to wrestle with mathematical ideas and relationships that are inherently part of the task.

While the level of cognitive demand is a critical consideration in selecting a task worthy of discussion, there are other characteristics that you should also consider when selecting a task. Specifically, you need to consider the following: the number of ways that the task can be accessed and solved, the extent to which justification or explanation is required, the different ways the mathematics can be represented and connected, and opportunities to look for patterns, make conjectures, and form generalizations. These characteristics are a hallmark of rich mathematical tasks and help ensure that students will have the opportunity to engage in the mathematics practices/processes (e.g., make sense of problems and persevere in solving them, reason abstractly and quantitatively, construct viable arguments, use repeated reasoning) that are viewed as essential to developing mathematical proficiency. When sizing up the potential of a task, keep in mind the questions shown in Figure 2.3. These questions will help you in selecting rich tasks that will make engagement in key mathematical practices and processes possible.

Figure 2.3 • Questions to help you *size up* the richness of a task

- Are there multiple ways to enter the task and to show competence?
- Does the task require students to provide a justification or explanation?
- Does the task provide the opportunity to use and make connections between different representations of a mathematical idea?
- Does the task provide the opportunity to look for patterns, make conjectures, and/or form generalizations?

Answering "yes" to each of these questions does not guarantee that students will engage in the mathematical practices. However, the use of the five practices, together with doing-mathematics tasks that have the characteristics described, will help ensure that this will occur. So rather than thinking about separate process goals, such as the Standards for Mathematical Practice advocated for in the Common Core State

Standards for Mathematics (National Governors Association Center for Best Practices & Council of Chief State School Officers, 2010), we encourage you to consider characteristics of tasks that will provide your students with the opportunities to engage in such processes.

For her lesson, Ms. Moran selected the Staircase task, shown in Figure 2.4, for several reasons. The task showed growth in two dimensions (i.e., the staircase was getting both taller and wider) and it could be solved in different ways and expressed in both recursive and explicit forms. The image of the growing staircase would provide students with an opportunity to concretely explore how the function was growing and how the stage number was related to the number of squares in the staircase for that stage. Ms. Moran also liked the fact that the questions provided scaffolding for students. The first two questions provided students with the opportunity to see how the staircase was changing and what a bigger staircase would look like if the pattern continued. To answer the third question, students would need to begin to move beyond the concrete and consider what the tenth staircase would look like given what had occurred with the first five staircases. The final question required students to generalize their findings in order to determine a function that would describe relationship between the total number of small squares in any stage and the stage number.

Figure 2.4 • The Staircase task

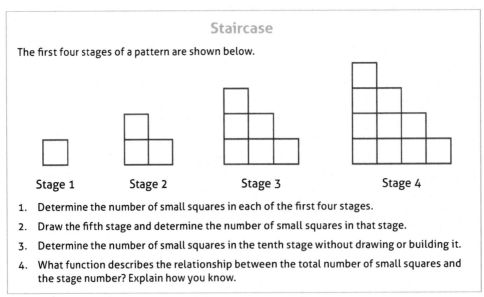

Staircase

The first four stages of a pattern are shown below.

Stage 1   Stage 2   Stage 3   Stage 4

1. Determine the number of small squares in each of the first four stages.
2. Draw the fifth stage and determine the number of small squares in that stage.
3. Determine the number of small squares in the tenth stage without drawing or building it.
4. What function describes the relationship between the total number of small squares and the stage number? Explain how you know.

 This task can also be accessed at **resources.corwin.com/5practices-highschool**

To ensure that students would have access to the task, Ms. Moran planned to provide students with a cup containing two different colors of square tiles they could use to build staircases at different stages, extra paper, markers, and physical and digital graphing resources. She would leave it up to the students to decide which, if any of these resources, would be useful. In addition to these material resources, Ms. Moran also decided that she would provide "human" resources by having students work on the task in groups so that they would have others with whom to confer.

When asked what students would say, do, or produce that would provide evidence of their understanding of the goals in the lesson through their work on this task, Ms. Moran indicated that students would do the following:

- state the number of square tiles in each of the stages (e.g., stage 4 has 10 square tiles, stage 5 has 15 square tiles, stage 10 has 55 square tiles);

- recognize that the staircase is growing in two dimensions—that it was getting both wider and taller;

- notice that the rate of change is not constant so it could not be linear;

- relate the stage number to the number of squares in a stage by making more familiar shapes from the squares in a particular stage; and

- make the connection that because the staircase was growing in two dimensions that the equation will contain a x^2 term.

Cori Moran's Attention to Key Questions: Setting Goals and Selecting Tasks

During her initial stage of lesson planning, Ms. Moran paid careful attention to the key questions. First, in setting her goals for the lesson, she clearly articulated what it was she wanted students to learn about mathematics as a result of engaging in the task. The specificity with which she stated her goals made it possible to determine what students understood about these ideas and to formulate questions that would help move her students forward. In addition to wanting her students to write a function that would describe the relationship between the number of squares in a stage and the stage number, she also wanted to make sure they understood what makes a function quadratic and how to recognize a quadratic function in different representational forms.

Second, she identified a high-level *doing-mathematics* task that aligned with her goals. Students could not solve the Staircase task by applying a known rule or procedure because the task required students to look for the underlying structure of the pattern of growth and use the identified pattern to generalize to other stages in the pattern. Ms. Moran *sized up* the task (see Figure 2.3) to ensure that it had several other important characteristics. Specifically, there were a number of approaches that students could use to enter the task (e.g., making a table showing the stage number and the number of squares in the stage, using square tiles to build specific stages, adding to or rearranging the square tiles in a stage to form a shape that could be more easily described) and the material and human resources that the teacher planned to provide would support their work. The task made it possible for students to use different representations— build a model, make a table, create an equation, and "explain how you know" (question 4). Finally, the task asked students to generalize their findings by describing the relationship between the stage number and the number of squares in the stage. Hence through their work on the task, students could learn important mathematics and engage in key practices.

The Staircase task, along with the resources the teacher made available to students, allowed all students to enter the task at some level. Rather than differentiating instruction by providing different students with different tasks, she selected one task and met the needs of different learners by providing resources for students to consider and questions that would challenge learners at different levels.

Finally, Ms. Moran indicated some things that she expected students to say and do that would provide evidence students were making progress on the ideas she wanted them to learn. By considering this evidence in advance of the lesson, she was ready to pay close attention to students' work for indications that they were making progress in their understanding.

Through her careful attention to setting goals and selecting a task, Ms. Moran's planning was off to a productive start and she was ready to engage in the five practices. In the next chapter we will continue to investigate her planning process as she anticipates what she thinks her students will do when presented with the task and how she will respond. We now turn our attention to the challenges that teachers face in setting goals and selecting tasks.

Part Two: Challenges Teachers Face: Setting Goals and Selecting Tasks

As we described in the chapter opening, setting goals and selecting tasks is foundational to orchestrating productive discussions. Setting goals and selecting tasks, however, is not without its challenges. In this section, we focus on four specific challenges associated with this practice, shown in Figure 2.5, that we have identified from our work with teachers.

Figure 2.5 • Challenges associated with the practice of setting goals and selecting tasks

CHALLENGE	DESCRIPTION
Identifying learning goals	Goal needs to focus on what students will learn as a result of engaging in the task, not on what students will do. Clarity on goals sets the stage for everything else!
Identifying a doing-mathematics task	While *doing-mathematics* tasks provide the greatest opportunities for student learning, they are not readily available in some textbooks. Teachers may need to adapt an existing task, find a task in another resource, or create a task.
Ensuring alignment between task and goals	Even with learning goals specified, teachers may select a task that does not allow students to make progress on those particular goals.
Launching a task to ensure student access	Teachers need to provide access to the context and the mathematics in the launch but not so much that the mathematical demands are reduced and key ideas are *given away*.

Identifying Learning Goals

Identifying learning goals is a challenging but critical first step in planning any lesson. It is challenging because we often focus on what students are going to be able to do as a result of engaging in a lesson, not on what they are going to learn about mathematics.

Consider, for example, the lesson that Michael Moore, one of our three featured teachers, was planning for his geometry students. When Mr. Moore initially planned the lesson, he indicated that he wanted students to "identify similar triangles and use their properties to solve problems." He selected the Floodlight Shadows task, shown in Figure 2.6, to accomplish this goal. Given time constraints, Mr. Moore planned to focus on questions 1 and 2 in one class period and reserve work on question 3 for the following day.

During a discussion about the lesson Mr. Moore was planning around the first two questions in the task, his colleagues pointed out that his goal was fairly broad. One of the teachers asked Mr. Moore if he could explain what he would be looking and listening for as students worked that would help him know if the students were meeting his goal. Mr. Moore first focused on the creation of the mathematical model of the geometric situation, since the creation of the model was what would allow students to start discussing similar triangles. Through the discussion with his colleagues, it became clear to Mr. Moore that the creation of a scale model or drawing was a critical step in moving students toward an exploration of similarity and should be a part of his goals. He explained that he wanted students to "see how those ideas actually show up in a model." As the conversation with his peers continued, Mr. Moore was able to clarify in detail what understandings of mathematics students would need to solve

Figure 2.6 • The Floodlight Shadows task

Floodlight Shadows

Eliot is playing football.

He is 6 feet tall.

He stands exactly half way between two floodlights.

The floodlights are 12 yards high and 50 yards apart.

The floodlights give Eliot two shadows, falling in opposite directions.

1. Draw a diagram to represent this situation.

    Label your diagram with the measurements.

2. Find the total length of Eliot's shadows.

    Explain your reasoning in detail.

3. Suppose Eliot walks in a straight line toward one of the floodlights.

    Figure out what happens to the total length of Eliot's shadows.

    Explain your reasoning in detail.

Source: This task is part of a carefully engineered lesson "Deducing Relationships: Floodlight Shadows" from the Mathematics Assessment Project, which can be downloaded for free from mathshell.org

 A link to this task can be accessed at **resources.corwin.com/5practices-highschool**

the Floodlight Shadows task. As a result, he was able to provide more specificity regarding what he wanted students to learn from the lesson and what he might be looking for in their work. Specifically, as a result of engaging in the lesson, Mr. Moore wanted his students to understand that

1. creating mathematical models of geometric situations is helpful in identifying key features that can be used to make mathematical arguments;

2. similar triangles are related in two ways: their corresponding angles are congruent, and the lengths of their corresponding sides are related by a common scale factor; and

3. justifying that two triangles are similar means making arguments about the ways in which corresponding angles are congruent, and corresponding sides are scaled using ideas such as corresponding parts of triangles and scale factor.

Mr. Moore also noted that the task had many features that would provide opportunities for his students to engage in the standards for mathematical practices (National Governors Association Center for Best Practices & Council of Chief State School Officers, 2010), including creating viable arguments using geometry properties as well as modeling with mathematics. With new clarity regarding what he wanted students to understand, Mr. Moore was now ready to anticipate how students would engage with the task and prepare questions that would help him illuminate what his students understood about these ideas as they worked through the lesson.

Why does this level of specificity matter? It matters because with this level of specificity, the teacher will be able to better listen for key student ideas and ask questions that draw students' attention to the meaningful features of the diagram without giving them a step-by-step recipe for determining similarity. When Mr. Moore interacts with his students as they work on the task, he can ask them where they see different triangles in the visual model. He can press them to consider how the triangles might be related, what features are the same across the triangles, and what features are different. He can also ask questions that aim to move students from judging the triangles as similar through visual inspection to creating a mathematical argument for that similarity using ideas about angle measures, side measures, and scale factor. By paying attention to how students will use the resources in the task and their visual diagrams to build rigorous similarity arguments, Mr. Moore will be able to determine what his students understand about the meaning of similarity in triangles and the relationships between similarity and dilations. This information will then help him in planning subsequent lessons in the unit to continue to develop the broader themes about dilations. (See Hunt and Stein [in press] for a description of three interconnected phases—defining a goal, unpacking the mathematics and refining the goal, and relating goals to pedagogy—that teachers can use individually or collaboratively to create and refine goals for student learning.)

While posting goals in the classroom has become commonplace, you might wonder if a goal at the level of depth and detail as the one Mr. Moore created is one that should be shared with students. You will often find that the mathematical goals you created to guide your decision making during a lesson need to be different from the mathematical goal you share with your students. The mathematical goal you choose to share with your students should focus their learning and communicate what is expected of them within the lesson without providing too much direction or guidance.

For the Floodlight Shadows task, for example, you might share the following goal with students: *Today, we will make mathematical arguments about relationships between triangles in a contextual situation.* A goal such as this explicitly connects to important aspects of prior knowledge by signaling that students will be doing work with triangles. The goal stops short of specifying that students will be determining similarity, so it leaves the question of what relationship exists between the triangles students will create as an open question for exploration. The goal also calls attention to making mathematical arguments a key mathematical practice at the heart of the lesson. On the whole, this goal focuses students on important content and processes that will be useful to them in the lesson, while still leaving significant exploratory territory for students to work within as they do the mathematics through engagement in the task.

Identifying a Doing-Mathematics Task

While doing-mathematics tasks provide the optimal vehicle for whole class discussions, not all curricular materials are replete with such tasks. Traditional textbooks tend to feature more procedural tasks that provide limited opportunities for reasoning and problem solving. While such resources do include *word problems*, they are often solved using procedures that have been previously introduced and modeled and require limited thinking. While standards-based texts (Senk & Thompson, 2003) contain some procedural tasks, they also include high-level tasks that promote reasoning and problem solving.

While there are many ways to provide high-level tasks to your students, such as finding tasks in other resources, adapting existing tasks, or creating your own task, using a curriculum that contains a wide variety of doing-mathematics tasks is the optimal choice for a number of reasons. First, it's simply a little bit less work for you as a teacher! But perhaps more importantly, standards-based curricula have been carefully crafted to develop important mathematical ideas with focus, rigor, and coherence. These curricula typically have thoughtful author teams made up of mathematicians and mathematics educators, undergo significant field testing and revision, and represent the current best thinking on ways to organize students' mathematical learning. The sampling of high school curricula, shown in Figure 2.7, contains a high number of doing-mathematics tasks; those marked with an asterisk have their genesis in the set of National Science Foundation–funded curricula of the mid-1990s.

Figure 2.7 • A sampling of high school curricula that contains high-level mathematics tasks

Commercially Available Curricula

- Contemporary Mathematics in Context (CORE-Plus)

  (https://www.mheducation.com/prek-12/program/core-plus-mathematics-20152015/MKTSP-QRE07M0.html)*

- Interactive Mathematics Program (IMP)

  (http://activatelearning.com/interactive-mathematics-program-imp/)*

Open Source/Free Curricula

- Open Up Resources High School Mathematics/Illustrative Mathematics

  (https://openupresources.org/math-curriculum/high-school/)

- MathMontana (formerly SIMMS Integrated Mathematics)

  (https://mathmontana.org)*

- Mathematics Vision Project

  (https://mathematicsvisionproject.org/)

If you are using a resource that does not include high-level tasks, what should you do? First and foremost, we encourage you to consider advocating for the adoption of a curricular resource with high-level tasks with your district during your next adoption cycle (or before!). In the meantime, in this section we explore three possible options for finding high-level tasks—adapt an existing task, find a task in another resource, or create your own task.

Adapting an Existing Task

Some textbook tasks either give students too much information and leave little for students to figure out on their own or ask students to simply recall and apply a previously learned rule. In such cases, you may want to consider adapting the task so as to provide more thinking opportunities for students. This section provides two examples of adapted tasks: the Binomial Expansion task shown in Figure 2.8 and the Heights of Dinosaurs task shown in Figure 2.9. Binomial Expansion is an example of a task with a fairly simple modification that provides opportunities for additional student reasoning. Heights of Dinosaurs is an example of a more extensive modification to remove unnecessary scaffolding and hence provide more opportunities for students to determine what to do and how to do it.

Grace Sullivan was working on a unit on quadratics, and she wanted her students to understand and be able to use a variety of representations and procedures for expanding and simplifying polynomials. She wanted students to feel comfortable using different methods, but also to understand why those methods worked and to be able to make connections between them. When she found the original Binomial Expansion task (shown in Figure 2.8), she was pleased to see that her textbook resource was also focusing on multiple representations. She decided to make a simple modification to the task—to ask students to compare two of the methods and relate them to the broader context of how the methods are helpful in determining the product.

Ms. Sullivan's modification of the task was relatively simple and did not require much time to complete. By asking students to compare two of the methods, she would be able to get additional information on how students were making sense of the different methods and of the broader concepts of multiplying binomials. For example, comparing the distributive property and FOIL methods would afford students the opportunity to see that FOIL isn't simply a memorized shortcut, but a double application of the distributive property. The algebra tile method would allow students to see that the binomial factors can be represented as the dimensions of a rectangle and the area can be connected to the products in any of the other three methods. The vertical method provides an important connection to whole-number multiplication, which brings conceptual understanding

TEACHING TAKEAWAY

If your textbook does not provide worthwhile tasks for discussion, you have options: adapt, find, or create your own!

Figure 2.8 • The Binomial Expansion task

Binomial Expansion Task—Original	Binomial Expansion Task—Modified
Show how to find $(3x + 4)(2x - 5)$ using each method:	Show how to find $(3x + 4)(2x - 5)$ using each method:
a. Distributive property	a. Distributive property
b. FOIL method	b. FOIL method
c. Vertical or column method	c. Vertical or column method
d. Algebra tiles	d. Algebra tiles
	Choose two of the methods a–d and for each of the selected methods describe: (1) the ways in which they are similar and different; and (2) how they both show the product.

Source: Holliday et al. (2005), *Algebra I*, p. 455, #2.

 This modified task can also be accessed at **resources.corwin.com/5practices-highschool**

and meaning to the other methods. By adding in a simple modification to the task, the opportunities to strengthen the understanding and build procedural fluency from conceptual understanding are heightened.

When George Jacobson saw the Heights of Dinosaurs task in the instructional materials for his Algebra II with Statistics course (Figure 2.9), he noticed that it walked students through a series of steps. He wondered if his students might get caught up in the mechanical details and lose the bigger mathematical idea—namely, in what ways does a data distribution help us understand what's typical in a data set? Mr. Jacobson decided to modify the task so that his students would be able to do more thinking and reasoning. Toward that end, he wanted to pose the question, "How tall was a compy?" at the start of the investigation rather than saving it until the end. This way, the question would motivate students' mathematical investigations.

Figure 2.9 • Heights of Dinosaurs task

Example 1: Heights of Dinosaurs and the Normal Curve

A paleontologist studies prehistoric life and sometimes works with dinosaur fossils. The table below shows the distribution of heights (rounded to the nearest centimeter) of 660 procompsognathids, otherwise known as compys.

Compsognathus (dinosaur image) created by Nobu Tamura, http://spinops.blogspot.com. CC BY 2.5
https://creativecommons.org/licenses/by/2.5/

The heights were determined by studying the fossil remains of the compys.

Height (cm)	Number of Compys	Relative Frequency
26	1	0.002
27	5	0.008
28	12	0.018
29	22	0.033
30	40	0.061
31	60	0.091
32	90	0.136
33	100	0.152
34	100	0.152
35	90	0.136
36	60	0.091
37	40	0.061
38	22	0.033
39	12	0.018
40	5	0.008
41	1	0.002
Total	660	1.000*

*The values above add to 1.002; this discrepancy is due to rounding.

Exercises 1–8

The following is a relative frequency histogram of the compy heights:

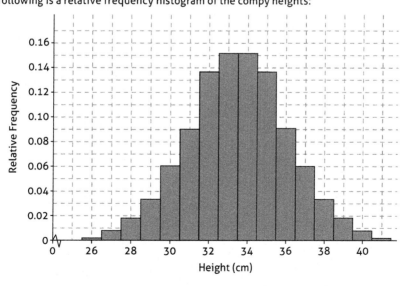

(Continued)

Figure 2.9 (*Continued*)

1. What does the relative frequency of 0.136 mean for the height of 32 cm?

2. What is the width of each bar? What does the height of the bar represent?

3. What is the area of the bar that represents the relative frequency for compys with a height of 32 cm?

4. The mean of the distribution of compy heights is 33.5 cm, and the standard deviation is 2.56 cm. Interpret the mean and standard deviation in this context.

5. Mark the mean on the graph, and mark *one* deviation above and below the mean.

   a. Approximately what percent of the values in this data set are within one standard deviation of the mean

      (i.e., between 33.5 cm – 2.56 cm = 30.94 cm and 33.5 cm + 2.56 cm = 36.06 cm)?

   b. Approximately what percent of the values in this data set are within *two* standard deviations of the mean?

6. Draw a smooth curve that comes reasonably close to passing through the midpoints of the tops of the bars in the histogram. Describe the shape of the distribution.

7. Shade the area of the histogram that represents the proportion of heights that are within one standard deviation of the mean.

8. Based on our analysis, how would you answer the question, "How tall was a compy?"

Source: Lesson 9: Using a Curve to Model a Data Distribution, Eureka Math. Copyright © 2016 by Great Minds. Allrights reserved.

Mr. Jacobson also felt that the task could be launched in a more engaging way. When students typically think of dinosaurs, they think of beasts far larger than humans. Yet the compy data show that these dinosaurs were closer in size to mid-sized birds. Mr. Jacobson remembered that these dinosaurs were featured in a memorable scene in the film *The Lost World: Jurassic Park II* and searched online for a video clip that might help to motivate the task. Inspired by the Three-Act Task format popularized by Dan Meyer (http://threeacts .mrmeyer.com) and Robert Kaplinsky (http://robertkaplinsky.com), the teacher thought that asking students to make observations, determine an inquiry of focus (i.e., how tall was a typical compy?), and decide what data they might need to have to answer that question would provide them with ownership and increase student motivation and engagement, rather than just handing students the compy height data set and having them get started.

Drawing on these ideas, Mr. Jacobson developed the Compy Attack! lesson. His slides and some notes about them are shown in Figure 2.10.

Figure 2.10 • Slides Mr. Jacobson prepared for launching the Compy Attack! lesson

COMPY ATTACK!

Act 1

This is a behind-the-scenes clip that describes how special effects were created for a scene from The Lost World: Jurassic Park II. The dinosaurs you see here are based on *procompsognathids*, or compys.
What do you notice?
What do you wonder about?

(likely responses: they're small, were they real, how quickly do they move, could they really eat a person, etc.)

If it doesn't explicitly come out, pose the question: How tall do you think the typical compy is? What information would we need to find out?

(Continued)

Figure 2.10 (*Continued*)

Act 1

What is the typical size of a compy dinosaur?
(Were they *really* the size in the movie, or was that just for effect?)

■ What information and tools would you need to make a decision?

The heights were determined by studying the fossil remains of the compys.

Height (cm)	Number of Compys	Relative Frequency
26	1	0.002
27	5	0.008
28	12	0.018
29	22	0.033
30	40	0.061
31	60	0.091
32	90	0.136
33	100	0.152
34	100	0.152
35	90	0.136
36	60	0.091
37	40	0.061
38	22	0.033
39	12	0.018
40	5	0.008
41	1	0.002
Total	660	1.00

Act 2

How tall is a typical compy?

Use the statistical tools you have at your disposal to make a determination.

Present the fossil data on compys.

Anticipated strategies:

- Create histogram (fairly straightforward based on the data)
- Find mean and standard deviation
- Find the median
- Take the modal values as typical (33–34 cm)
- Identify the boundary values for ±1SD, ±2SD of the mean
- Take into consideration the shape of the distribution – it is skewed? Is the mean the right measure to use?
  (draw a normal curve)

Act 3

Present your group's findings.
Were compys accurately portrayed in the movie?

Discuss what a reasonable typical value for the height of a compy might be. Show final produced clip, discuss whether what's shown on the screen accurately represents the creatures (31–36cm seems typical and the clip seems to accurately portray that typical size)
https://www.youtube.com/watch?v=uPQwNE4OsIE

Source: Adapted from Lesson 9: Using a Curve to Model a Data Distribution, Eureka Math. Copyright © 2016 by Great Minds. All rights reserved. Act 1 image source: THE LOST WORLD: JURASSIC PARK Compy Attack (Youtube) via Stan Winston School. Act 3 image *Source:* Dinosaur attack in Jurassic Park 2 (Youtube) via Richard Stenger.

This modified task can also be accessed at
resources.corwin.com/5practices-highschool

In comparing the original task to the modified task, you will see that Mr. Jacobson made the following changes:

- The question about the height of a typical compy ends Act 1 and motivates the investigation, rather than being the end point of the work.

- Rather than stepping students through a series of statistics calculations, the task asks them to use any statistical tools they choose to make their argument.

- Some additional motivation is provided for the launch and summary of the task using video clips.

- Students have multiple pathways available to them to identify what is typical and to justify their thinking.

By making these changes, Mr. Jacobson transformed a low-level task into a doing-mathematics task. In addition, his modified task has the additional characteristics we previously discussed—it can be entered and solved in several different ways, it requires students to use and make connections between different representations, it asks students to explain their thinking, and it asks students to generalize. (See Arbaugh, Smith,

Boyle, Stylianides, & Steele, 2019; Boyle & Kaiser, 2017; and Smith & Stein, 2018 for more insight on how to modify tasks.)

Finding a Task in Another Resource

You can find high-level doing-mathematics tasks in many print and electronic resources. The challenge is to find a task that meets your mathematical goals, is accessible to your students, has the potential to advance their learning beyond their current level, and fits with the content and flow of your curriculum.

For example, Michael Moore went to the Mathematics Assessment Project website (https://www.map.mathshell.org) to see if he could find a task that would help him reach the goals he had set for the lesson. He was familiar with the site and knew that it contained interesting tasks as well as complete lessons. He selected the Floodlight Shadows lesson, which included a detailed lesson plan. While he did not follow the plan as a script, it helped him think through how he wanted to orchestrate his lesson. By contrast, Kendra Nelson, who you will meet in the example that follows, selected the Triple Trouble task from a set of related lessons (Algebra II Lesson Set: Building Polynomial Functions) that the district had purchased. The advantage of this resource is that it contained a set of eight related tasks that as a collection had the potential to develop students' conceptual understanding of polynomial functions. So in addition to using the Triple Trouble task, Ms. Nelson could also consider the tasks that followed it in the sequence to continue the exploration of polynomial functions. (See Appendix A for a list of web and print resources that may be helpful to you in finding doing-mathematics tasks.)

Ms. Nelson's Algebra II class had been working with families of functions for most of the quarter. They had explored and compared linear, quadratic, and exponential functions, and Ms. Nelson was looking for a good bridge into the unit introducing polynomial functions. Unfortunately, most of what she found in her textbook strongly emphasized symbolic manipulation and did not provide students multiple entry points. She knew based on their previous work that her students brought a diverse set of skills to the table when it came to functions. Some students were extremely adept at graphing and making sense of a function visually, others focused on tables and numeric values, and several gravitated toward algebraic notation and manipulation. Ms. Nelson felt that the unit needed a broader variety of entry points that focused on making meaning of functions. As a result of engaging in this first lesson, Ms. Nelson wanted her students to understand the following:

- The key features of polynomial functions—x-intercepts/ roots, y-intercepts, local and absolute minima and maxima, and discontinuities—can be identified using multiple representations (equation, table, graph).

- The product of two or more polynomial functions is a polynomial function. The product function will have the same *x*-intercepts as the original functions.

- Two or more polynomial functions can be combined using addition, subtraction, or multiplication using their graphs or tables, because given two functions $f(x)$ and $g(x)$ and their associated numerical values, the sum, difference, or product of the two functions will be on the graph and the table as a specific value, *x*, and the values of the sum, difference, or product of the two functions, $f(x)$ and $g(x)$.

Ms. Nelson's district math leader suggested that she take a look through an ancillary print resource the district had purchased, which included sets of related lessons (including lesson guides) for some high school units. The Triple Trouble task (shown in Figure 2.11) was immediately compelling to Ms. Nelson. The task brought together a number of important elements that she expected would help students make a strong transition to thinking about polynomial functions. It began with two function families that were very familiar to her students—linear and quadratic. The task culminated in finding a new function, which would be cubic, that was the product of these two functions. Rather than jumping right into the symbolic work, the task asked students to evaluate four claims that fictional students made about the characteristics of $h(x)$.

Figure 2.11 • The Triple Trouble Task

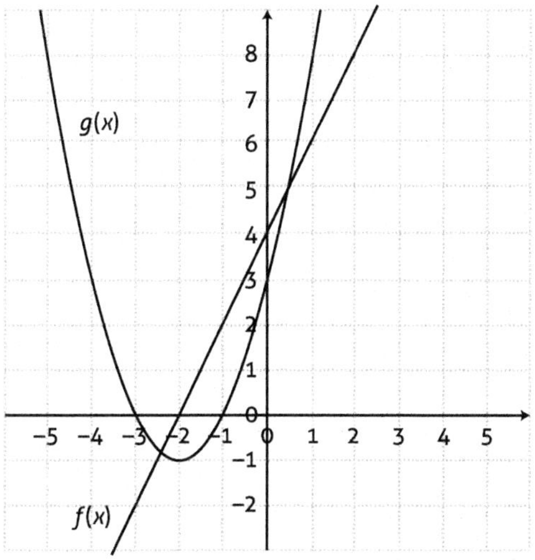

(Continued)

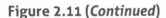

Figure 2.11 (*Continued*)

Consider the two functions shown in the graph. Let $h(x) = f(x) \cdot g(x)$.

1. David, Theresa, Manuel, and Joy are working in a group together to determine the key characteristics of $h(x)$. They each make a prediction. Decide whether you agree or disagree with each student's prediction. Use mathematics to justify your position.

   a. David: $h(x)$ will be a parabola.

   b. Theresa: $h(x)$ will have a y-intercept at (0, 12).

   c. Manuel: $h(x)$ will have negative y-values over the interval $-2 \le x \le -1$.

   d. Joy: $h(x)$ will have three x-intercepts.

2. Sketch a graph of $h(x)$ on the coordinate plane. Then identify key characteristics of the graph (zeros, y-intercept, maximum/minimum values, end behavior) and explain how each characteristic results from key characteristics of $f(x)$ and $g(x)$.

3. Determine the equation of $h(x)$. Justify your answer in terms of $f(x)$ and $g(x)$.

Source: Institute for Learning (2017). Lesson guides and student workbooks available at ifl.pitt.edu.

In working through the task on her own, Ms. Nelson identified a number of strategies that could be used to evaluate each of the four claims. Moreover, approaches that worked well for some claims were not as effective in evaluating other claims. For example, the first claim could be effectively argued from a conceptual understanding of functions, noting that a first-order (linear) function multiplied by a second-order (quadratic) function would result in a third-order (cubic) function, and therefore David's claim is wrong. The third claim about negative values between $x = -2$ and $x = -1$, in contrast, could be effectively justified by examining the range of the two functions over that interval and making a numerical argument about the products of negative and positive numbers, and therefore Manuel's claim is correct.

The second and third questions in the task would allow groups to draw together their observations from evaluating the claims into a more comprehensive picture of the function $h(x)$. The key features could be identified using a variety of the approaches that were useful in evaluating the claims in question 1. Finally, question 3 asks students to create the equation for $h(x)$. By positioning the more mechanical symbolic work at the end of the task, students would be more likely to make connections between the conceptual understanding of functions, the key features of the function as represented in the sketched graph, and the symbolic representation of the function. This would provide an excellent entry point into the broader unit on polynomials.

A note of caution here. There are many good tasks available electronically and in print (including those described in Appendix A) that could be interesting explorations for students. However, students develop an understanding of mathematical ideas as the result of engaging in

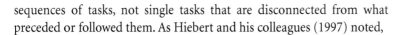

sequences of tasks, not single tasks that are disconnected from what preceded or followed them. As Hiebert and his colleagues (1997) noted,

> [The] teacher's role in selecting tasks goes well beyond choosing good individual tasks, one after another. Teachers need to select sequences of tasks so that, over time, students' experiences add up to something important. Teachers need to consider the residue left behind by sets of tasks, not just individual tasks. (p. 31)

Creating a Task

If you cannot find a task you want to use, you may decide to create one yourself. This was the case for Denise Hansen. Ms. Hansen's students were beginning a unit on probability. She wanted her students to understand the notion of sample space as the set of all possible outcomes and the Fundamental Principle of Counting as a way to determine the number of outcomes. This would lay the groundwork for the investigation of more advanced probability concepts in subsequent lessons. Specifically, through their work on the task, Ms. Hansen wanted students to understand that if one event could happen m different ways and another event could happen n different ways, then the number of outcomes for both events together would be $m \times n$.

While Ms. Hansen's textbook started the unit with students rolling dice and flipping coins, she decided that she wanted to select a context that students would immediately relate to. Toward this end, she created the Lunch Options task shown in Figure 2.12, which was based on the lunch menu in the school cafeteria that day. By starting with question 1, which students could solve by listing all the outcomes and counting, and ending with question 5 that could not be easily modeled or listed, Ms. Hansen was pressing students to generalize their findings so that determining the number of You Pick Two options would be a simple matter of multiplying $7 \times 19 \times 3$.

Figure 2.12 • Lunch Options task

Lunch Options

The Hot Entrée Combo in the cafeteria includes your choice of an entrée with 1 side and a drink for $6.50. Today's selections are shown below.

Entrée	Sides	Drinks
• Baked ziti with meat	• Steamed broccoli	• Milk
• Baked ziti with veggies	• Caesar salad	• Water
	• Garlic breadsticks	• Apple juice
	• Chicken soup	

(Continued)

Figure 2.12 (*Continued*)

1. How many different lunch combinations are there? Explain how you figured it out and how you know you have them all.

2. Suppose the combo also included a choice of 2 desserts: a peanut butter cookie or a chocolate brownie. How many different lunch combinations would there be then? How do you know?

3. Compare your answers to the first two questions. How are they different? Explain.

4. How many different combinations do you think you will have if you now add a choice of a peppermint or spearmint candy to your combo? Explain.

5. Panera Bread™ offers You Pick Two™, which includes a choice of 2 half portions from the following list: soup, macaroni, salad, and sandwich. You decide to have soup and a sandwich. There are 7 different soups and 19 different sandwiches. In addition, you can select a side of an apple, chips, or a baguette. Drawing on your work on the first four questions, determine how many different combinations you could put together.

 This task can also be accessed at **resources.corwin.com/5practices-highschool**

Because it cannot be solved by using a known rule or procedure, thus requiring students to reason and problem solve, Lunch Options is a doing-mathematics task. The task has other characteristics that make it a good choice for the lesson as previously described:

- It can be entered and solved in several different ways (e.g., make a list of possible combinations, model the situation, make a drawing, describe in words what is happening).

- It asks students to explain their thinking, not just provide an answer.

- The task provides the opportunity for students to make connections between a visual representation (tree diagram) and a numerical representation ($m \times n$).

- In order to answer question 5, students need to look back at their work on the first four questions, identify a pattern, and then use the pattern to determine the number of You Pick Two combinations.

While creating tasks is certainly an option, it is a challenging endeavor! If you decide to create a task yourself, we encourage you to ask others to review and solve the task so that you can identify any possible pitfalls before you give it to students. This is exactly what Ms. Hansen did with the Lunch Options task!

Ensuring Alignment Between Task and Goals

Another challenge teachers often face is making sure that there is alignment between the task and goals—that is, ensuring that the task they have selected as the basis for instruction provides students with the opportunity to explore the mathematical ideas that are targeted during the lesson.

As we described in Part One of this chapter, Ms. Moran was clear about what she wanted her students to learn about mathematics (not just what they would do) and she selected a high-level doing-mathematics task that was consistent with her learning goals. This combination of a high-level task and a clear learning goal is optimal for providing students with the opportunity to learn mathematics with understanding.

But what would it look like to have a mismatch, and what implications does this have for instruction and learning? Suppose, for example, you are teaching a lesson on exponential functions. You decide that you want students to understand that an exponential relationship, of the form $f(x) = ab^x$, has a rate of change that varies by a constant multiplicative factor; as the function's input values increase by 1 the output value changes by a constant factor (Goal B in the first row of Figure 2.2). You select the Evaluate the Functions task shown in Figure 2.13, which asks students to find the value of y give a value for x. This basic *naked numbers* task does not provide students the opportunity to develop an understanding of situations that can be represented by exponential functions, what "b" and "x" mean in context, or what it means for the output to change by a constant factor as the input increases by 1 unit. As a result, students may end up with correct or incorrect solutions but it would not be clear (to them or to you) whether they had a clear understanding of the targeted mathematical idea. In this situation, you have established a *learning* goal but have paired it with a low-level task that requires students to only apply their knowledge of exponents and the order of operations. If your goal had been for students to find values for y given values for a, b, and x (Goal A in the first row of Figure 2.2), then the low-level task would be a good match for this goal.

Figure 2.13 • Evaluate the Functions task

Evaluate each of the functions.

1. $f(x) = 4^x$ at $x = \dfrac{1}{2}$

2. $f(x) = \left(\dfrac{1}{2}\right)^x$ at $x = 5$

3. $f(x) = (10)2^x$ at $x = -2$

4. $f(x) = \left(\dfrac{1}{5}\right)\left(\dfrac{1}{3}\right)^x$ at $x = 3$

5. $f(x) = (-5)5^x$ at $x = 4$

If you want students to understand that an exponential function has a rate of change that varies by a constant multiplicative factor (as the function's input values increase by 1 the output value changes by a constant factor), then a better choice would be a task such as the one shown in

Figure 2.14. The Family Tree task provides a context for making sense of and modeling an exponential growth situation and is a good introductory task. Students are free to create drawings, graphs, or tables in order to explore growth from one generation to the previous one. In solving the task, students have the opportunity to discover that the number of "great" grandparents doubles every time you go back one additional generation and that the number of "great" grandparents can be found by multiplying 2 by the number of the of the generation (2^x). Through work on a problem such as the Family Tree, students can come to understand what an exponential function is and what each of the variables represents.

Figure 2.14 • The Family Tree task

Family Tree

Ramona was examining the family tree her mother had created using Ancestry.com, a website you can use to explore your genealogy. When examining a family tree, the branches are many. Ramona is generation "now." One generation ago, her 2 parents were born. Two generations ago, her 4 grandparents were born. Three generations ago, her great-grandparents were born. Four generations ago, her great-great-grandparents were born. Every time she went back another generation, another "great" was added!

1. How many of Ramona's great-grandparents were born 3 generations ago?

2. How many of Ramona's "great" grandparents were born 10 generations ago?

3. Explain how Ramona could figure out how many "great" grandparents were born in any number of generations ago.

4. Is the number of "great" grandparents in any generation a function of the generation? Why or why not? How do you know?

 This task can also be accessed at
resources.corwin.com/5practices-highschool

Ensuring alignment between your goals and task is essential and the foundation on which to begin to engage in the five practices. If you find that your task does not fit your goals, consider the ways in which you can modify the task in order to provide more opportunities for students to think and reason as we described previously.

Launching a Task to Ensure Student Access

Launching or setting up a task refers to what the teacher does prior to having students begin work on a task. While it is not uncommon to see teachers hand out a task, ask a student volunteer to read the task aloud, and then tell students what they are expected to produce as a result of the work on the task, research suggests that attention to the way in which the task is launched can lead to a more successful discussion at the end of the lesson. Jackson and her colleagues (Jackson, Shahan, Gibbons, & Cobb, 2012) describe the benefits of an effective launch:

> Students are much more likely to be able to get started solving a complex task, thereby enabling the teacher to attend to students' thinking and plan for a concluding whole-class discussion. This, in turn, increases the chances that all students will be supported to learn significant mathematics as they solve and discuss the task. (p. 28)

So what constitutes an effective launch? In Analyzing the Work of Teaching 2.1, you will explore Ms. Moran's launch of the Staircase task. We invite you to engage in the analysis of a video clip and consider the questions posed before you read our analysis. [NOTE: While the launch of a task occurs during instruction, it is planned for prior to instruction. Rather than describing what Ms. Moran intended to do, we decided to take you into her classroom so that you could see for yourself!]

Analyzing the Work of Teaching 2.1

Launching a Task

Video Clip 2.1
In this activity, you will watch Video Clip 2.1 from Cori Moran's Transition to College Math class. As you watch the clip, consider the following questions:

- What did the teacher do to help her students *get ready* to work on the Staircase task?

- What did the teacher learn about her students that indicated they were ready to engage in the task?

- Do you think the time spent in launching the task was time well spent?

 Videos may also be accessed at
resources.corwin.com/5practices-highschool

Launching a Task—Analysis

Ms. Moran began the lesson by showing students the images of the first four stages of the staircase on the interactive whiteboard and asking students what patterns they noticed. There are two aspects of this introduction that are important. First, by not immediately giving students access to the entire task, students' attention was focused only on the images and not on the questions they would subsequently have to answer. Second, the teacher cautioned students to "just take a second. Don't say anything right away." This gave students time to look closely at the images and make observations about the staircases and how they were growing and changing before ideas were made public. The focused yet open-ended nature of what students were asked to do provided all students with access to the task (everyone would be able to notice something) and their responses would help Ms. Moran determine whether students could identify key features of the growing figure that would help them in ultimately solving the task.

Two key ideas came up during the discussion of what students noticed that were critical in making sense of the problem. First, Nyleah explained that for stage 5, it would be "like 5 going across [width], 5 going up and down [height], and then 5 going down the stairs." She later generalized by saying, "Each stage is the amount of how many should be on the bottom and up and down and going down the stairs, too." At the teacher's request, Nyleah went up to the whiteboard to show exactly what she was referring to using stage 4 (see Figure 2.15). Nyleah's explanation made clear the parts of the staircase she was referring to.

Figure 2.15 • Nyleah's illustration of how the stage number related to the number of blocks in the stage

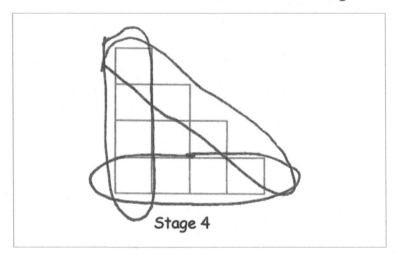

Stage 4

Next Elijah explained that the stage number was the same as the number of blocks on the bottom row. Araia, building on Elijah's explanation, further clarified: "The number of the stage is how many blocks you're adding. So stage 3, you add 3 blocks. Stage 4, you add 4 blocks … " This comment connected the bottom row of a stage that Elijah referred to as the number of blocks that were added from the previous stage.

The observations made by students could ultimately help them in recognizing that the growth was not linear—since the amount added on to each successive stage was not the same—and the staircases were growing in two dimensions, with both the width and height increasing at each new stage. Ms. Moran concluded the launch by describing the materials students would have access to and telling students that they were now going to explain and describe the patterns they noticed in their groups. The launch made it clear to Ms. Moran that students were attending to features of the staircases that would help them in reaching the goals of the lesson.

Was the time spent launching the task time well spent? We could argue that it was essential to ensuring that students were able to make sense of how the staircases were growing and thus positioning students to be ready to generalize the growth they were observing. Too often, students are given a task and do not understand some aspect of it. When this occurs, the teacher then ends up moving from one group to the next answering questions that could have been clarified with a more comprehensive launch.

Jackson and her colleagues (2012) list "four crucial aspects to keep in mind when setting up complex tasks to support all students' learning" (p. 26):

1. Key Contextual Features of the Task
2. Key Mathematical Ideas of the Task
3. Development of Common Language
4. Maintaining the Cognitive Demand

Ms. Moran's launch embodied many of the features described by Jackson and colleagues. The teacher (1) made sure that students could describe a staircase at a particular stage in terms of its shape and the number of squares that were been added to the previous staircase; (2) made sure that students recognized that a staircase had two dimensions (although they did not state this explicitly); (3) let students use common language to describe the dimensions (i.e., bottom, up and down) but made sure that these terms were understood by relating this verbal description to the visual of the staircase; and (4) ensured that the cognitive demand of the task was maintained by not suggesting a pathway to follow or giving away too much information.

> **TEACHING TAKEAWAY**
>
> A comprehensive launch ensures all students understand the entirety of the task, so that time is not spent later answering clarifying questions from groups or individuals.

While Ms. Moran's launch was appropriate given the task she had selected, other tasks might require different types of launches. For example, in launching the Floodlight Shadows task, Mr. Moore wanted to make sure that students had a basic understanding of shadows and how they changed when the distance from the light source changed. He started the lesson by darkening the room, standing on his desk with a high-power flashlight and shining the light on a student volunteer, and asking questions about what was happening and why. This, he felt, would position students to engage in the task. As Mr. Moore explained,

> *The most important part of understanding this task is the shadows and why shadows are formed. I'll really focus on when shadows are formed—we're talking about light and light that's being blocked out, and really, hopefully planting that seed a little bit into their mind of the role that the light plays in their diagram.*

Mr. Jacobson decided to launch the Compy Attack! lesson by showing students a short clip of a movie and asking students what they noticed and wondered about from their viewing of the video. He felt that this would motivate students, get them interested in solving the task, and raise authentic questions, some of which they would ultimately answer. While launches can take many forms, as a teacher you need to make sure that students understand the context of the task and are clear on what they are expected to do.

Perhaps the most challenging part of launching a task is making sure that you do enough to ensure that students understand the context and what they are being asked to do but not so much that there is nothing left for students to figure out. For example, in the Lunch Options task (Figure 2.12), you would not want to show students how to create a tree diagram or give them the Fundamental Principle of Counting. Either of these actions would lower the demand of the task by providing a strategy for students to use and limit their opportunity to figure out what to do and how.

Conclusion

In this chapter, we have discussed the importance of setting clear goals for student learning and selecting a task that is aligned with the goal, and we have described what is involved in this practice and the challenges associated with it. Our experience tells us that if you do not take the time to seriously consider Practice 0 as a first step in carefully planning your lesson, the remainder of the practices will be built on a shaky foundation.

Ms. Moran's work in setting a goal and selecting a task provided a concrete example of a teacher who thoughtfully and thoroughly engaged in this practice. Engaging in this practice in a deep and meaningful way does not happen overnight. It takes time and practice. As she said, "I think it's really important to really plan, plan, plan… It's important work. And I think it just gets better and better as you work with these practices."

Mr. Moore's efforts to determine what students would learn during the lesson and to ensure that the goals and tasks align made salient the challenges that teachers can face and overcome when engaging in this practice. Working with colleagues helped him make progress on Practice 0.

Setting Goals and Selecting Tasks—Summary

Video Clip 2.2
To hear and see more about setting goals and selecting tasks, watch Video Clip 2.2.

online resources 🔖   Videos may also be accessed at
resources.corwin.com/5practices-highschool

In the next chapter, we explore the first of the five practices: *anticipating*. Here, we will return to Ms. Moran's lesson and consider what it takes to engage in this practice and the challenges it presents.

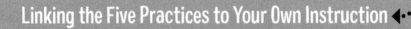

Linking the Five Practices to Your Own Instruction

SETTING GOALS AND SELECTING TASKS

Identify a mathematical idea that you will be teaching sometime in the next few weeks. Working alone or with your colleagues, do the following:

1. Determine what it is you want students to learn about mathematics as a result of engaging in the lesson. Be as specific as possible. It is okay to indicate what students will do during the lesson, but do not stop there!

2. Select a high-level cognitively demanding *doing-mathematics* task that is aligned with your goals. Make sure that there are different ways to enter and engage with the task. Identify resources that are likely to help students as they work on the task.

3. Identify what students will say and do that indicates that they are meeting the goals you have established.

4. Plan a launch that takes into account the four crucial aspects identified by Jackson and her colleagues.

Reflect on your planning so far. How does it differ from how you have previously thought about goals and tasks? In what ways do you think the differences will matter instructionally?

" It can be challenging to anticipate what a high school student is going to do when given a really rich task. But thinking about the different ways helps me be more ready to listen to students and understand where they're coming from. "

—MICHAEL MOORE, HIGH SCHOOL MATHEMATICS TEACHER

CHAPTER 3

Anticipating Student Responses

Now that you have identified a learning goal and have settled on a task that aligns with that goal, it is time to explore the next practice, anticipating student responses. Anticipating student responses takes place before instruction, during the planning stage of your lesson. This practice involves taking a close look at the task to identify the different strategies you expect students to use and to think about how you want to respond to those strategies during instruction. Anticipating helps prepare you to recognize and make sense of students' strategies during the lesson and to be able to respond effectively. In other words, by carefully anticipating student responses *prior* to a lesson, you will be better prepared to respond to students *during* instruction.

Smith and Stein (2018) explain anticipating in the following way:

> [Anticipating involves making] an effort to actively envision how students might mathematically approach the instructional task or tasks that they will work on and consider[ing] questions that could be asked of the students who used specific strategies. This involves much more than simply evaluating whether a task is at the right level of difficulty or of sufficient interest to students, and it goes beyond considering whether or not they are getting the "right" answer.

Anticipating students' responses involves developing considered expectations about how students might mathematically interpret a problem, the array of strategies—both correct and incorrect—that they might use to tackle it, and how those strategies and interpretations might relate to the mathematical concepts, representations, procedures, and practices that the teacher would like his or her students to learn. (p. 10)

In this chapter, we first unpack anticipating into its key components and illustrate what this practice looks like in an authentic high school classroom. We then explore what we have learned is challenging for teachers about this practice and provide an opportunity for you to explore anticipating in your own teaching practice.

Part One: Unpacking the Practice: Anticipating Student Responses

What is involved in anticipating student responses? This practice involves getting inside the problem (thinking about different ways students might solve the task), planning to respond to students using assessing and advancing questions, and preparing to notice key aspects of students' thinking in the midst of instruction. Figure 3.1 highlights the components of this practice along with key questions to guide the anticipating process.

Figure 3.1 • Key questions that support the practice of anticipating student responses

WHAT IT TAKES	KEY QUESTIONS
Getting inside the problem	How do you solve the task?
	How might students approach the task?
	What challenges might students face as they solve the task?
Planning to respond to student thinking	What assessing questions will you ask to draw out student thinking?
	What advancing questions will help you move student thinking forward?
Planning to notice student thinking	What strategies do you want to be on the lookout for as students work on the task?

Getting Inside the Problem

The first step is to get inside the problem! Many teachers find it useful to start by thinking about their own approach. How do you solve the task? You will want to think generally about the approach you use and at a detailed level about steps in your process (which may be different from someone else's). Next, consider how students might approach the task. You might investigate the problem using a different representation or think about how manipulatives might shape the way students explore the task. Do some approaches move students more easily toward the learning goals you established? You could also think about whether the task has different entry points. Often when students begin a task by working on different parts of the problem, their solutions look different (Lambert & Stylianou, 2013). Finally, as you explore these various approaches, keep in mind any challenges you think students will face as they solve the task. Are certain parts of the task likely to be difficult for students? Do you expect that students who use certain approaches will face particular kinds of challenges? Where do you think students might get stuck?

In Analyzing the Work of Teaching 3.1, we return to the Staircase task (Figure 2.4) that Ms. Moran selected for her students. In this activity, you will engage in solving and thinking deeply about the task. We will then look at the strategies that Ms. Moran anticipated her students would use in solving the task.

Analyzing the Work of Teaching 3.1

Getting Inside a Problem

Solve the Staircase task in at least two different ways. Then consider the following questions:

- What did you need to know to solve the task?
- What do you think might be challenging for students about this task?

Getting Inside a Problem—Analysis

While there are several ways *you* might approach this problem, we will explore two possible methods that involve geometric solutions—*doubling the staircase to make a rectangle* and *dividing the staircase into triangles.* When doubling the staircase to make a rectangle, you join two staircases from Stage *n*, one of which has been rotated 180 degrees. Figure 3.2 illustrates this process for Stage 3.

Figure 3.2 • Doubling the staircase in Stage 3 to create a 3 × 4 rectangle

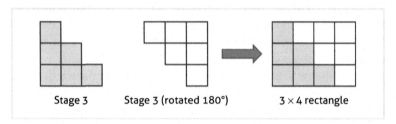

Stage 3   Stage 3 (rotated 180°)   3 × 4 rectangle

The resulting rectangle will have length n and width $(n+1)$. To find the area of the staircase in Stage n, you simply take half of the area of the $n \times (n+1)$ rectangle. This relationship can be represented by $A = \dfrac{n(n+1)}{2}$, where A is the total number of small squares in the stage (or the area of the staircase at the stage) and n is the stage number.

Another approach involves dividing the staircase for any stage into one large triangle and several smaller triangles. The large triangle can be found by drawing a diagonal through an imagined square encompassing the staircase. Figure 3.3 illustrates this decomposition for the staircase in Stage 3, with the large triangle shaded in green and each of the smaller triangles shaded in blue.

Figure 3.3 • Dividing the staircase in Stage 3 into triangles

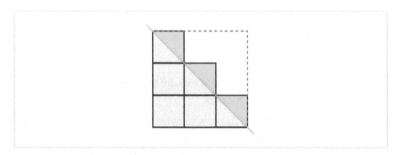

Notice that both the base and the height of the large triangle are n, where n is the stage number; thus, the area of the large triangle is $\dfrac{1}{2}n^2$. Each of the small triangles has area $\dfrac{1}{2}$ (the base and height of each small square is 1). Because there are n small triangles, the combined area of all the small triangles is $\dfrac{1}{2}n$. The area, A, of a staircase at Stage n (or the number of blocks at the stage) would then equal the area of the large triangle plus the area of the small triangles or $A = \dfrac{1}{2}n^2 + \dfrac{1}{2}n$.

In order to use the strategy of doubling the staircase to make a rectangle, you would need to consider composing two of the same staircases into a single shape that would make it easier for you to compute the area. Similarly, to use the strategy of dividing the staircase into triangles, you would need to know that it could be helpful to decompose the staircase into familiar shapes so that you can compute the area of each shape and add them together. You would also need to know the formulas for area of triangles and rectangles, that the base and height of the staircase is n for Stage n, and that there are n "stair steps" along the diagonal.

High school students may be challenged by this task if they do not have previous experience using geometric approaches to solve visual pattern tasks. In looking at the staircases, students may recognize that each staircase increases by 1 along the height and the width but may not know how to use that information to find a generalized solution. In addition, some students may attempt to use a table to identify a pattern, particularly if they have successfully used this approach to identify linear relationships. Deriving a quadratic equation from a table is, however, not as straightforward (Rhoads & Alvarez, 2017). Instead, what may be notable to students is the recursive relationship—that is, that the number of squares in successive staircases increases by the stage number.

Ms. Moran did the task herself and asked two colleagues how they would solve it. She also found a couple of potential solutions online. Through this process, Ms. Moran identified several possible methods for solving the Staircase task that she thought her students might use (see Figure 3.4).

To start, Ms. Moran thought that students might identify a recursive pattern that would allow them to determine the number of squares in Stage n if they knew the number of squares in Stage $(n-1)$. For example, students could determine the number of squares in Stage 5 by adding 5 to the number of squares in Stage 4 (Solution A, Figure 3.4). Ms. Moran explained that because of their previous work with linear functions, students were used to looking at the difference in growth between successive steps in a function: "I think they might start with a table and be drawn to the pattern of growth by adding 2, then growth of adding 3, growth of adding 4, and so on." Because a recursive pattern describes the relationship only between successive terms, it is considered more limited than an explicit form of the equation that allows one to determine the value of a function for any term (Lannin, 2004).

Ms. Moran also identified several geometric solutions that students might try. As described previously, Ms. Moran thought students might "double it and get a rectangular shape, knowing that then the staircase is half of it" (Solution B, Figure 3.4) or they might "see it as a larger triangle with smaller triangles" (Solution C, Figure 3.4). Ms. Moran explained that both colleagues she asked to solve the task used a third

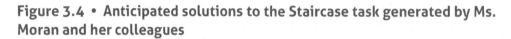

Figure 3.4 • Anticipated solutions to the Staircase task generated by Ms. Moran and her colleagues

A. Identify the Recursive Pattern

Stage number	Number of squares	Number of squares added to get next stage
1	1	
2	3	1 + 2 = **3**
3	6	3 + 3 = **6**
4	10	6 + 4 = **10**

Student uses a table or visual inspection of staircases to determine that the number of squares in a stage is the number of squares in the previous stage plus the stage number.

B. Double the Staircase to Create a Rectangle

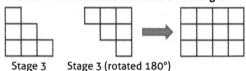

Stage 3   Stage 3 (rotated 180°)

Student creates the $n \times (n+1)$ rectangle by putting two copies of the same staircase together.

Student finds the area of the original staircase by taking $\frac{1}{2}$ of the area of the resulting rectangle.

Area of staircase in Stage $n = \dfrac{n(n+1)}{2}$

C. Divide the Staircase Into Triangles

Student draws a diagonal through the staircase to create one large triangle and several smaller triangles.

Student uses $A = \frac{1}{2}(bh)$ to determine the area of a large triangle. Since base and height are the same as the stage number, $A = \frac{1}{2}n^2$.

Student determines that the area of each small triangle is $\frac{1}{2}$ and that the number of small triangles is the same as the stage number. This means that the combined area of the small triangles is $\frac{1}{2}n$.

Total area = $\frac{1}{2}n^2 + \frac{1}{2}n$

D. Rearrange the Staircase Into a Rectangle

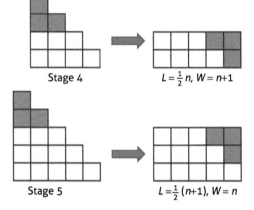

Stage 4 $L = \frac{1}{2}n,\ W = n+1$

Stage 5 $L = \frac{1}{2}(n+1),\ W = n$

Student rearranges the squares in a staircase to create a rectangle. Student determines the area of the original staircase by calculating the area of the resulting rectangle. Student uses a slightly different approach for even-number stages and for odd-number stages.

Area = $\frac{1}{2}n(n+1)$

E. Suggest Growth Is Exponential

Student recognizes that the difference in the number of squares in each stage is not constant and that the growth is not linear.

Because the amount of each staircase keeps getting bigger, the student decides that the growth must be exponential.

geometric method, rearranging the existing squares in a staircase to create a rectangle (Solution D, Figure 3.4): "They moved the squares to make a rectangle and got one pattern with even staircases and another pattern with the odds." For example, with an even stage number, you can move the squares in the upper half of the staircase to the right side of the staircase and create a rectangle with area of $\frac{1}{2}n(n+1)$.

Finally, Ms. Moran thought that her students might make a connection to exponential functions. Rather than recognize the function as quadratic, Ms. Moran believed students might "jump to exponential" once they realized that the function was not linear (Solution E, Figure 3.4).

Planning to Respond to Student Thinking

With your ideas about potential student solutions in mind, the next step is to think about how you will respond to students. We have found two kinds of questions to be particularly useful in supporting students' work (Figure 3.5). Assessing questions help to draw out students' thinking about a problem and are a valuable way for you to investigate what a student understands or why a student decided to take a particular approach. Rather than infer what students are doing or thinking from glancing at their work, assessing questions prompt students to explain their reasoning to you. Franke and colleagues (2009) explain that such questions are important because they help teachers "to more fully understand student thinking and, therefore, to make more informed instructional decisions" (p. 390). Asking students, "Can you tell me what you did?" can often be a good initial assessing question. You can then move to more specific questions that ask students to explain particular parts of their solution strategy and will help you to confirm, for example, whether or not students understand the reasoning behind their approach.

Figure 3.5 • Key characteristics of assessing and advancing questions

ASSESSING QUESTIONS	ADVANCING QUESTIONS
• Are based closely on the work students have produced • Clarify what students have done and what students understand about what they have done • Give the teacher information about what students understand	• Use what students have produced as a basis for making progress toward the target goal of the lesson • Move students beyond their current thinking by pressing students to extend what they know to a new situation • Press students to think about something they are not currently thinking about

Advancing questions have a different purpose. They are intended to help move students' thinking forward toward the lesson goals. But rather than telling students what to do next, advancing questions are designed to build on what students currently understand and encourage them to "think about something they are not currently thinking about" (Smith & Stein, 2018, p. 44). Advancing questions are not designed as hints. Instead, they ask students to consider particular aspects of their solution or strategy in a new way or to consider how their strategy applies more broadly.

During the anticipating stage, you will want to prepare both assessing and advancing questions that you will be able to use during instruction. One useful strategy is to prepare assessing and advancing questions for each of the student solutions that you anticipate. The assessing questions will help you establish what students know. Sometimes these questions will help confirm what you think a student is doing; other times these questions will help to clarify when the student's intentions are not clear to you. The advancing questions will help students move beyond where they currently are. This could include asking students to examine the limitations in their current approach or generalize their approach to other situations.

⏸ PAUSE AND CONSIDER

Select two solution strategies from Figure 3.4 for the Staircase task and write a few assessing questions for each approach. In addition to general questions that ask students to "Tell me what you did?" identify one or two more specific questions. Next, come up with a few advancing questions for each of the two strategies.

	Assessing Questions	Advancing Questions
Solution Strategy		
Solution Strategy		

Ms. Moran created a monitoring chart (see Figure 3.6) where she listed the strategies she had anticipated and then developed assessing and advancing questions for each of the strategies identified in Figure 3.4 as well as for the case of students who are not able to get started with the task. (Other features of a monitoring chart, shown in Figure 3.6, will be discussed in the next section of this chapter.) For example, for Solution A in which students use a recursive pattern for identifying the number of squares in a stage, her assessing questions aim to uncover what students understand about the relationship between the stage number and the number of squares in the staircase. The question "How would you describe the number of squares at Stage 5?" may help Ms. Moran gain information about whether students understand the staircase in Stage 5 as growing directly from Stage 4 or growing independent of the previous staircase. Asking about the number of squares at Stage 10 will help her assess whether students must rely on Stage 9 to produce an answer, or if they have another way to calculate the number of squares at Stage 10. If students clearly illustrate a recursive relationship between subsequent staircases, Ms. Moran will be in a good position to ask the advancing question, "What if you did Stage 50? Or Stage 100? Would you want to use that pattern?" This question builds directly on the approach students have used, while encouraging them to extend beyond a recursive relationship to determine the number of squares at a given stage.

Consider also the assessing and advancing questions for Solution B. Here students double the staircase to create an $n \times (n+1)$ rectangle. Ms. Moran's assessing questions first ask for general information about how the students used this approach: "What have you noticed so far?" She wants to understand both what students did and what students understand about the relationship between their strategy and the task. "What shape are you creating? Why?" will help her assess whether students understand why creating a rectangle is helpful and how doing so might help them make progress on the task. Ms. Moran also has advancing questions prepared that she can use if appropriate—"How can you relate the stage number to the shape you've created?" and "Using what you noticed, what would the equation be for the nth stage?" These questions are designed specifically to build on students' understanding of the relationship between doubling the staircase for a particular stage, to promote their thinking about this process in a more general way. If students have already produced the generalized equation $A = \frac{n(n+1)}{2}$, then Ms. Moran will ask "How does this equation relate to the staircase?" This question will prompt students to think explicitly about where and how the values of n, $n + 1$, and $\frac{1}{2}$ appear in the original staircase. (As you can see in Figure 3.6, Ms. Moran describes the anticipated strategies in her monitoring chart in detail. You may find it is sufficient to provide an overview of each strategy in monitoring charts that you create for your own use.)

Figure 3.6 • Assessing and advancing questions developed by Ms. Moran as shown in her monitoring chart

SOLUTION STRATEGY	ASSESSING QUESTIONS	ADVANCING QUESTIONS	WHO AND WHAT	ORDER
Students Cannot Get Started	• What have you noticed so far? • How many tiles were needed for Stage 1? For Stage 2? • What is the task asking you to figure out?	• Can you try building the staircase for Stage 5? How would you get started? • What do you notice about how the staircases grow at each stage?		
Solution A. Identify the Recursive Pattern Student uses a table or visual inspection of staircases to determine that the number of squares in a stage is the number of squares in the previous stage plus the stage number.	• What have you noticed so far? • How would you describe how the staircases grow? • If you had Stage 3, what would you do to find the number of squares in Stage 4? • How would you describe the number of squares at Stage 5? At Stage 10?	• What if you did Stage 50? Or Stage 100? Would you want to use that pattern? • Is there a way to use the tiles to help you visualize what's happening with the pattern?		
Solution B. Double the Staircase to Create a Rectangle Student creates the $n \times (n+1)$ rectangle by putting two copies of the same staircase together. Student finds the area of the original staircase by taking $\frac{1}{2}$ of the area of the resulting rectangle. Area of staircase in Stage $n = \frac{n(n+1)}{2}$	• What have you noticed so far? • What shape are you creating? Why? • Can you describe how this works for Stage 3? For Stage 4?	• How can you relate the stage number to the shape you've created? • (If equation) How does this equation relate to the staircase? • (If no equation) Using what you noticed, what would the equation be for the nth stage?		

SOLUTION STRATEGY	ASSESSING QUESTIONS	ADVANCING QUESTIONS	WHO AND WHAT	ORDER
Solution C. Divide the Staircase Into Triangles Student draws a diagonal through the staircase to create one large triangle and several smaller triangles. Student uses $A = \frac{1}{2}(bh)$ to determine the area of a large triangle. Since base and height are the same as the stage number, $A = \frac{1}{2}n^2$. Student determines that the area of each small triangle is $\frac{1}{2}$ and that the number of small triangles is the same as the stage number. This means that the combined area of the small triangles is $\frac{1}{2}n$. Total area $= \frac{1}{2}n^2 + \frac{1}{2}n$	• What have you noticed so far? • What shape are you creating? Why? • How did you figure out the number of squares in the large triangle? In the smaller triangles? • How does this work for Stage 3? For Stage 4?	• How can you relate the stage number to the different triangles? How is the size of the large triangle related to the stage number? How are the small triangles related to the stage number? • (If equation) How does this equation relate to the staircase? • (If no equation) Using what you noticed, what would the equation be for the nth stage?		
Solution D. Rearrange the Staircase Into a Rectangle Student rearranges the squares in a staircase to create a rectangle. Student determines the area of the original staircase by calculating the area of the resulting rectangle. Student uses a slightly different approach for even-number stages and for odd-number stages. Area $= \frac{1}{2}n(n + 1)$	• What have you noticed so far? • What shape are you creating? Why? • How does this shape relate to the stage number of the staircase? • Can you do the same process with another stage?	• Would your process work better for Stage 3 or Stage 4? Why? • (If equation) How does this equation relate to the staircase? • (If no equation) Using what you noticed, what would the equation be for the nth stage?		

(Continued)

Figure 3.6 (Continued)

SOLUTION STRATEGY	ASSESSING QUESTIONS	ADVANCING QUESTIONS	WHO AND WHAT	ORDER
Solution E. Suggest Growth Is Exponential Student recognizes that the difference in the number of squares in each stage is not constant and that the growth is not linear. Because the amount each staircase grows keeps getting bigger, the student decides that the growth must be exponential.	• Why do you think the pattern is exponential? • How would you describe the growth in the staircases? • What does it mean for a function to be exponential?	• $y = 3^x$ is an exponential function. How does the growth in $y = 3^x$ relate to the growth you identified in the staircase pattern?		
Other				

Planning to Notice Student Thinking

So far, we have focused on identifying the strategies you expect students to use in class as well as how you can respond when students use these strategies during class. The practice of anticipating also involves preparing yourself to notice what students are doing in the midst of instruction. Classrooms are often a whirlwind of activity! As the teacher, there is much for you to attend to—Are students on task? Do they have the materials they need? Are students collaborating productively? How much time is left in the period? Sherin and van Es (2009) explain that the ability to notice students' mathematical thinking in the midst of all that is taking place is a key component of teaching expertise today. In particular, teachers need to be able to sift through all the *noise* of the activity to identify what is important in what students are doing and saying.

Planning to notice involves preparing yourself to attend to those aspects of the lesson that you expect to be significant, while also being open to new ideas that might arise. Preparing a monitoring chart prior to instruction is a valuable approach for doing this (see Figure 3.6). The monitoring chart is a place where you can organize the strategies you anticipate that students will use along with the corresponding assessing and advancing questions for each strategy. Teachers often find it useful to list *Other* as a final strategy to remind them to be on the lookout for additional approaches that students might use. The monitoring chart also includes a *Who and What* column as a reminder to prepare to notice not just which strategies are being used but also who is using them. (We will discuss how to use the *Who and What* and *Order* columns in Chapters 4 and 5, respectively.) (A blank copy of the monitoring chart can be found in Appendix B.)

In addition to preparing yourself to be aware of how students will approach the task, you may want to also identify key ideas that you think are particularly important to keep track of as the lesson unfolds. For example, as Ms. Moran prepared for instruction, she had in mind a few key aspects of students' thinking that she planned to be on the lookout for. First, she was on the lookout for students who seemed aware that the staircases grew in two dimensions, as she thought this would be key to recognizing that the growth could be represented by a quadratic function. In addition, she planned to pay attention to those students who identified a recursive pattern in the growth and ask questions that would encourage them to consider an explicit pattern as well. Ms. Moran was also concerned that students with no experience with geometric solutions might not consider decomposing the staircases in any of the ways she and her colleagues had imagined. As needed, she planned to invite students to consider how they might use the square tiles she had distributed to visualize the relationship between the stage number and the number of squares in a given staircase.

TEACHING TAKEAWAY

A monitoring chart helps keeps track of the work you anticipated and the questions you prepared *in advance* of the lesson but also helps you stay focused, intentional, and actively listening *during the lesson*!

Cori Moran's Attention to Key Questions: Anticipating

As Ms. Moran anticipated what her students would do, how she would respond to them, and what she would be on the lookout for, she kept her focus on the key questions. She approached this work by first *getting inside the problem* and identifying different solution strategies that she thought her students might use. Ms. Moran then created assessing and advancing questions for each of these strategies. Her assessing questions were designed to draw out students' thinking, while the advancing questions were intended as prompts to move students' thinking forward. Finally, Ms. Moran prepared herself to notice students' responses during instruction by developing a monitoring chart (shown in Figure 3.6). Her monitoring chart included the key strategies she anticipated students would use, assessing and advancing questions for each, as well as a column labeled *Who and What* where she planned to record what students did in class. Let's now look at some of the key challenges teachers face as they anticipate students' responses.

Part Two: Challenges Teachers Face: Anticipating Student Responses

As we described at the beginning of the chapter, anticipating what students are likely to do in a lesson, how you will respond, and what you will keep track of during the lesson is foundational to orchestrating productive discussions. Anticipating, however, is not without its challenges. In this section, we focus on three specific challenges associated with this practice, shown in Figure 3.7 that we have identified from our work with teachers.

Figure 3.7 • Challenges associated with the practice of anticipating students' responses

CHALLENGE	DESCRIPTION
Moving beyond the way *you* solve a problem	Teachers often feel limited by their own experience. They know how to solve a task but may not have access to the array of strategies that students are likely to use.
Being prepared to help students who cannot get started on a task	Teachers need to be prepared to provide support to students who do not know how to begin work on the task so that they can make progress without being told exactly what to do and how.
Creating questions that move students toward the mathematical goals	The questions teachers ask need to be driven by the mathematical goals of the lesson. The focus needs to be on ensuring that students *understand* the key mathematical ideas, not just on producing a solution to the task.

Moving Beyond the Way YOU Solved the Problem

You may, at times, feel limited by your own experiences—you know one way to solve a task and cannot imagine other ways to do it. Why do you need more than one solution method? When students are presented with a high-level task, one for which "a predictable, well-rehearsed approach or pathway is not explicitly suggested by the task, task instructions, or a worked-out example" (Smith & Stein, 1998, p. 348), students must determine a course of action based on their prior knowledge and experiences. Since their prior knowledge and experiences are different from yours, they are likely to think about the situation in very different ways. By anticipating what students are likely to do *prior* to a lesson, you will be better positioned to support students *during* the lesson.

In exploring this challenge, we begin by examining the algebra lesson planned by Matthew Harmon. Mr. Harmon explained what the class had been working on and what the lesson was intended to accomplish:

> *We've put in a lot of work trying to build that idea of linearity. We have also introduced the concept of equivalent equations. I'm really hoping that this task kind of highlights that a little bit more. I think with where they're at developmentally, they should be a little bit more ready to see that just in terms of understanding what an equation represents and what it can do.*

Specifically, as a result of engaging in the lesson, he wanted his students to understand the following:

1. Patterns can be described and generalized by finding the underlying structure of the pattern and relating two variables that are changing at the same time.

2. Patterns that grow by a constant rate are linear.

3. There are different but equivalent ways of describing and representing the same pattern.

4. Connections can be made between different representational forms—tables, graphs, equations, words, and pictures.

Mr. Harmon selected the Toothpick Hexagons task, shown in Figure 3.8, as the basis for his lesson for several reasons. First, the task was aligned with his lesson goals, providing students with the opportunity to explore a linear growth pattern, represent the pattern in some way, and generalize the pattern beyond the cases they could physically build. Second, all students could access the task. The task was stated simply and clearly. Parts a and b of the task could be solved by counting and building, which would provide students with a basis for making a connection between the number of hexagons and the number of toothpicks. Third, students could demonstrate success in different ways. As Mr. Harmon explained, "I'm expecting some students to go right to an equation because we have been working on writing equations. But I do believe that students will be able to solve this task without being able to write an equation in abstract form." While he wants to move all students toward algebraic generalizations, this task would give him a chance to "see where students are at in their understanding."

Figure 3.8 • The Toothpick Hexagons task

Toothpick Hexagons

A row of hexagons can be made from toothpicks as follows.

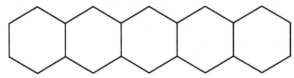

a. How many toothpicks do you need to have a row of 5 hexagons? Explain how you found your answer.

b. How many toothpicks do you need to have a row of 9 hexagons? Explain how you found your answer.

c. How many toothpicks do you need to have a row of 100 hexagons? Explain how you found your answer.

d. Write a generalization that can be used to find the total number of toothpicks when given the number of hexagons. Explain your generalization using the diagram.

e. How long would the row of hexagons be if you had 356 toothpicks to use? Explain how you found your answer.

f. What can you say about the relationship found in this pattern?

g. Create a graph of this pattern. Are there any more observations you can make after viewing the graph?

Source: Developed by the Milwaukee Mathematics Partnership (MMP) with support from the National Science Foundation under Grant No. 0314898.

Mr. Harmon began the practice of anticipating by solving the task himself. He then conferred with colleagues in order to gain additional insight regarding how students might solve the task. Although the task could be solved by creating a table, he felt that students would be drawn to using the diagram, pictures, or physical models of the hexagon rows to solve the task, as shown in Figure 3.9. In fact, providing students with toothpicks to use to build subsequent hexagon rows might encourage a visual approach.

Figure 3.9 • Complete and correct solutions to the Toothpick Hexagons task generated by Mr. Harmon and his colleagues

Solution A

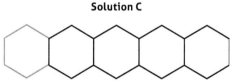

You would need 6 toothpicks to build each hexagon if they were not connected.

Since they are connected, you have overcounted because you only need 1 vertical side between hexagons, not 2.

You then need to subtract the ones that were double counted, represented by blue arrows. The number of sides you need to subtract is 1 less than the number of hexagons.

$y = 6x - (x - 1)$

Solution B

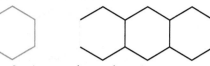

The first hexagon (orange) requires 6 toothpicks

The rest of the hexagons $(x - 1)$ only need 5 toothpicks (blue).

$y = 6 + 5(x - 1)$

Solution C

Each hexagon requires 5 toothpicks plus 1 for the last vertical side in the row.

$y = 5x + 1$

Solution D

There are 4 toothpicks on the top and bottom of each hexagon (orange).

Each hexagon also has a vertical side (blue) that will require toothpicks plus 1 toothpick at the end. So we need $4x$ for the top and bottom and $x + 1$ for the sides.

$y = 4x + x + 1$

In addition to considering what complete and correct solutions would look like, Mr. Harmon and his colleagues also thought about solutions that were incomplete or incorrect. They determined that students might

  i. have trouble starting the task.

 ii. miscount the number of toothpicks and therefore have trouble determining the pattern.

iii. try to count the number of toothpicks in a row with 100 hexagons (question c in Figure 3.8).

 iv. recognize the recursive nature of the pattern—add 5 more toothpicks with each additional hexagon—but not be able to find the number of toothpicks in a row without knowing the number of toothpicks in the previous row.

The key factor in Mr. Harmon's anticipating is that he did not have to *go it alone.* By working in collaboration with colleagues, he was able to expand on the set of ideas he was able to come up with on his own. As he explained, "The more you can anticipate, the more you can efficiently move throughout a class of a lot of different groups and try to get the most out of them all."

Michael Moore's Floodlight Shadows task, shown in Figure 2.6, lent itself to a different sort of anticipating since the task has two parts—first draw and label a diagram and then find the total length of the shadows—and success in part 1 is necessary in order to be successful in part 2. Recall that Mr. Moore's instructional goals focused on students creating mathematical models of the situation, understanding the ways in which triangles can be categorized as similar, and justifying that similarity using mathematical argumentation.

PAUSE AND CONSIDER

How might anticipating student solutions be different with Mr. Moore's Floodlight Shadows task as compared to Mr. Harmon's Toothpick Hexagons task?

As he began to anticipate, Mr. Moore noted that the construction of a visual model that represented the situation (see Figure 3.10) was a critical first step in successfully engaging with question 2 in the Floodlight Shadows task. He imagined that students might create diagrams that were more or less useful. If students did not attend to the relative size of the floodlights and the distance between floodlights, the triangles needed to make progress on the task might not be readily visible or might not appear to be similar. The visual model did not have to be exactly to scale for students to make progress, but it needed to be relatively true to the distance relationships in the task.

Figure 3.10 • Visual model for question 1 of the Floodlight Shadows task

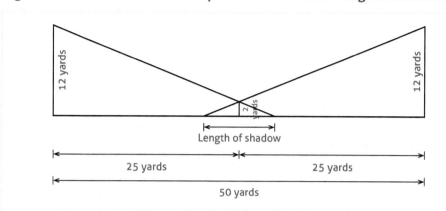

To gain entry into question 2, Mr. Moore knew that groups would need to construct a diagram that represented the key distance relationships and clearly showed the triangles. From that point, he anticipated that students would state that the triangles were similar (or assume it) and then prove that corresponding angles of the triangles were congruent by using nested right triangles (see Strategy A—Proof, Figure 3.11) or by using vertically oriented triangles (see Strategy B—Proof, Figure 3.11). They could then find the total length of the shadows using one of three approaches: using the fact that corresponding sides of similar triangles are in proportion (see Strategy A—Length of Shadow, Figure 3.11), using the fact that the sides of similar triangles are related by a scale factor (see Strategy B—Length of Shadow, Figure 3.11), or using the fact that triangles that are similar are related by a dilation (see Strategy C—Length of Shadow, Figure 3.11). Mr. Moore determined that there would be six different combinations that students might come up with, matching each proof strategy with one of the strategies for finding the total length of the shadows. (We have illustrated a subset of those combinations in Figure 3.11.)

Figure 3.11 • Visual models, proofs, and methods for finding the length of the shadows for question 2 of the Floodlight Shadows task

Strategy A: Using similar nested right triangles to prove similarity and proportions to find the length of the shadows

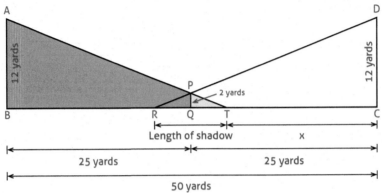

Proof

Prove ΔATB ~ ΔPTQ

∠ATB ≅ ∠PTQ reflexive

∠ABT = 90° and ∠PQT = 90° so ∠ABT ≅ ∠PQT

ΔATB ~ ΔPTQ. If two angles of one triangle are congruent to two angles of another triangle, then the triangles must be similar.

Length of Shadow

Length of $\overline{BT}$ is 50 – x and the Length of $\overline{QT}$ is 25 – x

$\frac{2}{12} = \frac{(25-x)}{(50-x)}$ —corresponding sides of similar figures are proportional

x = 20

25 – 20 = 5

So the shadow $\overline{QT}$ is 5 yards.(You can then prove that ΔDRC ~ ΔPRQ using the same argument. So $\overline{RQ}$ is also 5 yards.) So the entire shadow is 10 yards.

Strategy B: Using similar triangles oriented vertically to prove similarity and scale factor to find the length of the shadows

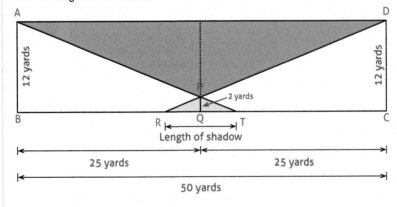

Proof

Prove ΔAPD ~ ΔRPT

∠APD ≅ ∠RPT vertical angles

∠DAP ≅ ∠PTR alternate interior angles

ΔAPD ~ ΔRPT. If two angles of one triangle are congruent to two angles of another triangle, then the triangles must be similar. The corresponding sides of similar triangles are related to a scale factor.

Length of Shadow

The scale factor between the two triangles can be found by looking at the altitudes. Triangle RPT has a height of 2. Triangle APD has a height of 12 (length of $\overline{AB}$) – 2 (length of $\overline{PQ}$), or 10. This indicates that the scale factor between the two triangles is 5. So the length of $\overline{RT}$ has to be $\frac{1}{5}$ the length of $\overline{AD}$. $\overline{AD}$ measures 50 yards, so the shadow is 10 yards.

Strategy C: Using similar nested right triangles to prove similarity and dilation to find the length of the shadows

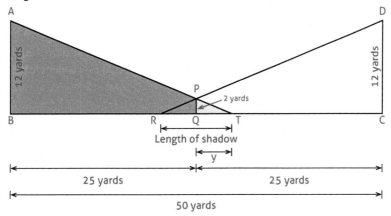

Proof

Prove ΔATB ~ ΔPTQ

∠ATB ≅ ∠PTQ reflexive

m∠ABT = 90° and m∠PQT = 90° so ∠ABT ≅ ∠PQT

ΔATB ~ ΔPTQ. If two angles of one triangle are congruent to two angles of another triangle, then the triangles must be similar.

Length of Shadow

The two triangles are similar and thus are related by a dilation. The center of the dilation would be T. Because we know that $\overline{PQ}$ measures 2 yards and $\overline{AB}$ measures 12 yards, we can tell that the dilation is a factor of 6.

The length of $\overline{BT}$ is 25 + y. Because of the scale factor, we also know that $\overline{BT}$ is 6 times the length of $\overline{QT}$. 6y = 25 + y, which leads to y = 5. The total length of the shadow is 10.

In summary, Mr. Moore anticipated that students would

Part 1

- Create a visual model that represents distance and triangles.
- Create a visual model that does not capture some aspect of the situation and/or does not identify appropriate triangles.

Part 2

- Prove that the triangles are similar using nested triangles or vertically oriented triangles, and find the length of the shadows using proportions, scale factors, or dilations.
- Assume that the triangles are similar but do not prove it, and find the length of the shadows using proportions, scale factors, or dilations.
- Prove that the triangles are similar using nested triangles or vertically oriented triangles, but do not find the length of the shadows.

While Mr. Harmon and Mr. Moore both engaged in anticipating, the nature of the tasks they used and the goals they had for student learning led them to do so in different ways. In comparing the structure of Mr. Moore's anticipating to Mr. Harmon's, we reflect on how the task and goals influenced the way the anticipating unfolded. Mr. Harmon's toothpick task afforded students several different discrete ways to make sense of and generalize the pattern. Mr. Harmon's goal was to foster those different solution paths and, through a whole class discussion, be able to identify the similarities and differences in them. Moreover, Mr. Harmon intended for students to express the equivalence of their solutions through algebraic manipulation as an important coda to the lesson. Mr. Harmon's anticipating focused on identifying discrete solution paths and comparing them through a whole class discussion, consistent with his goals related to equivalence. Mr. Moore's task had a single important mathematical idea as the cornerstone—the notion of similarity, and how one builds arguments for it. His anticipating focused on the key components needed to build toward the argument of similarity, with the whole class discussion focused on making those building blocks explicit.

So what can you do to anticipate multiple possible solution paths? A first step is to consider different ways to represent the situation. The diagram shown in Figure 3.12 describes five different ways to represent a mathematical idea—visual, symbolic, verbal, contextual, or physical.

Figure 3.12 • Different ways to represent a mathematical idea

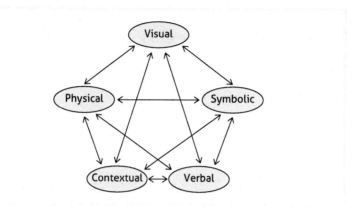

In order to illustrate how this diagram might be helpful in anticipating solution strategies, let us consider the Cycle Shop task shown in Figure 3.13.

Figure 3.13 • The Cycle Shop task

The Cycle Shop

You work for a small business that sells bicycles and tricycles. Bicycles have one seat, two pedals, and two wheels. Tricycles have one seat, two pedals, and three wheels.

On Monday, there are a total of 24 seats and 61 wheels in the shop. How many bicycles and how many tricycles are in the shop? Show all your work using any method you choose and explain your thinking.

 This task can also be accessed at
resources.corwin.com/5practices-highschool

PAUSE AND CONSIDER

How could you solve the Cycle Shop task shown in Figure 3.13 using visual, physical, and symbolic representations?

Visual:

Physical:

Symbolic:

Your first instinct in solving this problem may have been to create two linear equations and solve them using either substitution or elimination (see the Symbolic/Algebraic solutions, Figure 3.14). However, students who have not been formally taught these procedures, or who have been taught them but do not remember how to use them, will use one of several other ways to solve the problem as shown in Figure 3.14.

Figure 3.14 • Different ways of representing the relationships in the Cycle Shop task

Visual—Draw a Picture

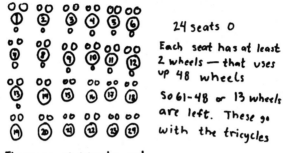

24 seats 0
Each seat has at least
2 wheels — that uses
up 48 wheels
So 61-48 or 13 wheels
are left. These go
with the tricycles

There are 13 tricycles and
11 bicycles

Visual—Create a Graph

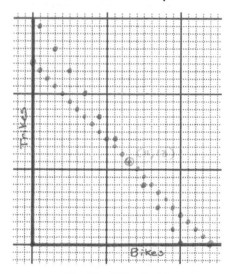

2b + 3t = 61 b + t = 24

Physical—Manipulatives

I made 24 columns to represent my seats.

I took 61 chips to represent my wheels.

Then I put 2 chips in each column, so this used up 48 wheels. So now I have 24 bikes with 2 wheels each. But I had 13 wheels left to distribute, so I used those to make 13 trikes by adding another wheel. So now I have used up 61 wheels on 24 seats. So I have 13 trikes and 11 bikes.

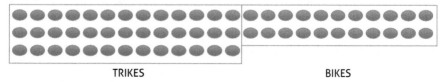

TRIKES   BIKES

(Continued)

Figure 3.14 (*Continued*)

Symbolic/Verbal—Guess and Check	Symbolic/Verbal—Make a Table

Symbolic/Verbal—Guess and Check

Start with a guess of bikes and trikes that totals 24, then figure out the number of wheels. If the guess is too many wheels, then lower the number of trikes and increase the number of wheels.

For example:

$1B + 23T = 24$ seats

$2W + 69W = 71$ wheels Too many

$5B + 19T = 24$ seats

$10W + 57W = 67$ wheels Too many

$10B + 14T = 24$ seats

$20W + 42W = 62$ wheels Close

$11B + 13T = 24$ seats
$22W + 39W = 61$ wheels

Symbolic/Verbal—Make a Table

Start with 1 bike and 23 trikes and find the total number of wheels; continue with 2 bikes and 22 trikes and continue the table until you get 61 wheels when you have 24 total bikes and trikes.

For example:

Number of Bikes	Number of Trikes	Bike Wheels	Trike Wheels	Total Wheels 61
1	23	2	69	71
2	22	4	66	70
3	21	6	63	69
4	20	8	60	68
5	19	10	57	67
6	18	12	54	66
7	17	14	51	65
8	16	16	48	64
9	15	18	45	63
10	14	20	42	62
11	13	22	39	61

Symbolic/Algebraic—Elimination

$2b + 3t = 61 \rightarrow 2b + 3t = 61$
$b + t = 24 \rightarrow -2b + {^-}2t = {^-}48$
$\overline{ t = 13}$

$b + 13 = 24$
$b = 24 - 13$
$b = 11$

13 trikes, 11 bikes

Symbolic/Algebraic—Substitution

$b + t = 24$
$b = 24 - t$

$2b + 3t = 61$
$2(24 - t) + 3t = 61$
$48 - 2t + 3t = 61$
$48 + t = 61$
$t = 61 - 48$
$t = 13$ trikes
$b + 13 = 24$
$b + 13 - 13 = 24 - 13$
$b = 11$ bikes

Source: These solutions appear in Steele and Smith (2018).

The point is to think through what students might do so that you are prepared to deal with a range of different strategies that are likely to appear during the lesson and to ask students questions that will assess what they currently understand and advance them toward the goal of the lesson. This level of anticipating will also help you think about the resources that you need to make available to students so they can pursue various pathways. For example, if you want students to be able to create physical models of the situation, you need to provide materials they could use for this purpose. If you want students to feel free to make a graph, you should have grid paper available for them to use. If you want students to draw a picture, you should provide paper and colored pencils or markers.

While you may not be able to generate an array of strategies yourself, consider ways to collaborate with others. You may be able to work with a colleague who teaches the same grade level or a different grade level, in or outside of your building. If you do not have math-teacher colleagues to help generate and discuss an expanded set of solutions to a particular task, consider one of the following options:

- Ask your friends (either face-to-face or virtually) to solve the task. Adults who are not mathematics teachers may produce solutions that approximate what students will do!

- Post a question on Twitter, My NCTM (https://my.nctm.org/home), or other social media outlets. This will give you access to a community of educators, many of whom will be eager to respond!

- Take photos of solutions students produce to a particular task the first time you teach it, and add to it every time you use the same task. Over time, you will have a robust collection of approaches to consider as you prepare for subsequent lessons. (This will also be a great resource to share with colleagues who are using the task for the first time.)

Being Prepared to Help Students Who Cannot Get Started

Regardless of how carefully you set up or launch the lesson, there is often a student who is unsure how to begin the task. Boston, Dillon, Smith, and Miller (2017) argue,

> When a student can't get started on a problem, it generally isn't the case that he or she has no relevant knowledge to bring to bear on the situation. It is more often that, for some reason, the student is unable to connect what he or she does know with the current task. (p. 205)

The inability to get started could be due to a reading comprehension issue, lack of familiarity with the context of the problem, or a lack of confidence in their ability to engage with a task for which a strategy is not provided.

TEACHING TAKEAWAY

Be prepared to help students who do not know how to get started on a problem by eliciting what they understand about the task rather than by suggesting specific steps to try or by having another student show them what to do.

Common approaches to this challenge include suggesting a strategy for the student to use or pairing the student who can't get started with a student who knows how to begin. While these approaches give the student something to do, they provide you with no insight regarding what the student understands about the task, do nothing to build the student's capacity to persevere in the face of struggle, and probably add to the student's self-perception as someone who cannot do mathematics. When students move forward based on someone else's thinking, it is unlikely that they will be able to retain and appropriately use a strategy they do not understand. Therefore, it is critical to have a plan in place regarding how to support students who struggle to get started.

PAUSE AND CONSIDER

What questions could you ask a student who could not begin the Toothpick Hexagons task (Figure 3.8)?

Mr. Harmon anticipated that some students in his class might have trouble getting started on the task, so he planned questions that would provide him with insight regarding what students understood about the problem. He planned to begin by asking students what they noticed about the problem. He hoped to hear students say things like "you have a row of five hexagons," "the hexagons are made up of toothpicks," and "we have to find the number of toothpicks in a row of 5 hexagons, 9 hexagons, and 100 hexagons." From here, he planned to ask students, "Can you count the number of toothpicks in the row of 5 hexagons?" If students could answer this correctly, he would then ask, "Can you build or draw a row of 6 hexagons? How many toothpicks will that take?" Once he had established that students had a basic understanding of how the hexagon rows were created and how to count the toothpicks in a row, he planned to ask students to explore rows of different numbers of hexagons and see if they notice a pattern. At that point, he planned to leave the students to explore this on their own and to return later to check on their progress.

The goal is to be able to support students' productive struggle—finding ways to support students so that they can move forward on their own

steam. Warshauer (2015) argues that while telling students what to do or providing them with directed guidance helps them to move forward, it tends to lower the cognitive demand of the task and limit students' opportunities to learn.

Creating Questions That Move Students Toward the Mathematical Goal

The questions that teachers ask students during a lesson need to be driven by the mathematical goals. You need to first determine what students know in comparison to what you ultimately want them to learn and then ask questions that move them toward the goal. You will not ask all students the same set of questions because they are not all thinking about the problem in the same way, and your questions will be driven by the different solutions they have produced.

In preparation for his lesson, Mr. Harmon created a series of assessing and advancing questions that he planned to ask his students, based on the approaches he anticipated they would use (see Figure 3.9).

 PAUSE AND CONSIDER

Review solution B in Figure 3.9 and iii in the list of incomplete or incorrect solutions on page 65. What questions could you plan to ask students who produced these solutions, given the lesson goals (shown below)?

1. Patterns can be described and generalized by finding the underlying structure of the pattern and relating two variables that are changing at the same time.

2. Patterns that grow by a constant rate are linear.

3. There are different but equivalent ways of describing and representing the same pattern.

4. Connections can be made between different representational forms—tables, graphs, equations, words, and pictures.

Two of the strategies that Mr. Harmon anticipated students would use, and the questions he planned to ask about those approaches, are shown in Figure 3.15. The first assessing question he plans to ask each student is, "What have you figured out so far?" By asking this question (or some variant), the teacher is honoring the student's thinking by giving the student the opportunity to explain what he or she has done, not assuming that he knows what the student is thinking, and laying the foundation on which to build subsequent questions. The remaining assessing questions are intended to elicit more details on what the student understands about the solution the student has produced should they be needed.

Figure 3.15 • Two strategies and related questions Mr. Harmon anticipated

STRATEGY	ASSESSING QUESTIONS	ADVANCING QUESTIONS
The first hexagon (orange) requires 6 toothpicks. The rest of the hexagons $(x-1)$ only need 5 toothpicks (blue). $y = 6 + 5(x-1)$	• What have you figured out so far? • What do the variables in your equation represent? • Does your equation give you the same answer for parts a and b that you got by counting? • Where do you see the different components of your equation $(6, x-1, 5)$ in the diagram?	• What is the rate of change? • What do you think the graph of your equation will look like? Why?
Try to count the number of toothpicks in a row with 100 hexagons.	• What you have figured out so far? • How many toothpicks were there in the row of 5 hexagons? • How many toothpicks were in the row of 9 hexagons? • Can you figure out the number of toothpicks in a row of 10 hexagons without building and counting them?	• Is there a relationship between the number of hexagons in a row and the number of toothpicks it takes to build them? Do you see a pattern? • Could you use this pattern to describe the number of toothpicks in a row of 100 hexagons without counting?

Even if a student produces a correct equation and a clear explanation (as shown in the first row of Figure 3.15 and Solution B in Figure 3.9), Mr. Harmon will be interested in what this student *understands* and would not equate answering the questions posed in the task with understanding.

Toward this end, he plans to ask the student three additional assessing questions, each of which corresponds to the goals he had targeted in the lesson. Note that he is not explicitly targeting Goal 1 (i.e., patterns can be described and generalized by finding the underlying structure of the pattern and relating two variables that are changing at the same time) in these questions since the student has written a generalization in the form of an equation, but he wants to determine what the student understands about the equation.

- *What do the variables in your equation represent?* By asking this question, the teacher is making sure that the student is clear on what the x and y in the equation mean in the context of the problem. The teacher might expect a student to indicate that x represents the number of hexagons in a row and y represents the number of toothpicks in a row of hexagons. This would signal to the teacher that the student can connect a symbolic and contextual representation (Goal 4).

- *Does your equation give you the same answer for parts a and b that you got by counting?* By asking this question, the teacher is ensuring that the student has checked to see that the equation produces the same answers for parts a and b that they had previously determined. This relates to Goal 1, since it sends the message to the student that they should look for ways to verify and confirm the identified pattern.

- *Where do you see the different components of your equation (6, x – 1, 5) in the diagram?* By asking this question, the teacher is checking to see if the students can make a connection between the diagram of a hexagon row and the equation (Goal 4).

Armed with answers to these questions, Mr. Harmon is then positioned to advance the student's thinking by asking about the rate of change and what a graph of the equation would look like (Goal 2). Determining the rate of change would require the student to simplify the equation $y = 6 + 5(x - 1)$ to $y = 5x + 1$, thus producing an equivalent equation that could subsequently be discussed (Goal 3).

The approach of counting the number of toothpicks in a row of 100 hexagons (shown in the second row of Figure 3.15) is not a productive path to follow since it is unlikely to lead to either a verbal or symbolic generalization. The goal of the questions posed to this student is to help the student see the pattern (i.e., when a hexagon is added to a row, 5 more toothpicks are needed) and then find the underlying structure of the pattern (i.e., the relationship between the number of hexagons and the number of toothpicks).

Toward that end, the teacher will begin by asking the student, "How many toothpicks were there in the row of 5 hexagons?" and "How many toothpicks were in the row of 9 hexagons?" in order to confirm that the student is able to accurately count the toothpicks. At this point, the teacher may ask, "Can you figure out the number of toothpicks in a row of 10 hexagons without building and counting them?" This question will focus the student on how a 9-hexagon row is different from a 10-hexagon row, establishing that there is an increase of 5 toothpicks.

In order to advance the student beyond a recursive generalization, the teacher will then ask the student, "Is there a relationship between the number of hexagons in a row and the number of toothpicks it takes to build them? Do you see a pattern?" and leave the student to pursue this. Should the teacher have time to return to see what progress the student has made, he may ask the student to use the pattern to describe the number of toothpicks in a row of 100 hexagons.

TEACHING TAKEAWAY

Posing questions carefully crafted around your lesson's mathematical goals *and* students' work will tell you what students understand, not just how well they perform.

The bottom line is that the lesson goals need to drive the questions you ask. If your goal is for students to understand a mathematical relationship, then the questions you ask need to focus on getting students to recognize and articulate the relationship. Being satisfied with an answer such as "$y = 6 + 5(x - 1)$" in the Toothpick Hexagons task or "the shadow is 10 yards long" in the Floodlight Shadows task without further probing tells you nothing about what the student understands. Some students are good at finding answers but do not know why they are doing it or what it means.

It is important to note that while the teacher establishes specific learning goals for the lesson, students will be at different places in their learning based on their prior knowledge and experiences. Therefore, students are asked questions that help them make progress *toward* the goals based on their current understanding. All students may not enter the whole class discussion having made the same amount of progress on the task. This is not imperative. What is important is that the conversation provides the opportunity for students to extend and solidify their own understandings. The discussion should provide an opportunity for learning, not just a chance for students to report out what they have done.

Conclusion

In this chapter, we explored the components of the practice of *anticipating* and focused on a set of challenges that teachers often face when engaging in this practice. Anticipating is critical to planning a lesson because it provides the teacher with the opportunity to think deeply about what students are likely to do and how they will respond. This in-advance-of-the-lesson thinking eliminates much of the on-the-fly decision making that often is required in teaching. While you will not be able to anticipate everything that students will do, our experience tells us that you may be able to anticipate much of what will happen, especially if you do not plan alone.

Ms. Moran's work on anticipating provides insight into what a teacher needs to consider as he or she engages in the process. In planning her lesson, Ms. Moran thought deeply about what students were likely to do when presented with the task, including identifying aspects of the task she thought would be challenging for students, and the questions that she would ask students to assess their thinking and to move them toward the goals of the lesson. In addition, she identified specific aspects of student thinking that she planned to be on the lookout for during the lesson. This level of preparation before the lesson is likely to have a positive impact on the quality of the lesson itself because she has thought deeply about the mathematics she wants students to learn, the task, and what her students are bringing to the task.

By examining the work of Mr. Harmon around the Toothpick Hexagons task and Mr. Moore around the Floodlight Shadows task, we saw that while there are challenges associated with anticipating, collaborating with colleagues can go a long way in addressing the challenges. Mr. Harmon's work also makes clear how important it is to never lose sight of the lesson goals—they should serve as a resource throughout the lesson and a way of evaluating students' learning.

Anticipating Student Responses— Summary

Video Clip 3.1
To hear and see more about anticipating student thinking and using the monitoring tool to plan your responses, watch Video Clip 3.1.

Videos may also be accessed at
resources.corwin.com/5practices-highschool

We now invite you to apply what you have learned from your work in this chapter to your own teaching practice by engaging in the Linking the Five Practices to Your Own Instruction activity. We encourage you to find one or more colleagues with whom to collaborate on this activity. As one teacher commented, "A best practice for anticipating strategies for a specific task is to sit with a team of teachers to identify all of the possible inroads, rather than completing this as a teacher in isolation" (Smith & Stein, 2018, p. 49).

Linking the Five Practices to Your Own Instruction

ANTICIPATING

Identify a mathematical idea that you plan to teach sometime in the next two weeks.

1. Specify a clear goal for student learning and select a high-level task that is aligned with your learning goal.

2. Anticipate—get inside the problem, plan to respond, and plan to notice. If possible, get input from colleagues either virtually or face-to-face in order to gain additional insights into the task, its solutions, and its challenges.

3. Create assessing and advancing questions that are driven by your goals for the lesson but build on where students are in their thinking.

4. Produce a monitoring chart you can use to record data during the lesson that includes possible solutions, assessing and advancing questions that are driven by your goals, and questions you can ask students who cannot get started.

" One of the benefits of monitoring is really seeing the thoughts that kids are having, being able to assess what they're doing, hearing them explain, and asking questions. It's just great to have kids know that they're going to be accountable for their work, and that they're going to have to explain what they're thinking about. "

—MICHAEL MOORE, HIGH SCHOOL MATHEMATICS TEACHER

CHAPTER 4

Monitoring Student Work

The next practice we explore is monitoring students' work. Having carefully selected a goal and corresponding task, and anticipated the different strategies students will use, we now turn to instruction. How do you, as the teacher, keep track of what students are doing and saying, as the lesson unfolds in your classroom? Monitoring involves paying close attention to students' ideas and methods as they relate to your goals for the lesson. With many students working at the same time, this can be quite challenging. Who is using what strategy? How far did they get? Monitoring also involves asking students questions both to clarify their thinking and to move their thinking forward. Interacting with students during instruction in ways that productively move the lesson forward is complex work. The practice of monitoring is designed to help you manage this complexity by having a clear, focused lens for attending to and keeping track of students' thinking.

Smith and Stein (2018) describe monitoring in the following way:

> *Monitoring is the process of paying attention to the thinking of students during the actual lesson as they work individually or collectively on a particular task. This involves not just listening in on what students are saying and observing what they are doing, but also keeping track of the approaches that they are using, identifying*

those that can help advance the mathematical discussion later in the lesson, and asking questions that will help students make progress on the task. This is the time when the assessing and advancing questions that you created prior to the lesson will come in handy. These questions include those that will make students' thinking explicit, get students back on track if they are following an unproductive or inaccurate pathway, and will press students who are on the right course to think more deeply about why things work the way that they do. (p. 54)

In this chapter, we first describe key aspects of monitoring and illustrate what this practice looks like in an authentic high school classroom. We then discuss what aspects of monitoring are challenging for teachers and provide an opportunity for you to explore monitoring in your own teaching practice.

Part One: Unpacking the Practice: Monitoring Student Work

What is involved in monitoring students' thinking? This practice involves tracking the thinking of students in your class and asking questions to uncover what students understand (assessing questions) and to move students' thinking forward (advancing questions). Figure 4.1 highlights the components of this practice along with key questions to guide the process of monitoring.

Figure 4.1 • Key questions that support the practice of monitoring

WHAT IT TAKES	KEY QUESTIONS
Tracking student thinking	How will you keep track of students' responses during the lesson?
	How will you ensure that you check in with all students during the lesson?
Assessing student thinking	Are your assessing questions meeting students where they are?
	Are your assessing questions making student thinking visible?
Advancing student thinking	Are your advancing questions driven by your lesson goals?
	Are students able to pursue advancing questions on their own?
	Are your advancing questions helping students to progress?

In the next sections, we illustrate the practice of monitoring by continuing our investigation of Ms. Moran's implementation of the Staircase task. As you view video clips from her class and read the descriptions of what took place, consider how Ms. Moran's attention to the key questions may have shaped her teaching.

Tracking Student Thinking

Once your students begin working on the task, you will want an efficient and productive way to follow what they are doing. Who is making progress? Who has questions? Who is feeling stuck? Tracking the diversity of students' thinking during instruction is complex work. Kazemi, Gibbons, Lomax, and Franke (2016) emphasize that it is not sufficient to wait for students to complete the task in order to check their progress. Instead, teachers need a way to "gain insight into student thinking that [is] manageable" during "face-to-face conversations with students" during class (p. 184).

The monitoring chart you developed during the anticipating phase can be a valuable resource for tracking student thinking. As you observe and talk with your students, you can quickly note what strategy students are using and record it in the *Who and What* column of your monitoring chart. This is where listing the anticipated strategies on your monitoring chart really comes in handy! You may also want to note anything particularly interesting that a student is doing—a question or variation in a strategy or a connection between two strategies, for example. Indicating when students are using a strategy that was not anticipated is equally important, both for the day's lesson and for the future, particularly if those strategies have the potential to illuminate the mathematical goals of the lesson. There is typically little time to make elaborate comments on the monitoring chart during instruction. Still, making some notes throughout the lesson can help you stay abreast of what is happening. Many teachers choose to print their monitoring chart before the lesson and take notes by hand as the lesson progresses. Others prefer to annotate an electronic version of the monitoring chart during instruction. Either way, the monitoring chart can help you quickly reference how students are thinking about the task.

As you track students' responses, you want to make sure that you are circulating throughout the classroom. Some teachers opt to move in a designated pattern around the room as a way to ensure they check in with each student during the lesson. Having students work in groups can increase collaboration and make it easier to touch base with more than one student at a time (Horn, 2012). Using the monitoring chart can help you keep track of which students you have spoken with as well as how many times you have visited each group. It may be hard, at times, to pull yourself away from a group that is having a particularly interesting discussion. Or you may find yourself spending extra time with students who are having trouble getting started with the task. In either case, making a plan for how you will circulate among and keep track of students as you monitor their thinking is an important consideration. Ms. Moran explained that the monitoring chart is an important part of her planning, and

> **TEACHING TAKEAWAY**
>
> Taking quick notes on your monitoring chart can help you track which students use which strategies.

> **TEACHING TAKEAWAY**
>
> Using the monitoring chart can help you track your interaction with students, in terms of both what students are doing and with whom you have spoken.

using it during instruction is a key part of how she teaches: "When I'm walking around, I have my monitoring chart and I use it to keep track of things, where groups are at and who I need to come to back to." Electronic teacher dashboards can also be a resource as you monitor student thinking. For example, the Desmos platform allows teachers quick access to individual students' work on the graphing calculator and geometry tool (Danielson & Meyer, 2016). This can provide valuable information about how individual students approach the task and can help you decide who you might need to talk with as you make your way around the room.

 **PAUSE AND CONSIDER**

How do you track students' ideas during instruction?

How do you circulate among your students as they are working?

What techniques might help you more effectively track student thinking in your classroom?

Assessing Student Thinking

As you monitor students' progress, you want to interact with students in ways that take them from where they are now and move them toward the lesson goals. Jacobs and Philipp (2010) highlight the importance of this goal when they explain that teaching that "builds on children's ways of thinking can lead to rich instructional environments and gains in student achievement" (p. 101).

To start, be on the lookout for those strategies that you anticipated that students might use. Once you recognize that a student is using one of the anticipated approaches, you can examine the assessing questions you designed for that approach. The assessing (and advancing) questions in the monitoring chart are not meant to be a script. Rather, they are intended as a reference for you to use to help you consider what questions you want to ask particular students. For example, when Ms. Moran sees a student using a recursive pattern, she does not automatically ask, "How would you describe the number of squares in Stage 5?" Instead, she looks at what this particular student is doing or saying and decides what question is appropriate to ask.

When selecting an assessing question to use in class, there are two main considerations. First, aim to meet students where they are in their current thinking about the task. Ball, Lubienski, and Mewborn (2001) emphasize that "sizing up students' thinking and responding" depends on the details of what a student is doing (p. 451). Be sure to ask about the students' ideas, about what they have written or drawn. Using students' own terminology can often be helpful. Be aware that what you anticipated students might do is not always what they end up doing. Asking students specific questions about their work is an important way to uncover how they are thinking about the task and their solution. As Ms. Moran explained, "As much as I plan and as much as I anticipate, students always surprise me." Matthew Harmon echoed this point, saying, "There's always going to be a new method that you never would have thought of." Assessing questions are important because they can help you uncover what students are doing, whether or not that aligns with what you anticipated.

> ### TEACHING TAKEAWAY
> Look and listen *carefully*. Modify your planned assessing questions in real time based specifically on what students are doing and saying, rather than what you thought they would do or say.

Second, assessing questions are most useful when they make students' thinking visible in ways that can then help you move their thinking forward toward the lesson goals. Ms. Moran described the value of assessing questions: "They help me be sure I know where students are, what concepts are strong, and what goals are getting reached." You want to understand not only *what* students did but *why* they did it. Understanding the reasons behind a student's strategy often provides the clues you need to help a student reconsider her position or move deeper into the task.

What does this look like in practice? In Analyzing the Work of Teaching 4.0, you will explore how students in Ms. Moran's class begin to make sense of the Staircase task. We encourage you to look at the student work and consider the questions posed before you read our analysis.

Analyzing the Work of Teaching 4.0

Exploring Student Problem-Solving Approaches

After launching the Staircase task, Ms. Moran gave students time to work on the task in their groups, with each group sharing a single copy of the task. Here you will investigate the work of two groups of students: Maya, Taylor, and Collin in one group and Mae and Isabel in the other group.

Maya, Taylor, and Collin's Work

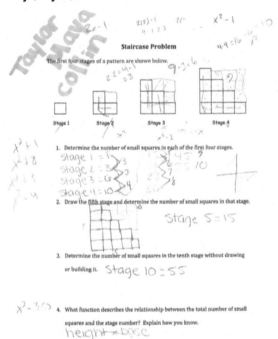

online resources ► A full-size scan of this image can be accessed at
resources.corwin.com/5practices-highschool

Mae and Isabel's Work

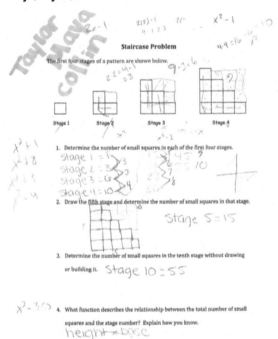

online resources ► A full-size scan of this image can be accessed at
resources.corwin.com/5practices-highschool

As you examine the students' written work, consider the following questions:

1. What can you infer from their written work about how these groups of students are thinking about the task?

   - What do Maya, Taylor, and Collin's responses to each of the four questions reveal about their understanding of the task?

   - What does Mae and Isabel's table reveal about their understanding of the task?

2. What strategies are these two groups of students using? Can you identify each strategy as one listed on Ms. Moran's monitoring chart? (See Figure 3.6)

3. What assessing questions would you want to ask these students in order to be sure that you understand their reasoning about the problem?

Exploring Student Problem-Solving Approaches—Analysis

There is a lot to see in Maya, Taylor, and Collin's work! First, they have made a variety of notations in the four figures shown at the top of the task sheet. They have drawn vertical and horizontal lines in the left columns and bottom rows of the staircases, which may indicate that they were investigating the growth of the figures along these dimensions. They have also created larger squares around each staircase and on Staircase 3 seem to have crossed out the small squares that are not part of that staircase. In responding to question 1, the students have made a table of sorts, listing the stage number and total number of small squares for staircases in Stages 1–4, as well as the total number of small squares for staircases in Stages 5–10. They also wrote the difference in the number of small squares between subsequent stages, from a difference of 2 between staircases in Stages 1 and 2 to a difference of 10 between staircases in Stages 9 and 10. This recursive approach of adding the stage number to the previous stage (Solution A, Figure 3.4) is likely the source of their answer to question 3 about the total number of small squares in the staircase at Stage 10. For question 2, Maya, Taylor, and Collin have drawn the fifth staircase and also lightly drawn additional small squares to create a 5×5 square, similar to the staircases at the top of the sheet. It may be that they were beginning to explore a geometric solution to the task as well. On the left side of the page they have written a number of equations: $x^2 + 1, x^2 + 2, x^2 + 3$, and more. Perhaps these students understood that the figures increased along two dimensions and thus the equation representing the relationship between the total number of small squares and the stage number would be quadratic—and they were trying to find an equation that produced the total number of small squares they had already calculated. Their response to question 4, "height × base," provides further evidence that they understood that the pattern involves two-dimensional growth.

What might Ms. Moran want to ask Maya, Taylor, and Collin to help understand their work? She might want to ask how they determined their answer to question 3: "Can you tell me how you found that Stage 10 has 55 squares?" This would give her insight into whether they did in fact use a recursive strategy to determine this. Or she might want to ask about the 5 × 5 square they have drawn: "Can you tell me what you did here on question 2?" or "What do these additional squares represent?" Ms. Moran could also explore the equations they have written by asking, "Can you tell me about these equations?" Each of these questions would help Ms. Moran begin to assess how Maya, Taylor, and Collin approached the task.

Mae and Isabel have created a table for the staircases at Stages 1–6 with x as the stage number and y as the number of cubes or small squares. On the line that separates these values, they have written the difference between the stage number and the number of small squares for Stages 1–4. Their table also lists the differences in the number of small squares in a staircase from one stage to the next. It may be that Mae and Isabel used recursion (Solution A, Figure 3.4) to identify the values in the table, for example, determining that Stage 6 has 21 squares because it is 6 more than the 15 squares in Stage 5. In addition, next to each row in the table, Mae and Isabel have written a multiplication expression in which the product equals the number of small squares in the corresponding stage. For example, next to Stage 2, we see the expression 1 × 3, whose product 3 is the number of cubes in Stage 2. Next to Stage 4, we see 2 × 5, with 10 being the number of cubes in Stage 4. What is this pattern? Could it be that Mae and Isabel have identified a numeric pattern that is similar to the geometric pattern in Solution D (Figure 3.4), in which one multiplies half of the length ($\frac{1}{2}n$) by one more than the width ($n + 1$) to find the total number of squares? If so, why have they reversed these values and written 7 × 3 for the last expression?

There can be a great deal to process in the moments of instruction. Effective assessing questions help students articulate their ideas and give you insight into how they are making sense of the task. What might you ask Mae and Isabel to help them reveal their thinking? Potential assessing questions include "What does the expression 1 × 3 mean?" "How does 1 × 3 relate to the stage number? To the number of squares?" "How did you determine these expressions?"

In Analyzing the Work of Teaching 4.1, you will investigate what Ms. Moran does to support Mae and Isabel as they continue to work on the Staircase task.

Analyzing the Work of Teaching 4.1

Assessing Student Thinking

Video Clip 4.1

In this video, you will listen as Ms. Moran talks with Mae and Isabel. You examined Mae and Isabel's written work earlier in Analyzing the Work of Teaching 4.0. Take a moment and remind yourself of their approach.

Mae and Isabel's Work

x stage	y # of cubes		
1	1	2	.5 × 2
2	3	3	1 × 3
3	6	4	1.5 × 4
4	10	5	2 × 5
5	15		2.5 × 6
6	21		7 × 3

Since they created the table you saw in Analyzing the Work of Teaching 4.0, Mae and Isabel have continued to explore the pattern they discovered. As Ms. Moran approaches, there is a 3×7 rectangle created from square tiles on Mae's desk. In addition, Mae is writing on her paper "Stage 10—5×11."

As you watch Video Clip 4.1, consider the following questions:

1. What assessing questions does Ms. Moran ask Mae and Isabel?

2. How do her assessing questions help Ms. Moran make sense of how Mae and Isabel are thinking about the problem?

3. How do her assessing questions help Ms. Moran diagnose challenges these students are facing?

 Videos may also be accessed at
resources.corwin.com/5practices-highschool

Assessing Student Thinking—Analysis

As Ms. Moran approaches Mae and Isabel, we hear Isabel state, "So then Stage 10 would be 5 times 11. Okay, we figured out how to get them." Ms. Moran's assessing questions are intended to help the teacher understand what it is that Mae and Isabel have figured out. Ms. Moran first asks Mae to "draw it out" for her with Stage 10. When Mae responds that "a smaller one would probably be easier," Ms. Moran adjusts her question and asks, "Could you use what you discovered for Stage 2?" Mae begins to do so, then hesitates and says, "I know how to explain it without the cubes." In response, Ms. Moran suggests that Mae draw a picture of what's happening with the pattern. Mae responds, "I know how to do it without a picture, just with words and numbers." Ms. Moran then says, "Okay, so explain it in words for me."

This dialogue between Ms. Moran and Mae is significant. Ms. Moran's assessing questions change in response to Mae's comments, yet the goal of wanting to help Mae express her thinking remains the same. As the conversation continues, Mae provides an overview of their idea: "Every time, you get to two numbers [that] you multiply to get the number of cubes." She explains further: "You have one number that's half of the stage. You have the other number [that's] one more than the number that the stage is." Ms. Moran now follows up with several assessing questions intended to uncover how Mae and Isabel came up with this idea, beginning with "What were you thinking that led to this?"

Throughout this conversation, Ms. Moran's questions aim to uncover her students' thinking—she is not asking them to think differently; rather her goal is to better understand how they approached the problem. Having assessed Mae and Isabel's understanding, Ms. Moran writes the following notes in her monitoring chart next to Solution D (Figure 3.4): "Mae and Isabel: table/square tiles, Stage 10 is 5 × 11, explain in words $\frac{1}{2}n \times (n+1)$, no equation."

It is worth noting that in her conversation with students, Ms. Moran does not always use the assessing questions she had prepared in advance word-for-word, and in addition, she uses several assessing questions that she had not prepared in advance. This is to be expected! Developing assessing questions prior to instruction helped Ms. Moran get her head around how she might draw out students' thinking in specific cases. In the moment, however, as she interacts with students, she also develops new questions based on what students are doing and saying.

Advancing Student Thinking

Once you have an idea of how students are thinking about the problem, the next step is to advance their thinking. For some students, this might involve helping them reconsider what the task is asking them to do. For other students, it might mean encouraging them to consider a special case or pressing them to be able to explain why an approach was successful. Once again, your monitoring chart can be a resource as you decide how to help move students' thinking forward, as you select from or adapt the assessing questions you anticipated earlier.

As you choose an advancing question to use, you want to make sure that the question is driven by your goals for the lesson, and not just a way to help students produce an accurate solution. For example, for the Staircase task, the teacher's goal is not simply for students to identify an equation that represents the relationship between the staircases and the number of squares; her goal is for them to do so in a way that relates to an understanding of how quadratic functions grow and the different ways that such growth can be represented. Similarly, Mr. Harmon explained the need to have "advancing questions that drive precisely towards the goal of the lesson" and that "having a clear math learning goal is the thing that permeates the conversations you have and the questions you ask." As you select advancing questions, you will want to keep your goals for the lesson clearly in mind.

Another important feature of advancing questions is that they usually cannot be answered immediately. Instead, an effective advancing question should prompt students to think, explore, or reconsider ideas about the task. As Ms. Moran explained, "When an advancing question works well, you can see the students' heads go down and you can walk away and you know they're continuing their work. They're not even looking at you as they're working, as you're walking away."

This ability for students to pursue an advancing question is key. Thus, as you pose advancing questions, you will want to gauge students' initial reaction. Do they begin working? Can you see them thinking, mulling something over? Often that's how you will be able to tell if they were ready for that advancing question.

Of course, what is most essential is that your advancing questions prompt students to move forward in their thinking. After you ask an advancing question, you will want to give students time to work but will also want to check back in with the group to see how they have progressed. Michelle Musumeci, a teacher with whom we have worked, explained that in her experience,

> ....
> **TEACHING TAKEAWAY**
> You can often gauge the effectiveness of an advancing question by noticing whether students immediately begin to explore it!

I think you need to leave the students to think for a while and then go back and see what they've come up with. If they're still stuck, maybe that wasn't the right advancing question, and you need to try another one. And if they have moved forward, then possibly, you can move them forward even further, or you could ask more assessing questions to see what their thinking is at this point. (Smith & Sherin, 2019, p. 76)

While advancing questions are designed to help students make progress, it is important that you take time during the lesson to check whether or not they have successfully done so.

What does this look like in practice? In Analyzing the Work of Teaching 4.2 and 4.3, you will explore how Ms. Moran's use of advancing questions helps students make progress on the Staircase task. We encourage you to view the video clips and consider the questions posed before you read the analysis.

Analyzing the Work of Teaching 4.2
Advancing Student Thinking—Part One

Video Clip 4.2

In this video clip, Ms. Moran talks with the group that includes Aidan, Micki, Emily, and Erin. Their written work is provided below. What can you infer about how these students might be thinking about the task?

Aidan, Micki, Emily, and Erin's Work

Staircase Problem

The first four stages of a pattern are shown below.

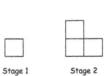

Stage 1   Stage 2   Stage 3   Stage 4

1. Determine the number of small squares in each of the first four stages.

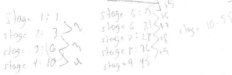

2. Draw the fifth stage and determine the number of small squares in that stage.

Next, watch Video Clip 4.2 in which Ms. Moran talks with Aidan, Micki, Emily, and Erin about their approach to the task.

As you watch the clip, consider the following questions:

1. What advancing questions does Ms. Moran ask Aidan, Micki, Emily, and Erin? What goals were the advancing questions targeting?

2. Is there evidence that the advancing questions can or cannot be pursued by the students?

```
online
resources
```
Videos may also be accessed at
resources.corwin.com/5practices-highschool

Advancing Student Thinking, Part One—Analysis

When Ms. Moran approaches Aidan, Micki, Emily, and Erin, she begins by asking general assessing questions in order to explore how they are thinking about the task. She first asks, "So, what are you guys noticing here?" Aidan responds that from Stage 1 to Stage 2, "The area is going up by 2. And then from Stage 2 to [Stage] 3, it's gone up by 3." As he speaks, Aidan refers to the table they created that lists the stage number and total number of small squares in each stage, along with the increase in the number of small squares from one stage to the next. Aidan then says, "So there's a constant number that we're going up each time." Ms. Moran asks about this idea of "adding by a constant" and Emily clarifies that "whatever the stage number is, is what you're going up by." Ms. Moran continues to assess this approach by asking about a specific case: what did they need to know to move from Staircase 3 to Staircase 4? At this point, Ms. Moran seems clear about the group's use of recursion to find the total number of squares (Solution A, Figure 3.4) and turns to another part of their work.

Ms. Moran next points to the figure labeled Stage 4 and once again asks a general assessing question: "What did you guys do here?" Aidan responds by explaining that they were exploring "making a full square, just to make it easier" to find the area, but that the edges of the figure are "not a straight line." Up until now, Ms. Moran had only been aware of the group's focus on a recursive solution, and yet she knew that recursion would not allow them to describe a general relationship between the stage number and the number of small squares at any given stage. Aidan's comments, however, provided an opening to a geometric solution. Having previously anticipated Solution C (Figure 3.4) in which students divide the figure into triangles, Ms. Moran is ready to seize on Aidan's comment and try to advance the group's thinking. She does so in two ways. First, she asks them to extend their thinking by considering using the diagonal: "What if you did draw that straight even line there? What shape would you have?" Ms. Moran is aware that the diagonal can be used to create triangles and encourages the students to extend their thinking to triangles. Second, she asks a general, but very important, advancing question: "How can you relate the figure to the figure number?" In doing so, Ms. Moran addresses one of her lesson goals, which is for students to see that quadratic growth can be expressed in both recursive and explicit forms. In particular, Ms. Moran's question suggests that rather than use the previous stage number to find the area of the current staircase, the students should see if they can relate the area of a staircase directly to the current stage number.

As Ms. Moran leaves the students, we can see that they begin to talk among themselves. While not shown in this video, Aidan, Micki, Emily, and Erin do find an equation that relates the number of small squares in a staircase to the stage number. You will have an opportunity to explore their thinking again in Analyzing the Work of Teaching 4.6.

Next, in Analyzing the Work of Teaching 4.3, you will explore Ms. Moran's interactions with another group of students as they work on the Staircase task.

Analyzing the Work of Teaching 4.3

Advancing Student Thinking—Part Two

Video Clip 4.3

In this video clip, Ms. Moran visits Araia, Kyle, Esme, and Adreana's group to discuss their progress on the Staircase task. Here is a copy of the students' work so far. What can you infer about how they might be thinking about the task?

Araia, Kyle, Esme, and Adreana's Work

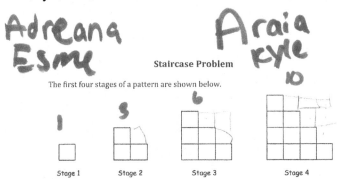

As Ms. Moran approaches the group, you can see that Araia has created a 5×5 square consisting of 15 blue and 10 yellow squares.

Next, watch Video Clip 4.3 in which Ms. Moran talks with Araia, Kyle, Esme, and Adreana.

As you watch the clip, consider the following questions:

1. What advancing questions does Ms. Moran ask the students? What goals were the advancing questions targeting?

2. Is there evidence that the advancing questions can or cannot be pursued by the students?

Videos may also be accessed at
resources.corwin.com/5practices-highschool

Advancing Student Thinking, Part Two—Analysis

When Ms. Moran approaches Araia, Kyle, Esme, and Adreana, she begins by asking a general assessing question: "So, what did you guys figure out here?" Araia then explains that they have been looking at the "amount missing" for Stages 1–5, which is the number of small squares needed to create a larger square as represented by the yellow squares for Stage 5. Ms. Moran continues to assess their strategy, asking why they decided to create a square. Araia responds that with the square "it's just easier to picture" and that their "goal right now is to try to find the equation." Ms. Moran then pursues a line of assessing questions intended to see how they understand their progress on this goal of finding an equation. "And how does this one [referring to the figure on Araia's desk] relate to that figure number?" she asks. Here Ms. Moran is asking how the figure Araia has created on her desk relates to Stage 5 (see Figure 4.2). Esme responds that "the other half [referring to the yellow squares] is from the previous stage" and "so maybe it's like x^2 minus the previous one." As the conversation continues, Ms. Moran seems to learn two things from her assessing questions: first, the students understand that the growth is two-dimensional ("this is 5 × 5"), and second, their process involves recursion—the blue squares represent the current stage number and the yellow squares are "just one less" or "the stage previous."

Figure 4.2 • Staircase 5 (in blue) combined with Staircase 4 (in yellow) as seen on Araia's desk

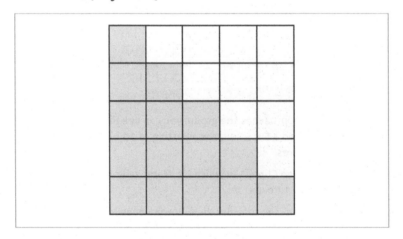

At this point, Ms. Moran is ready to try to advance the students' thinking. She is aware that the recursive solution they are using will not lead directly to an explicit equation. Yet she also understands that the geometric approach they are using, of adding small squares to make a shape that is "easier to picture," could be fruitful. Thus, she asks, "What if you use the same stage? You're saying you did the previous [stage]. What if you use the same stage?" Araia then adds another column of yellow squares to the figure on her desk (Figure 4.3). Ms. Moran clarifies, "So this right here, the blue is stage?" Araia responds, "Five," and indicates that the yellow squares also represent Stage 5.

Figure 4.3 • Staircase 5 (in blue) combined with another Staircase 5 (in yellow) as seen on Araia's desk

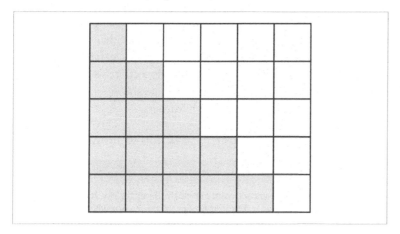

Ms. Moran then asks a final advancing question: "How does that relate to your original figure?" She walks away, leaving Araia, Kyle, Esme, and Adreana to consider this further. As Ms. Moran walks away, we hear Araia exclaim, "6 × 5 is 30 and this is 15, divided by 2 … there's our equation" along with "oh" and "yeah" from the others in the group, suggesting that Ms. Moran's advancing question was in fact effective. (In fact, when Ms. Moran returned to this group later, she found that they did not write a generalized equation for this approach, and instead were exploring a different strategy after talking with another group about their method.)

Cori Moran's Attention to Key Questions: Monitoring

Once students begin working on a task, it is essential that the teacher carefully monitor their progress. To do this, Ms. Moran tracks her students' thinking by paying close attention to what her students do and say. Because she has already listed the strategies she anticipated students will use on her monitoring chart, she can quickly note who is doing what as she circulates throughout the classroom. Using assessing and advancing questions allows Ms. Moran to draw out and make sense of students' ideas, as well as to try to move students' thinking forward.

We now take a look at key challenges teachers face as they monitor students' progress during instruction.

Part Two: Challenges Teachers Face: Monitoring Student Work

Although you can prepare for monitoring prior to the lesson by setting goals, selecting a high-level task, and anticipating what students will do and how you will respond, as we discussed in Part One, monitoring occurs *during* instruction. Collecting as much information as you can about what students are doing and thinking—and providing them support to help them make progress—arms you with data that will be vital to making decisions regarding the whole class discussion. Monitoring, however, is not without its challenges. In this section, we focus on three specific challenges associated with this practice, shown in Figure 4.4, that we have identified from our work with teachers.

Figure 4.4 • Challenges associated with the practice of monitoring

CHALLENGE	DESCRIPTION
Trying to understand what students are thinking	Students do not always articulate their thinking clearly. It can be quite demanding for teachers, in the moment, to figure out what a student means or is trying to say. This requires teachers to listen carefully to what students are saying and to ask questions that help them better explain what they are thinking.
Keeping track of group progress—which groups you visited and what you left them to work on	As teachers are running from group to group, providing support, they need to be able to keep track of what each group is doing and what they left students to work on. Also, it is important for a teacher to return to a group in order to determine whether the advancing question given to them helped them make progress.
Involving all members of a group	All individuals in the group need to be challenged to answer assessing and advancing questions. For individuals to benefit from the thinking of their peers, they need to be held accountable for listening to and adding on, repeating and summarizing what others are saying.

Trying to Understand What Students Are Thinking

Students are not always very articulate when they are asked to explain their thinking. They often use nonacademic language to describe things (e.g., "I did the opposite"), make vague references (e.g., "I put *this* over *that*."), and have difficulty providing a concise description of what they have done. In addition, students may come up with ways of solving problems (both correct and incorrect) that you had not anticipated. And even when you think that you know exactly what a student is thinking because their work resembles what *you* did, you could be dead wrong!

Trying to understand what students are thinking can be challenging work for a teacher, yet it is critical for teachers to make an effort to do so. If students have arrived at a correct solution, you will want to know how they got there so you can determine whether the process they used makes sense, always works, and how (or if) it might connect to more standard approaches. If students have arrived at an incorrect solution, you will want to know what led to the result so that you can provide an opportunity for students to consider some aspect of the task they may have not attended to. It would be easier for the teacher to just tell students that they are wrong and provide them with a new pathway to pursue or ask students to use a more standard or recognizable approach, but such *help* is short term. It may allow students to get a correct answer to the problem at hand using a standard method, but since students are moving forward based on the thinking of the teacher rather than their own thinking, it is not clear whether students will have access to the strategy the next time they are presented with a similar problem. Telling students what to do or how to do it does not help build their capacity to figure things out on their own or develop their identities as capable mathematics doers.

Assessing questions help make student thinking visible. Once student thinking is clear, then the teacher is in the position to help move the thinking forward. According to Boston, Dillon, Smith, and Miller (2017),

> *Questions are the only tool that teachers have to determine what students know and understand about mathematics. Specifically, purposeful questions should reveal students' current understandings; encourage students to explain, elaborate, or clarify their thinking; and make mathematics more visible and accessible for student examination and discussion.* (p. 71)

In Analyzing the Work of Teaching 4.4, you will have the opportunity to make sense of the thinking of students in Mr. Harmon's class. (Recall that Mr. Harmon's algebra students were working on the Toothpick Hexagons task, shown in Figure 3.8.)

Analyzing the Work of Teaching 4.4

Determining What Students Are Thinking—Part One

Video Clip 4.4

CONTINUED

CONTINUED FROM PREVIOUS

In Video Clip 4.4, you will visit the small group that includes Alexander, Jordyn, and Neveah. Alexander and Jordyn have written the equation $y = 5x + 1$ on their paper, while Neveah has written $y = 6 + 5(x - 1)$.

As you watch the video clip, consider the following questions:

1. What are the students thinking?

2. What does the teacher do in order to be sure he understands what students are thinking?

3. Why does the teacher suggest that the students graph the two equations?

 Videos may also be accessed at resources.corwin.com/5practices-highschool

Determining What Students Are Thinking, Part One—Analysis

As the video begins, Alexander and Jordyn are explaining their equation $y = 5x + 1$ to Nevaeh. Alexander explains that 1 is "our y-intercept," so "you put the 1 toothpick and then you add 5 and keep adding 5." He then comments that "we could use 6 as our y-intercept, but that's for another equation."

As Mr. Harmon approaches the group, he hears the end of the discussion regarding 6 as the "y-intercept." In an effort to better understand what they thought 6 represented, the teacher asks, "Could you write that equation? You're saying it's possible to start with 6." Alexander then points Mr. Harmon to the equation that Neveah has written, $y = 6 + 5(x - 1)$. Mr. Harmon likely realizes that while 6 is not the y-intercept in the equation $y = 6 + 5(x - 1)$, it could serve as an initial value for students as they model the equation. Not wanting to make assumptions about what the students understand, Mr. Harmon asks, "So the starting value for this one [pointing to Neveah's equation] is what?" Neveah then responds, "Six."

At this point, Mr. Harmon is aware that these students have two correct equations for finding the number of toothpicks when given the number of hexagons. However, it is not clear to Mr. Harmon whether the students understand that 6 is not the y-intercept or that the two equations are in fact equivalent. To explore this, he first asks, "What's consistent in both equations?" Alexander responds, "The slope." Since Mr. Harmon is still not sure that students recognize that two equations that represent the same situation must be equivalent, he next asks an advancing question intended to prompt students to further explore the relationship between the equations: "Could you draw both graphs?" Mr. Harmon suspects that graphing both equations might highlight for the students that while the starting values in their equations are different, the *y*-intercepts and rates of change in the graphs of the equations are the same. Mr. Harmon makes a note to be sure to raise a question during the whole group discussion regarding the domain of the function. He wants to be sure that students realize that the *y*-intercept has no meaning in this context, the *x*-values of the function in this context are limited to the natural numbers, and therefore the graph of the function begins with the point (1, 6) and is discrete rather than continuous.

Mr. Harmon made a number of important moves during his brief interaction with the small group. First and foremost, he asked questions that assessed students' understanding of the equation $y = 6 + 5(x - 1)$ and how it was the same as or different from the first equation $y = 5x + 1$. His advancing question, pressing students to compare the two solutions, addressed a key goal of the lesson—that there are different but equivalent ways of describing and representing the same pattern.

In Analyzing the Work of Teaching 4.5, you will explore one small group's work on the Floodlight Shadows task and their discussion with Mr. Moore.

Analyzing the Work of Teaching 4.5

Determining What Students Are Thinking—Part Two

Video Clip 4.5

In Video Clip 4.5, you will visit the small group that includes Zachary, Jerry, and Izzy. Students in the group produced the drawing and work shown, which served as the basis for their discussion with each other and ultimately with Mr. Moore. Before watching the video, consider the following: What might the students' written work reveal about their thinking?

CONTINUED

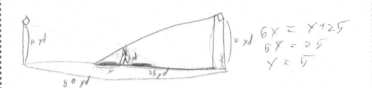

CONTINUED FROM PREVIOUS

As you watch the video clip, consider the following questions:

1. How are these students thinking about the task? What assumptions do they make?

2. What does the teacher do to understand the students' thinking, to make sure they are all on the same page, and to help move them forward?

online resources → Videos may also be accessed at resources.corwin.com/5practices-highschool

Determining What Students Are Thinking, Part Two—Analysis

The drawing produced by Zachary, Jerry, and Izzy, while not drawn to scale, provides a useful model of the information given in the problem. They have labeled the height of the floodlights and the length of the football field in yards and converted Eliot's height of 6 feet to 2 yards. In addition, they have labeled the distance from Eliot to one of the floodlights as 25 yards, since he is exactly halfway between the floodlights. Finally, they have drawn triangles, indicated where the shadows fall, and labeled the length of $\frac{1}{2}$ of the total shadow as x. However, it is not clear from their written work where they got the equation $6x = x + 25$ or what it represents in the context of the problem.

As we drop in on the small group discussion, Zachary has identified nested triangles $\triangle ABC$ and $\triangle DBE$ (see Figure 4.5) and is explaining that if Eliot is 2 yards tall ($\overline{DE}$) and the floodlight is 12 yards tall ($\overline{AC}$), then $\triangle ABC$ must be six times larger than $\triangle DBE$. He then states that $6x = x + 25$, and Jerry adds that this is because "the big triangle" ($\triangle ABC$) is six times larger than "the small triangle" ($\triangle DBE$). Zachary then explains further that in the equation $6x = 25 + x$, x represents the length of side $\overline{BE}$ and $25 + x$ represents the length of side $\overline{BC}$. He solves the equation and concludes that $x = 5$ yards and therefore the entire shadow length is 10 yards.

Figure 4.5 • Zachary, Jerry, and Izzy's drawing with labels added

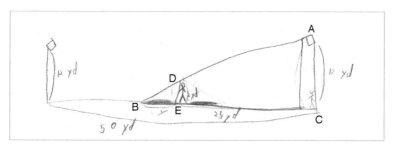

What is missing from Zachary's explanation is a discussion of *why* he can claim that ΔABC is six times the size of ΔDBE. While it is correct that *if* the large triangle (ΔABC) is six times the size of the small triangle (ΔDBE), then the corresponding sides of the two triangles must be related by the same scale factor, this relationship—corresponding sides of triangles are related by a scale—exits *if and only if* the two triangles are similar. Zachary appears to have taken similarity as a given when in fact it must be proven (something that Mr. Moore anticipated). He cannot *assume* that the triangles are similar.

When Mr. Moore joins the group, he asks, "How is it going?" This is an open invitation for the group to explain what they have been working on and is an opportunity for the teacher to just listen closely to how students are thinking about the problem. Zachary repeats the explanation he provided to his group. After Zachary indicates that ΔABC was six times the size of ΔDBE, Jerry mentions "similar triangles"; this is the first time the students have used this label to describe the relationship between the two triangles. At this point, Mr. Moore draws Izzy into the conversation by asking her to explain "what $x = 5$ is telling us." Izzy's explanation, that 5 yards is the length of one shadow and that the total length of both shadows is 10 yards, provides Mr. Moore with evidence that Izzy has some understanding of what Zachary and Jerry have been discussing.

Before leaving the group, Mr. Moore asks a critical question: "How do we know that we have similar triangles?" This is a key question for students to pursue, since their conclusion about the relationship between the corresponding sides of the triangles is only valid if the triangles are similar and one of the learning goals for the lesson was for students to justify that the triangles were similar by proving that corresponding angles are congruent. While Mr. Moore might have raised the question earlier in his interaction with the group, by waiting until the students had fully explained their thinking and confirming that the group members appeared to be on the same page, it was clear to him what students understood, what was missing in their argument, and what they needed to consider next.

Keeping Track of Group Progress

When you have students working in groups, it is important to keep track of which groups you have visited, what they are doing, and what you have left them to work on. Without a method of tracking this information, it is easy to forget to return to a group or to miss a group completely. To address this challenge, some teachers move around the room in a defined pattern so they know where they have been and where they need to go next. You could start with the group closest to the door and move counterclockwise on your initial pass around the room. Some teachers put a small colored dot on the table with each visit to a group so that they can easily tell which groups they have visited and how many times they had been there. Alternatively, you could give each group a number tent, list the group numbers on the bottom of your monitoring chart, and place a check next to the group number on the monitoring chart each time you visit the group.

Once you have checked the progress of each group, however, you may find that given time limitations it is more important to revisit some groups than others. For example, if you encountered a group that had trouble getting started or was struggling to move forward, you would want to make sure that they were able to move beyond the impasse they had encountered. Also, if you found that a group had started to use a strategy that you had planned to share but had not yet completed their work, you might want to check in with them again to see what progress they had been able to make.

While the *Who and What* column of the monitoring chart can be used to record what a group is doing, it is also important to keep track of the advancing question you encouraged the group to pursue when you left them. Asking advancing questions is critical in moving students forward, but you need to make sure that the question you asked is having the desired effect. You could track this by highlighting the question on your monitoring chart and indicate the group to whom you asked the question next to it. Alternatively, you could jot the question on the sticky note next to the group number if you used the sticky note approach. Elizabeth Brovey, a former teacher and current coach, indicates that she takes notes but also holds the group responsible for telling her what they were asked to do. As she described it,

> I have to keep track of what I told them to work on, so I try to take notes. But the other thing I do is when I come back I make them say, "What was it I was asking you to work on?... I told you guys, what did I ask you to do before I left?" And they have to tell me. So that's not just about them. That's about me too. 'Cause I also have to honor the frame that I've given them. (Conversation with Elizabeth Brovey, September 11, 2015)

In Analyzing the Work of Teaching 4.6, you will return to Ms. Moran's class where students continue to work on the Staircase task. You will observe Ms. Moran as she visits Aidan, Micki, Emily, and Erin a second time and consider what progress, if any, they have made.

Analyzing the Work of Teaching 4.6
Following Up With Students

Video Clip 4.6

When Ms. Moran first visited Aidan, Micki, Emily, and Erin (see Analyzing the Work of Teaching 4.2), she noted that they had found the recursive pattern but were struggling to find a way to easily calculate the number of small squares in larger staircases without knowing the number of squares in the previous staircase. Students had enclosed the staircase for Stage 4 (shown below) in a square but had not found a way to make productive use of it. Eventually students drew a diagonal across the square to create a large triangle and smaller triangles on the steps of the staircase. Ms. Moran challenged the group to see if they could relate the staircase to the stage number.

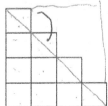

Stage 4

In Video Clip 4.6, Ms. Moran returns to the group to see what progress they have made.

As you watch Video Clip 4.6, consider the following questions:

1. Did the advancing question students were left with help them move forward?

2. What does the teacher do to push their thinking further?

Videos may also be accessed at
resources.corwin.com/5practices-highschool

At the end of her first visit to the group that included Aidan, Micki, Emily, and Erin, Ms. Moran challenged the students to relate the triangles formed by the staircase cut by the diagonal of the square to the stage number. Prior to Ms. Moran's arrival at the group, Emily explains how she counted the pieces (see Figure 4.6): the 6 whole squares in the staircase (blue), the 4 triangles in the staircase below the diagonal (green), and the 4 triangles in the staircase above the diagonal (pink). While this method produced the correct number of small squares in the Stage 4 staircase, there is nothing generalizable about Emily's method—she does relate the stage number to the number of pink triangles, but she does not seem to recognize that the green triangles are also half the stage number or that the green and pink triangles together give you the same number of squares as the stage number and she has not come up with a way to determine the number of whole squares without counting.

Figure 4.6 • A visual model showing the way Emily counted the small squares

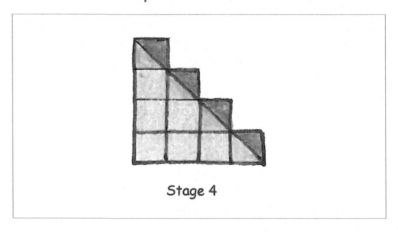

Stage 4

Aidan then explains an alternative method, using Stage 8:

> So we just did 8 × 8 [length and width of the square]. And then …
> which was 64 [area of the whole square] and we divide it by 2,
> which got to 32 [area of the triangle in blue formed by the red
> diagonal]. And then we took, x is the stage number, so we took the
> stage number and then basically divide it by two [which gives the
> area of the small yellow triangles], I guess, which is four … and then
> add that to 32, which we got as 36. (See Figure 4.7)

Figure 4.7 • A visual model showing the way Aidan found the number of small squares in the staircase for Stage 8

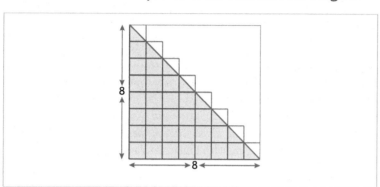

Ms. Moran clarifies that Aidan is describing a method for finding the number of small squares in the staircase at Stage 8. Following his explanation, she asks the group if they can connect the number of squares in Stage 4 to the image of the staircase at Stage 4. In asking the group to apply their method to another stage number, she is challenging them to move beyond the specifics of one stage to see if they can apply the method to another stage and begin to generalize for any stage. She wants the students to realize that although they have used three variables—length, width, and stage number—the three variables all represent the same quantity.

The advancing question posed to students at the end of Ms. Moran's first visit challenged students to relate the triangles formed by the staircase cut by the diagonal of the square to the stage number. Aidan's explanation of how to find the number of small squares in a Stage 8 staircase provides evidence that they had made considerable progress in accomplishing what they had been asked to do. They were now positioned to refine their description and create an equation that could be used more generally.

Involving All Members of a Group

The purpose of having students work in groups is so they can serve as resources for each other as they engage in solving challenging problems (Horn, 2012). But getting students to actually work together requires more than just telling them to do so. The teacher needs to set clear expectations regarding group work and to reinforce these expectations through her interactions with small groups. For example, if one student in the group has a question, the teacher might indicate that she will only answer a question if no one in the group can so that students see members of the group as a first source of support. When the teacher begins a discussion with one member of a group, she needs to bring in other group members to make sure they are following the discussion.

There is limited value in having student desks pushed together if they are not benefiting from what their peers have to contribute. Mr. Harmon describes how he ensures that all of the group members are invested in the work of the group:

> So when I'm interacting with a group, my tendency is generally to try and bring out voices that aren't as forthcoming. So a lot of times, I'll come up to the group and the person who's talking is the person who is generally doing the thinking. And so I'll try and steer the direction towards someone else to try and elicit their understanding. Maybe ask them questions about what the person was talking about what they're referring to, where they can they point to those things in reference to the problem.

While involving all members of a group in a discussion is important, it is extremely difficult for several reasons. First, it takes time. The more time you spend with one group, the less time there is to visit other groups. Second, it is challenging enough for the teacher to understand some explanations without making sure that everyone else in the group understands it too. Hence, it may not be realistic to make sure that every student speaks every time you interact with a single group. What is important is that you set norms for working together that make clear what your expectations are and that you make an effort to ensure that members of the group are at a minimum paying attention to the discussion.

In Analyzing the Work of Teaching 4.7, you will drop in on Clairice Robinson's ninth-grade class as they work on the Cycle Shop task, discussed in Chapter 3 and presented again in Figure 4.8. As a result of engaging in this lesson, Ms. Robinson wants her students to understand the following:

1. Equations can be created that represent real-world constraints.

2. There is a point of intersection between two (unique nonparallel) linear equations that represents where the two equations have the same x- and y-values; this point is the solution to the system since it satisfies both equations.

3. A system of equations can be solved using different representations (i.e., tables, graphs, equations, pictures) and connections can be made between different representational forms, including the problem context.

Ms. Robinson consistently tells her students that when they work in groups, they need to work together—they need to explain their thinking, listen closely to the thinking of other members of the group, and ask questions when something is not clear. She stresses that every member of the group needs to be able to explain what the group is doing and thinking. As you explore the vignette, which depicts her interactions with one group, you will consider how she operationalizes her commitment to holding students accountable to working together.

Figure 4.8 • The Cycle Shop task

The Cycle Shop

You work for a small business that sells bicycles and tricycles. Bicycles have one seat, two pedals, and two wheels. Tricycles have one seat, two pedals, and three wheels.

On Monday, there are a total of 24 seats and 61 wheels in the shop. How many bicycles and how many tricycles are in the shop? Show all your work using any method you choose and explain your thinking.

Source: This version of the task appears in Steele and Smith (2018). The task was adapted from New York City Department of Education. (n.d.). The Cycle Shop. Retrieved from https://www.weteachnyc.org/resources/resource/high-school-algebra-cycle-shop/

 This task can also be accessed at
resources.corwin.com/5practices-highschool

Analyzing the Work of Teaching 4.7
Holding All Students Accountable

In the Cycle Shop Vignette, you will see Ms. Robinson's interactions with one small group in her class that consists of Kayla, Hailey, and Angel.

As you read the vignette, consider the following questions:

1. What aspects of monitoring do you see Ms. Robinson engage in as she interacts with Kayla, Hailey, and Angel?

2. What does Ms. Robinson do to ensure that all three students are involved in making progress on the task?

Cycle Shop Vignette

1	Ms. R:	So tell me what your group came up with.
2	Kayla:	We said that the answer was (11, 13).
3	Ms. R:	How did you get that?
4	Kayla:	We created two equations and then graphed them using Desmos.
5		*(Kayla points to the image on her computer screen, shown below.)*
6		

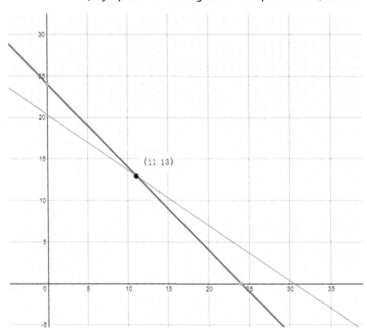

7   *Source:* Graph created with Desmos at desmos.com.

8	Ms. R:	What equations did you come up with?
9	Kayla:	$x + y = 24$ and $2x + 3y = 61$.
10	Ms. R:	Hailey, what do these equations mean?
11	Hailey:	24 is the number of seats and 61 is the number of wheels.
12	Ms. R:	Angel, what do x and y represent?
13	Angel:	x is the number of bicycles and y is the number of tricycles.
14	Ms. R:	So what does the equation $x + y = 24$ mean?
15	Angel:	It means that the number of bicycles plus the number of tricycles is 24.
16	Ms. R:	What does the equation $2x + 3y = 61$ mean? Hailey?
17	Hailey:	Each bicycle has two wheels, so $2x$ is the number of bicycle wheels.
18		Each trike has three wheels, so $3x$ is the number of trike wheels.
19		Altogether there are 61 wheels.
20	Ms. R:	So which line represents which equation? Kayla?
21	Kayla:	*(Referring to the color-coding on Desmos)* The red one is $x + y = 24$ and the
22		blue one is $2x + 3y = 61$.
23	Ms. R:	What does each of these lines represent in the context of this situation?
24		*(All three students shrug and remain silent. Ms. R waits 10 seconds.)* I want
25		the three of you to talk about this and see if you can explain what is going
26		on here. I will be back.
27		

28   *(Ms. R makes note of the question she posed and leaves students to pursue it while she talks*
29   *with other groups. She returns to check their progress. While the graph was not completely*
30   *accurate because it did not show discrete points, she knew this could be addressed later.)*
31   Ms. R: So what did you figure out? Angel?
32   Angel: The red line is $x + y = 24$.
33   Ms. R: What do the points on the line mean? I see that $(24, 0)$
34   is a point on this line. What does that mean? Hailey?
35   Hailey: I think it means that you could have 24 bicycles and no
36   tricycles and have 24 seats.
37   Ms. R: So what do all the points on the line represent? Kayla?
38   Kayla: Different ways to get 24 seats?
39   Angel: Oh, yeah. That's it! All the combinations that give you 24.
40   Ms. R: So what does the blue line represent? Hailey?
41   Hailey: All the combinations that give you 61 wheels?
42   Ms. R: Take a minute to discuss whether or not Hailey is right
43   and how you can be sure. I will be back.
44
45   *(Ms. R makes note of the question she posed and leaves students to pursue*
46   *it while she talks with other groups. She returns to check their progress.)*
47
48   Ms. R: So Kayla, what do you think?
49   Kayla: Hailey was right. We found two points on the graph $(20, 7)$ and $(8, 15)$ and
50   they both worked in the equation. So we think that all the points on the line
51                   $2x + 3y = 61$ would make the equation true. *(Angel and Hailey are both*
52   *nodding their agreement.)*
53   Ms. R: Okay, so why do the two lines cross at $(11, 13)$? What does that mean?
54   Angel: It means that it is the answer: 11 bikes, 13 trikes.
55   Ms. R: But why do the two lines cross here and nowhere else?
56   What exactly does that mean? I may not have time to
57   check in with you again, but I expect you to keep
58   working on this.
59   *(Ms. R makes note of the final challenge posed to the group. She did not have time to return the*
60   *group but felt that they had made sufficient progress to benefit from the whole group discussion.)*

Holding All Students Accountable—Analysis

Ms. Robinson's three interactions with Kayla, Hailey, and Angel highlight many of the aspects of monitoring that we have discussed in this chapter. She begins each visit to the group by offering an open invitation to students to describe their work (line 1: "So tell me what your group came up with."; line 31: "So what did you figure out?"; line 48: "So Kayla, what do you think?"). Following the students' explanation, she asks a series of assessing questions (lines 3, 10, 12, 14, 16, 20, and 56) that are directly connected to the explanations given by students and are intended to make students' thinking clearer and public. For example, when Kayla states that "We created two equations and then graphed them using Desmos" (line 4), Ms. Robinson asks "What equations did you come up with?" (line 8).

As a result of the assessing questions Ms. Robinson asked during her first visit to the group, she realized that while students had arrived at the correct answer of 11 bikes and 13 trikes, it was not clear that they understood how the graph related to the equations they had created or to the context of the problem. In order to press the trio to think about the connection between the different representations they had (i.e., equations, a graph, and the problem context), the teacher asks an advancing question (lines 23–26) intended to focus students on the relationship between the context and the graph. While students were subsequently able to explain that the lines represented all the combinations of 24 seats and 61 wheels (lines 35–41), the tentative nature of Kayla (line 38) and Hailey's (line 41) responses lead Ms. Robinson to asked students to explore the validity of Hailey's claim (lines 42–43).

In this short vignette, we see Ms. Robinson keeping track of the questions she leaves students to work on in her absence (lines 28–30, 45–46, and 59–60) so she will know what she needs to follow up on when she returns to the group. While the first advancing question (lines 23–26) did not result in much progress, students' response to the question made clear that they needed a more explicit directive to focus their attention on what the points on the line actually represented. The second advancing question (lines 42–43) was successful in moving students forward and evidenced by their explanation: "We found two points on the graph (20, 7) and (8, 15) and they both worked in the equation. So we think that all the points on the line would make the equation true" (lines 49–51). The understanding that a line represents all the points that satisfies the equation is critical to ultimately seeing that the point of intersection is the point that satisfies both equations at the same time. While the graph was not completely accurate because it did not show discrete points, this was something that Ms. Robinson knew would come out in the discussion. She felt that having the lines drawn at this point would help students better visualize the point of intersection and understand what the lines represented.

Perhaps what is most striking in Ms. Robinson's interactions with the group is the way in which she holds Kayla, Hailey, and Angel accountable for participating in the discussion. Ms. Robinson has stressed the need for students to work together and has made it clear that every member of the group needs to be able to explain what the group is doing and thinking. There are several instances of this in the vignette. While Kayla is the first to indicate what the answer is and how they got it, Ms. Robinson turns to Angel and Hailey to explain what each of the equations actually means. At the end of the first visit, Ms. Robinson makes it clear: "I want the three of you to talk about this and see if you can explain what is going on here" (lines 24–26). When she makes subsequent return visits to the group, she involves all three students in explaining what they have figured out.

The key to holding students accountable for working together is setting clear expectations regarding what you expect and then reinforcing these expectations through your actions and interactions.

Conclusion

In this chapter, we explored the practice of monitoring. This is perhaps one of the more challenging practices because the actual practice of monitoring takes place during instruction as the lesson is unfolding in real time. There is a lot to attend to as students work individually and in small groups, and it can be overwhelming. Our experience suggests that careful attention to anticipating prior to the lesson, including the preparation of a monitoring chart, can help make monitoring more manageable.

This was evident in the work of Ms. Moran. As a result of the care she took in planning the lesson (as described in Chapters 2 and 3), she entered the class with clarity about what she wanted students to learn and how she would support them in reaching the goals she set. She asked assessing questions that made students' thinking clear and public, asked advancing questions to move students forward in thinking about the mathematics of the lesson, and checked on their progress. She made notes as she interacted with groups so that she would be able to make purposeful decisions about who and what to highlight during the whole group discussion that would follow. (You can see Ms. Moran's annotated monitoring chart in Appendix C.) Ms. Moran's work during the monitoring phase makes salient that assessing and advancing questions occur in cycles—you assess, then you advance, you return, and you assess again, then you advance again. The intent is that each time you return to a group, you move them further toward the goal. While one visit to some groups may be sufficient, other groups may require multiple visits.

> **TEACHING TAKEAWAY**
>
> Assessing and advancing questions occur in cycles.

As you will note on Ms. Moran's monitoring chart, she managed to capture a great deal of what was going on while students worked on the task. Did she record everything that happened when she interacted with students as they worked on the task? No. She was able to capture sufficient detail about what students were doing to give her a good sense of what they understood and what they were struggling with. While we discussed in this chapter what would be ideal to try to capture on the monitoring chart, the reality is that you may not get every single thing. The point is to do the best you can to get an accurate picture of the ideas students have generated that will help you in achieving the goals for the lesson.

In our analysis of Mr. Harmon, Mr. Moore, and Ms. Robinson's interactions with small groups, we saw the importance of asking questions that help clarify what students are thinking. You cannot move students forward if you do not know where they are to start with. It is critical to use questions to make student thinking visible. Although sometimes this can be straightforward, other times this can require perseverance on the part of the teacher to get to the bottom of what a student is really thinking!

Because monitoring generally involves interaction with small groups of students, it is critical to consider how you can help build students' capacity to work together. Ms. Robinson's interactions with Kayla, Hailey, and Angel provide some insights on how to hold students accountable for working together, but getting students to work together productively will not happen overnight. This will require time, patience, and persistence on your part!

Your ability to effectively monitor will improve over time as you continue to do it, reflect on what went well and what did not, make midcourse corrections, and do it again. The key is to keep at it, even if the first few times are not as successful as you would like.

Monitoring Student Work—Summary

Video Clip 4.7

To hear and see more about monitoring student work using the monitoring tool, watch Video Clip 4.7.

 Videos may also be accessed at
resources.corwin.com/5practices-highschool

In the next chapter, we explore the next two practices: *selecting* and *sequencing*. There, we will return to Ms. Moran's lesson and consider what it takes to engage in these practices and the challenges they present.

Linking the Five Practices to Your Own Instruction

MONITORING

It is now time to teach the lesson you planned in Chapters 2 and 3! (Or if you prefer, select another lesson. Just make sure that you have engaged in Practice 0 and have anticipated student responses and questions before you begin.) We encourage you to video record the lesson so that you can reflect back on what occurred during the lesson.

1. Before teaching the lesson, consider how you are going to make sure you visit every group and remember the questions you leave groups to pursue. Also, consider whether there are any specific instructions you want to give students regarding your expectations for how you expect them to work in their groups.

2. As you teach the lesson, use your monitoring chart to keep track of the strategies students are using. Be sure you are checking in with every group and returning to groups to see if they are making good progress.

3. Following the lesson, use these questions to guide reflection on your monitoring:

   • Did you interact with each group in the class? If not, what could you do differently to ensure that you have a chance to check in with all of your students? Did you return to groups when you said you would to check on their progress?

   • To what extent did students use the strategies you had anticipated? What was unexpected?

   • To what extent were the assessing questions you anticipated in planning useful in your interactions with students? Did they help you make students' thinking clear and public?

   • To what extent were the advancing questions you anticipated in planning useful in your interactions with students? Did they help students make progress on the task?

   • To what extent were you able to involve all members of a group in the conversation? What might you do differently in the future to hear the voices of more students?

4. What did you learn about students' understanding of mathematics as a result of teaching the lesson?

5. What lessons have you learned about monitoring that will help you in planning and enacting the next lesson you teach?

"As I monitor the groups and see where they're at, I'm also thinking about the discussion and what ideas to share and what groups. The key for me is that with selecting and sequencing, I can make sure that the goals are highlighted in a way that helps really create a story for the students. "

—CORI MORAN, HIGH SCHOOL MATHEMATICS TEACHER

CHAPTER 5

Selecting and Sequencing Student Solutions

Once students have had the opportunity to explore the task individually or in small groups, and you as the teacher have monitored their discussions, the next step is to bring the class together for a whole group discussion of the key mathematical ideas of the lesson. To help ensure that the discussion is meaningful for all students, you will want to engage in the next two practices, selecting and sequencing student solutions.

Selecting and sequencing builds on the careful monitoring you did as students worked on the task. These practices involve choosing which solutions will be shared with the class, who will share those solutions, and the order in which the solutions will be shared. Selecting particular solutions to highlight provides you with an opportunity to help students move beyond the specific strategies they used to consider other approaches. In addition, being intentional about the order in which the solutions are presented provides an opportunity to build strategically on what students have done.

Smith and Stein (2018) describe selecting and sequencing in the following way:

> Selecting is the process of determining which ideas (what) and students (who) the teacher will focus on during the discussion. This is a crucial decision, since it determines what ideas students will have the opportunity to grapple with and ultimately to learn.

Selecting can be thought of as the act of purposefully determining what mathematics students will have access to—beyond what they were able to consider individually or in small groups—in building their mathematical understanding. (pp. 63–64)

Sequencing is the process of determining the order in which the students will present their solutions. The key is to order the work in such a way as to make the mathematics accessible to all students and to build a mathematically coherent story line. (p. 64)

In this chapter, we first unpack selecting and sequencing into their key components and illustrate what these practices look like in an authentic high school classroom. Next, we explore what we have learned is challenging for teachers about selecting and sequencing and provide an opportunity for you to explore these practices in your own teaching.

Part One: Unpacking the Practice: Selecting and Sequencing Student Solutions

Selecting and sequencing involve identifying the student work you wish to highlight, purposefully selecting individual presenters, and establishing a coherent storyline for sequencing students' presentations. Here we explore each of these components by looking inside Ms. Moran's classroom. Figure 5.1 highlights the components of these practices along with key questions to guide the processes of selecting and sequencing.

Figure 5.1 • Key questions that support the practices of selecting and sequencing

WHAT IT TAKES	KEY QUESTIONS
Identifying student work to highlight	Which student solution strategies would help you accomplish your mathematical goals for the lesson?
	What challenges did students face in solving the task? Were there any common challenges?
Purposefully selecting individual presenters	Which students do you want to involve in presenting their work?
	How might selecting particular students promote equitable access to mathematics learning in your classroom?
Establishing a coherent storyline	How can you order the student work such that there is a coherent storyline related to the mathematical learning goal?

Identifying Student Work to Highlight

The first step in selecting and sequencing is to identify the student work that you want to highlight for the class. As you monitored students' progress, you will likely have noticed a range of solutions that students produced and will have noted them on your monitoring chart. Remember that you intentionally chose a task that invited multiple approaches!

Having access to different solution strategies during the discussion has the potential to help students deepen their understanding of the mathematics involved in the task (Zbiek & Shimizu, 2005). To realize this, you want to identify those solution paths that put the key mathematical ideas in the spotlight and will therefore help you to achieve your lesson goals. As you review students' work on the task, look for similarities and differences among the paths students took to solve the task, while keeping in mind the mathematical features of students' solutions that are important for the class to consider.

You will also want to consider the challenges that students faced as they solved the task. Were there any common challenges that you want to highlight? Often, we shy away from discussing incorrect solutions with students when in fact there can be important benefits to discussing errors and false starts (Santagata & Bray, 2016). As Kazemi and Hintz (2014) explain,

> How we respond to errors and partially developed ideas sends important messages about taking risks. It is not easy for students to express their ideas if there is a high burden to be correct and understand everything the first time around. (p. 5)

As you consider which solution strategies to focus on with the whole class, keep in mind the potential value in discussing some of the difficulties that students may have encountered.

As she reviewed her monitoring chart, Ms. Moran could see that her students had solved the Staircase task in a number of different ways, as shown in Figure 5.2. All of the groups had initially started with some sort of recursive approach, describing the area of a staircase at one stage as it related to the area of the staircase with the previous stage (Solution I). The most common recursive approach was to illustrate this pattern in a table. In addition, some students demonstrated recursion visually by noticing that if you draw a square around a staircase, the part you "add on to make the square" is the staircase from the previous stage. One group of students tried to write an equation to represent recursion but only got as far as "y = stage x + ☐"; they seemed to be uncertain how to describe symbolically the number of squares in the previous stage.

As students tried to find ways to describe the area of a staircase without knowing the number of squares in the previous staircase, Ms. Moran recorded several additional strategies. Many groups understood the idea that the staircases were growing along two dimensions, and thus that the equation must involve an x^2 term (Solution II). She noted on her monitoring chart that one group used "guess and check" to try a series of equations, such as $x^2 + 1, x^2 + 2, x^2 + 3, x^2 + 4$, and so on, but with no success. A second group explained that the equation must be "x^2 minus something," since the area of the square encompassing the staircase would be x^2 and the area of the staircase is less than that.

Ms. Moran also observed a number of geometric solutions. One group created a rectangle composed of two of the same staircases and took "half of it" to find the area of the staircase, a solution she had anticipated (Solution III). Another group drew a diagonal line from the top left corner of the staircase to the bottom right corner, highlighting a large triangle under the diagonal and a set of small triangles above the diagonal, another solution that Ms. Moran had anticipated. This group also wrote an equation to represent their solution (Solution IV). In addition, Ms. Moran noted a pair of students who connected a numerical relationship in their table to the area of the staircase (Solution V). These students found that the number of squares at any stage could be represented by multiplication of "half of the stage number" with "one more than the stage number." Further, they found that they could rearrange the small squares in a staircase to reflect this pattern. These students wrote an equation to represent their approach. This solution was similar to one that Ms. Moran had anticipated in which students rearrange the small squares in a staircase into a rectangle (Figure 3.4, Solution D); however, in class, Ms. Moran noted that the students found the multiplicative relationship first, and then the geometric relationship.

Finally, Ms. Moran saw that some students produced a graph illustrating the relationship between the stage number and the number of small squares in a staircase (Solution VI). One group did so by plotting points from a table they had made. Another group used Desmos to produce a graph after having determined an equation and commented that the shape was a parabola. Even though Ms. Moran thought that some students might describe the growth of the staircases as exponential, she did not observe any students making this claim.

Figure 5.2 • Solutions produced by students as Ms. Moran noted on her monitoring chart

Solution I. Identify the Recursive Pattern

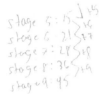

"Whatever the stage number is, is what you're going up by."

"If you make a square, then the part that's missing is the previous stage."

"It's y equals the stage number plus something."

Solution II. Explore Potential Equations Involving

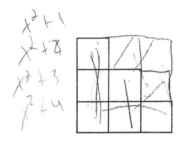

"The length and width are growing, so the equation has to have an x^2."

"It's got to be minus something, 'cause the staircase isn't the whole square."

Solution III. Double the Staircase to Create a Rectangle

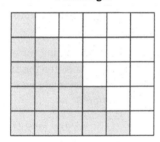

"It's length times width divided by 2 but for the length you add a row."

Solution IV. Divide the Staircase into Triangles

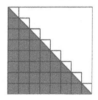

$$y = l \cdot w \, (\div 2) + \tfrac{1}{2} x$$

"You add the big triangle with the little triangles above the line."

Solution V. Connect the Numerical Relationship to the Area of the Staircase

$$(n \div 2)\,(n + 1) = y$$

"You multiply half of the stage number by one more than the stage number. So for Stage 6, it's 3×7."

Solution VI. Graph the Function

Source: Created with Desmos at desmos.com.

"We used the points from the table."

"We put our equation into Desmos."

In Analyzing the Work of Teaching 5.1, you will analyze the approaches taken by Ms. Moran's students in solving the problem and consider which strategies would be most useful in addressing the mathematical goals she had for the lesson.

Analyzing the Work of Teaching 5.1

Selecting Student Solutions

Consider the solutions shown in Figure 5.2 in light of Ms. Moran's goals for the lesson.

Goal 1: Quadratic functions may be characterized by two-dimensional growth.

Goal 2: Quadratic functions, unlike linear functions, do not have a constant rate of change.

Goal 3: Quadratic growth can be expressed in both recursive and explicit forms.

Goal 4: Quadratic growth can be modeled in a variety of ways—with a diagram in which width and height increase linearly, with a table where the second difference is constant, with a graph where the shape of a function is a parabola, and with an equation of degree 2.

- Which solutions do you think Ms. Moran might want to select in order to address her goals for the lesson?

- Solution II did not result in students determining correct equations to represent the relationship between the stage number and the area of the staircase. What might be the benefit of sharing one of these solutions?

Selecting Student Solutions—Analysis

The solutions produced by Ms. Moran's students address the lesson goals in several different ways.

Goal 1: Quadratic functions may be characterized by two-dimensional growth.

Central to Ms. Moran's goals for the Staircase task is for students to understand that quadratic functions can be modeled by two-dimensional growth. This goal is reflected in all six of the solutions she observed and most notably in Solution II, in which students explored the use of x^2 in their equations to indicate that the staircases grow both in length and width.

Goal 2: Quadratic functions, unlike linear functions, do not have a constant rate of change.

In addition, Ms. Moran wanted her students to understand that quadratic functions do not have a constant rate of change. Solution I, recursion, provides evidence of this goal, particularly in those cases where students made a table and noted that the difference from one stage to the next was increasing. Solutions II, VI, and V further emphasize this goal in that the equations produced represent quadratic functions.

Goal 3: Quadratic growth can be expressed in both recursive and explicit forms.

Expressing quadratic growth in a recursive form is reflected in Solution I, while expressing quadratic growth in an explicit form is reflected in the equations produced by students in Solutions IV and V. The pattern of growth identified in Solution III could also be written in explicit form, although Ms. Moran's students did not do so.

Goal 4: Quadratic growth can be modeled in a variety of ways—with a diagram in which width and height increase linearly, with a table where the second difference is constant, with a graph where the shape of a function is a parabola, and with an equation of degree 2.

Ms. Moran's final goal is for students to examine two-dimensional growth in multiple ways. As she explained, "There's so many ways to see two-dimensional growth. We can know it's quadratic from a table or equation or from building it. I really want students to think about what does x^2 mean in all these?" For many students, rather than a particular solution strategy, their initial examination of the staircases highlighted that both the length and width increased. More specifically, many students who used Solution I produced a table illustrating that the rate of change was not constant and those who used Solution VI explored this growth graphically. In addition, Solutions IV and V, and to some degree Solution II, involved the use of equations with a second degree term, further reflecting quadratic growth.

In Solution II, students attempt to determine the equation for the growth of the staircases but are unsuccessful in doing so. Still, students are exploring a critical feature of the explicit equation—that two-dimensional growth involves an x^2 term. Discussing this idea, as well as the challenges students faced in writing an equation to represent the growth of the staircases, has several potential benefits. For example, discussing whether the equation is of the form "$x^2 + \square$" versus "$x^2 - \square$" may prompt students to consider geometric approaches to the task. In addition, one group found that the equation worked for Stage 1 and Stage 2, but not for Stage 3. Discussing why this is the case and what it might mean about the growth of the staircase could provide further insights for students. Similarly, a teacher might want to explore Solution III with the class, perhaps after a discussion of Solution IV as a way to consider whether a similar approach might be used to write an equation corresponding to Solution III. In general, discussing incorrect thinking can potentially illustrate for students that the classroom is a place where all mathematical ideas are respected and where errors are a time for reflection and discussion.

After reviewing the solution strategies in light of her lesson goals, Ms. Moran decided that she wanted to highlight Solutions I, IV, V, and VI. She thought Solution I, recursion, would be a good way to highlight the two-dimensional growth of the staircases (Goal 1) and the increasing rate of change (Goal 2) as well as directly address Goal 3 (for the recursive form). She planned to use Solutions IV and V to address Goal 3 (for the explicit form). Having students explore Solution V would also allow Ms. Moran to address Goal 4 by highlighting the use of tables (Solution I), drawings (Solution IV), graphs (Solution V), and equations (Solutions IV and V) to explore two-dimensional growth.

Ms. Moran could have made other choices. For example, she might have decided to use Solution II to more explicitly address the two-dimensional growth of the staircase with the students, as well as to explore features of the explicit form of this growth. In addition, Ms. Moran might have chosen to highlight Solution III in class. In some ways, this solution reflects a simpler and more straightforward geometric solution than either Solution IV or V, and for that reason, Ms. Moran might have thought it would be more accessible for students during the class discussion. Furthermore, Ms. Moran might have decided not to address Solution I, particularly since the class had already addressed recursion in the launch of the task and Ms. Moran had purposefully used advancing questions to try to move students toward more explicit solutions. The point is, there is not just one *right way* to select the set of solutions that are shared during the whole class discussion. The key is ensuring that the selected solutions will make it possible for you to surface the mathematical ideas that are central to the lesson.

Purposefully Selecting Individual Presenters

Once you identify the solutions that you want to highlight, you will need to purposefully select students to present those solutions to the class. But how should you decide? One factor, of course, is which students produced the solutions that you want to share with the class. Having students present their own solutions can validate the importance of different kinds of mathematical thinking and help the class recognize their peers as valuable intellectual resources for learning mathematics (Aguirre et al., 2013; Jilk, 2016). In addition, because it is students' own work, they can authentically answer questions about the reasoning behind their representations and solution strategies (Imm, Stylianou, & Chae, 2008). Although you may find it more efficient and less messy to share a student's work yourself, doing so robs the student of the opportunity to be seen as an author of mathematical ideas, contributing both to a student's authority and identity. (See Aguirre et al. [2013] for a set of equity-based teaching practices that are intended to strengthen mathematics learning and the development of positive mathematics identities.)

> **TEACHING TAKEAWAY**
>
> There is not one way to select or sequence the set of solutions to be shared. The choice should be driven by your mathematical goals.

> **TEACHING TAKEAWAY**
>
> Be sure to allow students to share their own work so that they are seen as the author of their mathematical ideas and can answer questions about their reasoning.

Being purposeful about the students you select can also promote equitable access to mathematics learning in your classroom. Classroom discourse in the United States is often stratified with certain students contributing more frequently than others (Hung, 2015). In addition, students from diverse racial backgrounds are often considered not as good at mathematics as their White and Asian peers (Louie, 2017; Shah, 2017). Particularly troubling is recent research that shows that as early as elementary school, students are aware of racial stereotypes concerning who is good at mathematics and that such ideas get stronger in the middle school years and can persist throughout high school (McGee, 2013; Nasir, McKinney de Royston, O'Connor, & Wischnia, 2017).

Your choice of which students will present their solutions sends an important message about who and what is valued mathematically in your classroom. You will want to pay attention to who has recently had an opportunity to share their work with the class, and who has not; who might be comfortable sharing an incorrect or unusual solution, and who might benefit from sharing a solution that was used by many students in the class.

To be clear, decisions about what solutions to select and who to select as presenters are often closely related. Here, we have suggested that you first select the solutions you want students to share in class and then chose who should present those solutions. In practice, these decisions often happen in an integrated way. You may recognize that a particular student is more engaged than usual and decide to have her present her solution. Or you may recognize a solution as novel and interesting but realize the student who created it presented recently and decide to forgo that solution for a different one.

Two teachers with whom we have worked, Jennifer Mossotti and Michelle Saroney, explained their approach to selecting student presenters. Mrs. Mossotti explained that she makes a conscious effort to vary which students present in class. In addition, she often tells students in advance that she plans to have them present: "I'll give them a little tap on the shoulder and say, 'Do you mind saying this in front of the room?'" Mrs. Saroney described a similar process:

> As I walk around and make notes about what students are doing, I'll be trying to figure out who I want to come up. And I tend to let students know so they can be prepared to talk about that particular piece of their work. Also if a student's nervous, it helps that they're not put on the spot all of a sudden.

Mrs. Mossotti also explained that while she often asks students to present individually, she also finds it productive to ask students who have worked together to present together. She has found, particularly

TEACHING TAKEAWAY

Your choice of who will present can send strong messages about what and who you value. Do not miss these important opportunities to promote equity.

at the beginning of the year, that it can build students' confidence if they have "somebody who thought about it the same way up there" with them. In addition, she stated that she routinely looks to highlight "somebody who thinks about it different than everybody else. I like to put a spotlight on that student so that the rest of the kids can get access to different kinds of thinking." Clearly, there is much to keep in mind as you coordinate what ideas you want students to share in class and which students you want to present those ideas! (For more information about Jennifer Mossotti and Michelle Saroney's use of the five practices, see Smith and Sherin, 2019.)

A final consideration is the process through which students share their work. If a document camera is available in your classroom, students can share their own written work for the rest of the class to see. Projectors or interactive whiteboards, combined with cloud-based document systems, can make it easy to take pictures of student work using a phone or tablet and display them for the class to discuss, debate, and annotate. If these technologies are not available to you, you might ask students to re-create their solution on the board, or if there is time, you might ask them to prepare a poster to present to the class. In cases where students are completing their work electronically, you may be able to project the work directly for the class to view. A new feature on the Desmos platform called Snapshots allows teachers to capture images of students' work for later sharing with the class. (Snapshots is also a useful tool for selecting and sequencing student work! See http://blog.mrmeyer .com/2018/orchestrate-more-productive-mathematics-discussions-with -desmos-snapshots/ for further discussion of this feature.) As technology continues to advance, we may see more technologically based solutions for easy sharing of student work.

 PAUSE AND CONSIDER

How do you make decisions about which students should present in class? How do your decisions promote or constrain an equitable learning environment?

For the Staircase task, Ms. Moran decided to invite students to present in their groups as a way to recognize the collaborative work that students had done in class so far. Specifically, Ms. Moran decided to ask Elijah, Nyleah, Lauren, and John to present Solution I, recursion. While Ms. Moran had several groups to choose from, she wanted to leverage this group's use of both tables and visual models to explore recursion during the class discussion. In addition, John had not had an opportunity to present recently. In contrast, for Solutions IV and V, only one group of students had used each of those solutions—Aidan, Micki, Emily, and Erin used Solution IV, and Mae and Isabel used Solution V. In these cases, as explained above, Ms. Moran's choice of solution strategies to share and students to present those strategies was likely closely related. In fact, Ms. Moran explained that she was particularly pleased to have an opportunity to ask Mae and Isabel to present since "they were really confident about their equation." In addition, Ms. Moran noted that Aidan, Micki, Emily, and Erin's use of "length" and "width" as variables in Solution IV would provide an opportunity to "explore some strong concepts related to the visual pattern" even if they had not been "completely able to work out the equation." For Solution VI, Ms. Moran decided to have Mae and Isabel share the work they had done to graph their equation using Desmos. While Mae and Isabel's graph of the equation is correct, it does not represent the context of the problem since the domain of the function representing the staircases is limited to the natural numbers. Ms. Moran did not see this as a problem since it could be addressed in the discussion.

Establishing a Coherent Storyline

The final step in selecting and sequencing is to decide on the order in which students will present their solutions. Being intentional about the order provides you with an important opportunity to build a coherent storyline around the goals of the lesson. Just as the materials in a curriculum unit are carefully sequenced to build on each other in ways that support students' learning, you will want to be strategic in how you sequence students' presentations. One teacher we have worked with, Michelle Musumeci, explained it in the following way: "I'm trying to build almost like a story about this problem that moves us toward the goal so that we can make connections along the way." (You can explore a lesson from Michelle Musumeci's classroom in detail in Smith and Sherin, 2019.)

PAUSE AND CONSIDER

What factors do you think may be important to consider when deciding how to sequence students' presentations of solution strategies in class?

There are a number of issues you may want to consider in thinking about how to effectively create a story that brings students together and highlights the lesson goals. To build conceptual coherence, you might find it beneficial to move from the most concrete strategies to more abstract approaches. Some teachers find it productive to sequence solutions according to the representations used in order to make connections between them. For example, moving from a table to a graph can help students see how specific points from the table are located on the graph, or moving from a graph to an equation can highlight how the y-intercept and slope in the graph appear in the equation and vice versa.

Attending to the social organization of the classroom can also be an important consideration in thinking about how to sequence the class discussion (Horn, 2012). You may, for instance, choose to first share a solution strategy that many students used so that students will initially see work similar to their own being presented (Aguirre et al., 2017). Once students' own strategies are validated, they may be more interested in hearing about strategies that differ from their own. You will also want to think carefully about when and how to address incorrect strategies (this is explored further in Part Two of this chapter).

Whatever criteria you chose to use, it is important that you vary your approach over time. Students can become accustomed to routines, even when they are not made explicit. If students have a sense, for example, that you typically introduce the simplest strategies first, they may feel disappointed if they are asked to be the first presenter. Mixing up the criteria you use to sequence class discussions may also help to increase opportunities for all students to participate.

In thinking about how to organize the discussion of the Staircase task, Ms. Moran had in mind that "the story I wanted to tell" in the discussion was "where groups had been and where their work had taken them." Thus, she decided to begin with Elijah, Nyleah, Lauren, and John describing their use of recursion. As Ms. Moran explained, "I thought that's something that all groups could relate to, and it would be a good starting point to go back to where the beginning of the discussion had been." In this way, Ms. Moran would tie back to the launch where recursion had initially been introduced. Next, she planned to have Aidan, Micki, Emily, and Erin explain how they divided the staircases into triangles in order to find the area of the staircase (Figure 5.2, Solution IV). Ms. Moran believed that Aidan, Micki, Emily, and Erin's approach would be a good follow-up to recursion because the class could continue to explore the staircases visually but do so in a way that would lead to an explicit form. Next, Ms. Moran planned to have Mae and Isabel present Solution V, in which they identified a numerical relationship to the area of the staircase and then identified a way to visually represent that relationship as a rectangle.

Another reason Ms. Moran thought it was valuable to have Aidan, Micki, Emily, and Erin present their approach to the class before Mae and Isabel was because of differences in the equations that the groups had produced. Ms. Moran explained that "there was still some work to do around Aidan's group's equation" (Solution IV, Figure 5.2), and she planned to give the class time "to think about their variables, the l, w, and x" during the discussion. In contrast, Mae and Isabel had used a single variable for the stage number (Solution V, Figure 5.2), so Ms. Moran thought it best for "their equation to be discussed after Aidan's group." Finally, Ms. Moran planned to ask Mae and Isabel to share the graph of their equation (Solution VI) and to discuss what this graph might reveal about the relationship between the stage number and the area of the staircases.

Cori Moran's Attention to Key Questions: Selecting and Sequencing

As Ms. Moran prepared for her class to discuss the strategies students used to solve the Staircase task, she focused on the key questions. Using her monitoring chart, she reviewed students' solutions with the lesson goals in mind. What solutions would highlight the goal for students to understand that quadratic functions are characterized by two-dimensional growth? What solutions would highlight the different ways to represent two-dimensional growth? These questions were critical for Ms. Moran as she thought about which solutions she wanted to call attention to during the class discussion. In addition, she reviewed the challenges students faced as they worked on the task and considered whether it would be valuable to discuss those with the class as well.

Ms. Moran also gave careful attention to *who* would share these solutions with the class. She considered a number of factors, including who had recently presented, whether to have students present individually or in groups, and the kinds of supports she might want to offer students as they present. She kept in mind that her selection of presenters matters and could play a role in promoting an equitable learning environment for students in her class.

Finally, in deciding how to sequence the presentations, Ms. Moran attempted to create a coherent structure that would allow the learning goals to become visible for all students, even those who had not used those particular solution strategies. We now take a look at some of the challenges teachers face as they select and sequence students' solutions.

Part Two: Challenges Teachers Face: Selecting and Sequencing Student Solutions

You must purposefully select and sequence the solutions that will be shared in order to ensure that the goals of the lesson are met and that class time is used efficiently and effectively. Selecting and sequencing can be particularly challenging because, although you can give some consideration to what you would ideally like to share as you plan the lesson, the actual decisions about *what* is shared, *who* is going to share it, and *how* the solutions will be ordered are made during the lesson. In this section, we focus on five specific challenges associated with these practices, shown in Figure 5.3, that we have identified from our work with teachers.

Figure 5.3 • Challenges associated with the practices of selecting and sequencing

CHALLENGE	DESCRIPTION
Selecting only solutions that are most relevant to learning goals	Teachers need to select a limited number of solutions that will help achieve the mathematical goals of the lesson. Sharing solutions that are not directly relevant can take a discussion off track, and sharing too many solutions (even if they are relevant) can lead to student disengagement.
Expanding beyond the usual student presenters	Teachers often select students who are articulate and on whom they can count for a coherent explanation. Teachers need to look for opportunities to position each and every student as a presenter and help students develop their ability to explain their thinking.
Deciding what work to share when the majority of students were not able to solve the task and your initial goal no longer seems obtainable	Teachers may on occasion find that the task was too challenging for most students and that they were not able to engage as intended. This situation requires the teacher to modify her initial plan and determine how to focus the discussion so students can make progress.

CHALLENGE	DESCRIPTION
Moving forward when a key strategy is not produced by students	In planning the lesson, a teacher may determine that a particular strategy is critical to accomplishing the lesson goals. If the success of a lesson hinges on the availability of a particular strategy, then the teacher needs to be prepared to introduce the strategy through some means.
Determining how to sequence incorrect and/or incomplete solutions	Teachers often choose not to share work that is not complete and correct for fear that students will remember incorrect methods. Sharing solutions that highlight key errors in a domain can provide all students with an opportunity to analyze why a particular approach does not work. Sharing incomplete or partial solutions can provide all students with the opportunity to consider how such work can be connected to more robust solutions.

Selecting Only Solutions Relevant to Learning Goals

You may be tempted to have every group publicly share their work on a task in order to motivate students to produce a complete product, give all students an opportunity to share their thinking, or acknowledge students' efforts. While this approach is well intended, it often results in long, drawn-out discussions where similar solutions are repeated, mathematical ideas get lost, and students disengage. Limiting the number of solutions that are shared to those that will help you explicitly address the mathematics you are targeting in the lesson will allow you to make the best use of your instructional time and keep the class focused and engaged. One critical goal in selecting and sequencing solutions is to meaningfully build the mathematical storyline using students' own work and voices.

To illustrate ways to address this challenge, we take you to Martha Mulligan's calculus class. In the first month of the school year, Ms. Mulligan was introducing her students to derivatives. She began this work by having students explore derivatives qualitatively, using the $\frac{d}{dx} f(x)$ functionality within the Desmos graphing calculator to explore graphically how changing a function affects the derivative. The class also discussed relationships between the degrees of families of functions (e.g., linear, quadratic, cubic) and the degrees of their corresponding derivatives (e.g., constant, linear, quadratic). To move students' thinking past the initial exploration and toward the investigation of the derivative with specific functions, Ms. Mulligan set the following goals for her next lesson:

1. Understand that the key features of functions and their derivatives can be identified and related to their graphical, numerical, and symbolic representations.
   (related to AP Calculus standard EK 2.2A2)

2. Describe the ways in which key features of the graph of a function, such as the family (linear, quadratic, exponential), local and global maxima and minima, discontinuities, and periodicity, can be used to identify key features of the graph of the function's derivative. (related to AP Calculus standard EK 2.2A3)

To accomplish these goals, Ms. Mulligan selected the Sketchy Derivatives task designed by Desmos. While the original task consists of five challenges and two extensions, Ms. Mulligan chose to focus on the first three challenges, shown in Figure 5.4, since this portion of the task aligned with her goals for the lesson. (The other challenges were available to students who worked through the initial ones more quickly; the full task can be found at https://desmos.com by typing Sketchy Derivatives in the search bar.) Ms. Mulligan selected the Desmos task for a number of reasons. First, the use of the platform allowed students to be able to easily create and modify derivative sketches without having to start completely from scratch. The annotations students could make and the digital captures of their work also shed important light on the thinking processes in which students were engaged, giving the teacher access to students' thinking and work at various stages rather than just a finished written product. Students could also work within the Desmos system either by graphing the value of the rate of change point by point, or by using more general principles about the relationships between derivatives and their underlying functions (such as the derivative of a parabola being a line).

Figure 5.4 • The first three challenges in the Sketchy Derivatives task

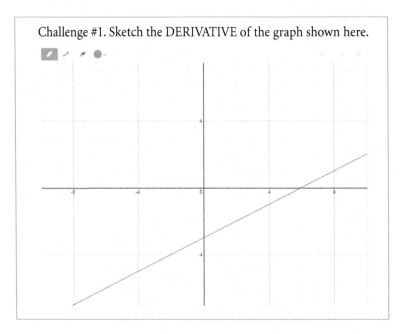

Challenge #1. Sketch the DERIVATIVE of the graph shown here.

Challenge #2. Sketch the DERIVATIVE of the graph shown here.

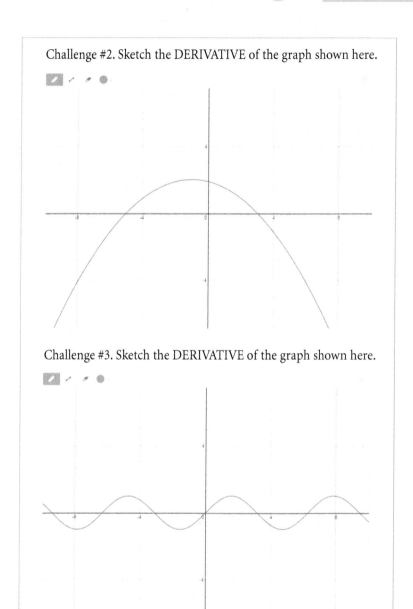

Challenge #3. Sketch the DERIVATIVE of the graph shown here.

Source: Activity by Desmos at teacher.desmos.com.

Ms. Mulligan had students work individually on the task, and then consult in pairs. After partner work time, she planned to have a whole class discussion that highlighted a number of key strategies and common pitfalls related to functions and their derivatives. As she monitored the class, she made note of the following pieces of student work:

Derivatives for Challenge 1

A. A horizontal line crossing the *y*-axis at $(0, 2)$ [Mohir]

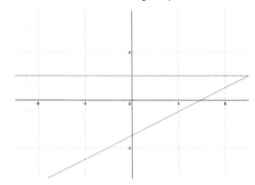

B. A horizontal line crossing the *y*-axis at $(0, -3)$ [Tatiana]

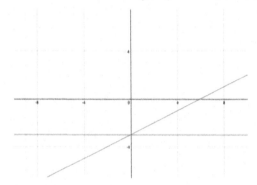

C. A horizontal line crossing the *y*-axis at $(0, \frac{1}{2})$, and side calculations seeking to find the slope between two points of the parent function [Callie]

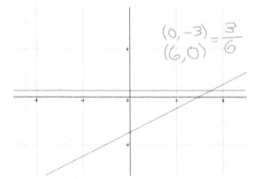

Source: Activity by Desmos at teacher.desmos.com.

Derivatives for Challenge 2

    D. A line with an *x*-intercept of $(-1, 0)$ and a negative slope [Gracelynn]

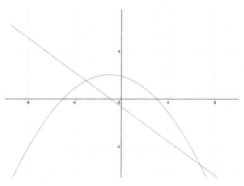

    E. A line with an *x*-intercept of $(-1, 0)$ and a positive slope [Celeste]

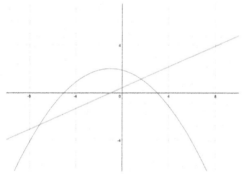

    F. A function resembling a cubic with a point of inflection at $(-1, 0)$ [Robert]

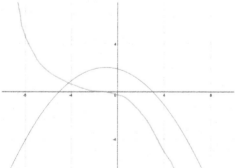

Source: Activity by Desmos at teacher.desmos.com.

Derivatives for Challenge 3

G. A periodic function with *x*-intercepts at each of the maxima and minima, with the intercepts marked on the graph [Cosima]

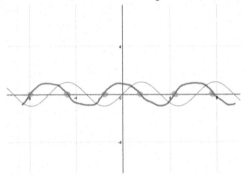

H. A periodic function reflected over the *x*-axis from the original, with points marked opposite the original function's maxima and minima [Linnea]

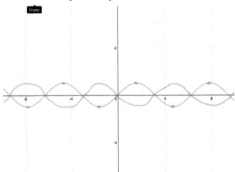

I. A periodic, piecewise linear "sawtooth" function with *x*-intercepts at each of the maxima and minima of the parent function, but with line segments drawn to connect the *x*-intercepts [Beau]

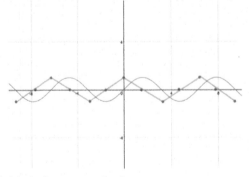

Source: Activity by Desmos at teacher.desmos.com.

In considering how best to address her goals, Ms. Mulligan selected Solutions A, E, D, C, and G in that order. She wanted to begin the discussion with a focus on the relationships between the original functions and their derivatives. She also felt that Solutions A and E would provide a bounded discussion of the key points that could be used to sketch the derivatives: the y-intercept in the function in Challenge 1, and the local maximum in Challenge 2. Solution E paired nicely with Solution D and helped to emphasize the importance of paying attention to the rates of change and individual points together—both solutions correctly incorporated the point $(-1, 0)$, but Solution E had positive values for the derivative where the original function had a negative rate of change, and vice versa. Solution D shows the accurate relationship between the rates of change of the quadratic function at different x-values and the positive and negative values of the derivative.

Ms. Mulligan then returned to the first function and shared Solution C. The specific slope calculations that the student made would serve to connect the value of the slope between two points to the value of the derivative function at those same points. While the student isn't explicit on how she used the coordinates to determine the slope, the teacher felt that sharing the work at this point in the sequence would highlight the relationship between the graph and the calculation of the slope. Finally, the class would consider the sinusoidal function with Solution G to highlight the strategy of using multiple maxima/minima points and analyzing the behavior of the function in between. This function was important—in the previous lesson, the class had worked with the relationship between the degree of the initial function and the degree of the derivative. By considering the sinusoidal function, students would have to bring a richer understanding of what the derivative function *means*, beyond just the procedural rule of reducing the degree of the function by 1.

While Ms. Mulligan could have selected a variety of the available solutions to share, or simply asked for volunteers, the five that she chose to share aligned most closely with her goals. Solutions A and E provided a focus on the first goal, understanding the nature of the derivative. Comparing Solutions D and C with E and A, respectively, made connections between the first goal, understanding the derivative, and the second goal relating to key features. Solution G made use of the key features to find the derivative of a function of a type that had not been previously explored.

So what do you do if there are *lots* of different solutions? How do you limit the solutions that are discussed to a manageable number? To answer this question, consider the Cycle Shop task shown in Figure 5.5.

Figure 5.5 • The Cycle Shop task

The Cycle Shop

You work for a small business that sells bicycles and tricycles. Bicycles have one seat, two pedals, and two wheels. Tricycles have one seat, two pedals, and three wheels.

On Monday, there are a total of 24 seats and 61 wheels in the shop. How many bicycles and how many tricycles are in the shop? Show all your work using any method you choose and explain your thinking.

Source: This version of the task appears in Steele and Smith (2018). The task was adapted from New York City Department of Education (n.d.). The Cycle Shop. Retrieved from https://www.weteachnyc.org/resources/resource/high-school-algebra-cycle-shop/

 This task may also be accessed at
resources.corwin.com/5practices-highschool

Like Clairice Robinson, featured in the vignette at the end of Chapter 4, as a result of engaging in a lesson around this task you want your students to understand the following:

1. Equations can be created that represent real-world constraints.

2. There is a point of intersection between two (unique nonparallel) linear equations that represents where the two equations have the same x- and y-values; this point is the solution to the system since it satisfies both equations.

3. A system of equations can be solved using different representations (i.e., tables, graphs, equations, pictures) and connections can be made between different representational forms, including the problem context.

Your students produced the strategies shown in Figure 5.6. In Analyzing the Work of Teaching 5.2, you will consider how you could select and sequence students' solutions in order to accomplish your goals for the lesson.

Analyzing the Work of Teaching 5.2

Selecting Solutions That Highlight Key Ideas

Review the student solutions to the Cycle Shop task shown in Figure 5.6. Keeping the goals for the lesson in mind (elaborated below), determine

1. which solutions you should select for the whole class discussion;

2. what each solution will contribute to the discussion; and

3. how you would sequence them in order to ensure that all students have access to the discussion.

Figure 5.6 • Solutions to the Cycle Shop task

Solution A

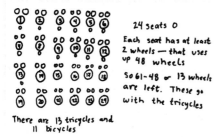

24 seats 0

Each seat has at least 2 wheels — that uses up 48 wheels

So 61-48 or 13 wheels are left. These go with the tricycles

There are 13 tricycles and 11 bicycles

Solution B

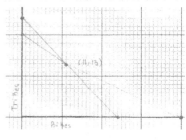

$2b + 3t = 61$
$b + t = 24$

Solution C

Start with a guess of bikes and trikes that totals 24, then figure out the number of wheels. If the guess is too many wheels, then lower the number of trikes and increase the number of wheels.

For example:

$1B + 23T = 24$ seats
$2W + 69W = 71$ wheels   Too many

$5B + 19T = 24$ seats
$10W + 57W = 67$ wheels   Too many

$10B + 14T = 24$ seats
$20W + 42W = 62$ wheels   close

$11B + 13T = 24$ seats
$22W + 39W = 61$ wheels

Solution D

Start with 1 bike and 23 trikes and find the total number of wheels; continue with 2 bikes and 22 trikes and continue the table until you get 61 wheels when you have 24 total bikes and trikes.

For example:

Number of Bikes	Number of Trikes	Bike Wheels	Trike Wheels	Total Wheels 61
1	23	2	69	71
2	22	4	66	70
3	21	6	63	69
4	20	8	60	68
5	19	10	57	67
6	18	12	54	66
7	17	14	51	65
8	16	16	48	64
9	15	18	45	63
10	14	20	42	62
11	13	22	39	61

Solution E

$b + t = 24$
$b = 24 - t$

$2b + 3t = 61$
$2(24 - t) + 3t = 61$
$48 - 2t + 3t = 61$
$48 + t = 61$
$t = 61 - 48$
$t = 13$ trikes

$b + 13 = 24$
$b + 13 - 13 = 24 - 13$
$b = 11$ bikes

Solution F

T: Tricycles
B: Bicycles

$2B + 3T = 61$
$B + T = 24$

Check:
$11 + 13 = 24$
$22 + 34 = 61$

$2B + 3T = 61$
$2B + 2T = 48$
———————
$T = 13$
$B = 11$

(Continued)

Figure 5.6 (*Continued*)

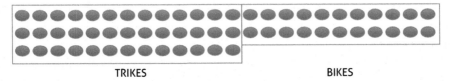

Solution G

Bike	Trike	Total Seats	Total wheels
1	1	2	5
2	2	4	10
5	5	10	25
12	12	24	24+36=60
13	11	24	26+33=59
11	13	24	22+39=61

Solution H

$$2b + 3t = 61 \qquad 1b + 1t = 24$$
$$2(24 + {}^-t) + 3t = 61 \qquad 1b = 24 + {}^-1t$$
$$48 + 2t = 61$$
$$-48 \qquad -48$$
$$\overline{}$$
$$2t = 13 \qquad t = 8 \div 2$$
$$t = 6\tfrac{1}{2} \text{ or } 7$$

Solution I

I made 24 columns to represent my seats.

I took 61 chips to represent my wheels.

Then I put 2 chips in each column, so this used up 48 wheels. So now I have 24 bikes with 2 wheels each. But I had 13 wheels left to distribute, so I used those to make 13 trikes by adding another wheel. So now I have used up 61 wheels on 24 seats. So I have 13 trikes and 11 bikes.

TRIKES   BIKES

Source: Solutions A–E and I appear in Steele and Smith (2018). Solutions F, G and H were taken from New York City Department of Education. (n.d.). The Cycle Shop. Retrieved from https://www.weteachnyc.org/resources/resource/high-school-algebra-cycle-shop/

Selecting Solutions That Highlight Key Ideas—Analysis

The Cycle Shop task can be solved using a number of different strategies. Figure 5.7 provides a summary of the strategies used by students who produced Solutions A–I.

Figure 5.7 • Strategies used by students

SOLUTION	STRATEGY	ANALYSIS
A	Draw a picture	The student fixed the number of seats at 24 and distributed wheels in sets of 2 to all 24 seats, then distributed the remaining wheels one at a time until all 61 wheels were used up.
B	Set up an equation and graph	The student accurately represented the problem with the two equations. While the graph shows the correct point of intersection, it shows the functions as continuous rather than discrete.
C	Guess and check	The student tried different combinations of bikes and trikes that would total 24 until they found the combination that resulted in 61 wheels.

SOLUTION	STRATEGY	ANALYSIS
D	Make a table	The student systematically tested combinations of bikes and trikes that would total 24 and for each combination found the number of wheels.
E	Set up an equation and solve algebraically	The student accurately represented the problem with the two equations and solved the system of equations using substitution.
F	Set up an equation and solve algebraically	The student accurately represented the problem with the two equations and solved the system of equations using elimination.
G	Make a table/ guess and check	The student tested combinations of bikes and trikes first not fixing the number of seats at 24 but ultimately using guesses to strategically identify the correct combination.
H	Set up an equation and solve algebraically	The student accurately represented the problem with the two equations and solved the system of equations using substitution. A distribution error resulted in the incorrect solution.
I	Build a concrete model	The student used 61 chips to represent the total number of wheels and distributed the wheels in sets of 2 in each of 24 columns and then distributed the remaining wheels one at a time until the wheels were used up.

There are a number of different ways that you could select and sequence the students' solutions. The challenge is to decide which subset of the nine solutions will help you accomplish your lesson goals, allow all students access to the discussion, and keep students interested and attentive. In determining a possible sequence, you need to keep in mind what you are trying to accomplish mathematically. Toward that end, it is critical to consider which solutions will help you best align with your lesson goals.

Goal 1: Equations can be created that represent real-world constraints.

Solutions B, E, F, and H include the correct equation.

Goal 2: There is a point of intersection between two (unique nonparallel) linear equations that represents where the two equations have the same x- and y-values; this point is the solution to the system since it satisfies both equations.

Solution B is the only solution that clearly shows the point of intersection of two linear equations. While the other solutions (with the exception of Solution H) show the correct answer, it is unclear as to whether students understand that this is the point at which two lines intersect when graphed. In addition, none of the algebra solutions explicitly shows that the solution of 11 bikes and 13 trikes satisfies both equations.

Goal 3: A system of equations can be solved using different representations (i.e., tables, graphs, equations, pictures) and connections can be made between different representational forms, including the problem context.

Solutions D and G use a table, although G is more of a guess-and-check strategy. Solutions B, E, F, and H use equations. Solution B includes a graph. Solutions A and I use a picture or model.

One possible sequence would be Solutions A, D, E, and B in this order. This sequence includes solutions that show equations (Solutions B and E) that represent the constraints in the problem (Goal 1), a solution (Solution B) that makes the point of intersection salient (Goal 2), and solutions that show four different representation (picture, Solution A; table, Solution D; equation, Solution E; and graph, Solution B) that can be connected (Goal 3). By ordering the solutions in this way—from picture to table to equation to graph—all students will have access to the discussion and the opportunity to engage with the key mathematical ideas at the heart of the lesson.

Specifically, Solution A shows the modeling of the context without any numbers and should be accessible to all students. The number of bikes and trikes pictured totals 24 and each "bike" is shown with 2 "wheels" and each "trike" with 3 "wheels." Solution D shows a systematic testing of combinations of 24. Solution E shows the two equations in symbolic form and an algebraic solution. The equations in Solution E can be connected to Solution A (bikes + trikes = 24 seats/large circles and 2 × bikes + 3 × trikes = 61 wheels/small circles) and to Solution D (the sum of the number of bikes and number of trikes in the first two columns is 24, and the number of bikes multiplied by two in the third column and the number of trikes multiplied by 3 in the fourth column give you the total number of wheels in the fifth column). By making connections across these three solutions, students have the opportunity to see how pictures, tables, and equations are connected.

Solution B shows the two equations and the graph. The graph shows the point of intersection (11, 13), which is the answer that students found in the previous solutions. In addition, the first two columns in the table in Solution D can be seen as points on the graph of the line b + t = 24. This strategy is critical to the discussion since it is the only one that clearly shows the solution as point of intersection of two linear equations. It provides the opportunity to discuss what the points on each line mean, what the point of intersection represents in context, and why using substitution (Solution E) gives you the *x*-coordinate of the point of intersection.

The solutions that you select and the sequence in which you order them depends on your lesson goals and on the solutions you have access to. The selecting and sequencing illustrated in this example represents the "concrete to abstract" approach discussed in Part One of this chapter. Given the nine solutions available, this approach makes sense. While some students were using algebraic equations, many were not. Since writing equations is a goal of the lesson, it may be necessary to start where students are (pictures, models, tables) and then move to more symbolic strategies and then make connections between them. Later in the chapter we will see a different example of sequencing where Mr. Harmon decides to begin his discussion with the solution strategies that were most commonly used by students.

Our point here is not that you should only select three or four solutions to share as we have illustrated in these examples, but rather that the number of solutions to be shared should be driven by your lesson goals and the time you have available for the discussion. Using this rule of thumb, not all students will be able to share each day. This should not be a concern as long as over time each and every student has the opportunity to share their work and their thinking, as we will discuss in the next section.

Expanding Beyond the Usual Presenters

While selecting solutions to be presented should be done based on the mathematical potential of the solution, a secondary consideration needs to be who will do the presenting. Over time all students need the opportunity to present in front of the class. This is an issue of equity! It is also important for the development of identity and being seen by one's peers as competent. While it is tempting to call on students who you know you can count on to give a coherent and articulate explanation, students do not improve their skills at presenting and explaining simply by listening to others do it. Further, always calling on the same students sends a clear message regarding who the teacher thinks is capable.

 PAUSE AND CONSIDER

Reflect on your practice of identifying presenters. Do you tend to call on the same students repeatedly? What could you do to provide more students the opportunity to improve their ability to explain their thinking and to be seen by the class as mathematically capable?

Consider, for example, the Lunch Options task created by Denise Hansen, presented in Chapter 2 and shown again in Figure 5.8. Through their work on the task, Ms. Hansen wanted her students to understand that if one event could happen m different ways and another event could happen n different ways, then the number of outcomes for both events together would be $m \times n$. After students had an opportunity to work on the task independently and in small groups, she was planning a whole class discussion that would feature several different possible strategies and ultimately lead to a discussion of the generalization.

Figure 5.8 • The Lunch Options task

Lunch Options

The Hot Entrée Combo in the cafeteria includes your choice of an entrée with 1 side and a drink for $6.50. Today's selections are shown below.

Entrée	Sides	Drinks
• Baked ziti with meat	• Steamed broccoli	• Milk
• Baked ziti with veggies	• Caesar salad	• Water
	• Garlic breadsticks	• Apple juice
	• Chicken soup	

1. How many different lunch combinations are there? Explain how you figured it out and how you know you have them all.

2. Suppose the combo also included a choice of 2 desserts: a peanut butter cookie or a chocolate brownie. How many different lunch combinations would there be then? How do you know?

3. Compare your answers to the first two questions. How are they different? Explain.

4. How many different combinations do you think you will have if you now add a choice of a peppermint or spearmint candy to your combo? Explain.

5. Panera Bread offers You Pick Two, which includes a choice of 2 half portions from the following list: soup, macaroni, salad, and sandwich. You decide to have soup and a sandwich. There are 7 different soups and 19 different sandwiches. In addition, you can select a side of an apple, chips, or a baguette. Drawing on your work on the first four questions, determine how many different combinations you could put together.

 This task may also be accessed at
resources.corwin.com/5practices-highschool

One solution that Ms. Hansen wanted to have shared during the whole class discussion was a tree diagram, since this solution provides a visual model for keeping track of different outcomes and clearly shows the total number of lunch combinations—thus answering the first question in the task. As it turned out, several different students in the class produced this solution. Who should Ms. Hansen select to present it during the whole group discussion?

Ms. Hansen was prepared to make this decision because prior to the lesson, she had reviewed monitoring charts from previous discussions (focusing on the *Who and What* and *Order* columns) and had made a short list on a sticky note of students who had not recently been featured prominently in a discussion. She looked at her Lunch Options monitoring chart to see who had produced a tree diagram then looked to see if any of those students were on her list. Ms. Hansen decided to have Kayla present her tree diagram (see Figure 5.9) since she had not had an opportunity recently to present her work during a whole class discussion. In addition, unlike many students, Kayla only produced a tree for one of the two entrée options. This, Ms. Hansen felt, was sure to generate a lively discussion about how Kayla calculated the total with only half the combinations!

Figure 5.9 • Kayla's solution to the Lunch Options task

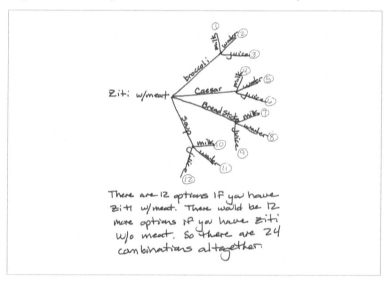

Keeping track of students who have not recently presented will help you in making decisions about which students to select when there are options and ensure that over time all students have the opportunity to be seen by their peers as capable and to develop positive mathematics identities. Of course, if none of the students on your list have produced the solution you want to feature, you should select someone else and continue to look for opportunities to involve the students on your list in some way. In addition to your physical record-keeping, digital supports like the EQUIP tool can help you keep track of patterns regarding which student voices are more or less present in your classroom (Herbel-Eisenmann & Shah, 2019; Reinholtz & Shah, 2018).

Once you have identified students to present, you should let the students know that you want them to share their solution. This will give the students a chance to practice their explanation in the safety of their group before giving it in front of the whole class. While this is particularly important for English Language Learners, it can help all students feel more confident about standing up in front of the class. In addition, a student may feel more comfortable presenting if he or she can do so with a partner. However, in this situation you need to make sure that the partner is not the one doing all the explaining!

In some cases, you may be able to include students who you would like to involve in the discussion, even if they have not produced the solutions you initially targeted. Consider, for example, what occurred in Marco Washington's algebra class. He wanted his students to understand the following:

1. An exponential relationship of the form $f(x) = ab^x$ has a rate of change that varies by a constant multiplicative factor; as the function's input values increase by 1 the output value changes by a constant factor.

2. Linear functions increase by a constant amount (additive) and exponential functions increase by a constant factor (multiplicative).

3. An exponential function can be represented in different ways and connections can be made among the representations.

Mr. Washington selected the Family Tree task (discussed in Chapter 2 and shown again in Figure 5.10) because he felt it would be accessible to all students, it aligned with his lesson goal, and it would challenge students to think and reason.

Figure 5.10 • The Family Tree task

Family Tree

Ramona was examining the family tree her mother had created using Ancestry.com, a website you can use to explore your genealogy. When examining a family tree, the branches are many. Ramona is generation "now." One generation ago, her 2 parents were born. Two generations ago, her 4 grandparents were born. Three generations ago, her great-grandparents were born. Four generations ago, her great-great-grandparents were born. Every time she went back another generation, another "great" was added!

1. How many of Ramona's great-grandparents were born 3 generations ago?

2. How many of Ramona's "great" grandparents were born 10 generations ago?

3. Explain how Ramona could figure out how many "great" grandparents were born in any number of generations ago.

4. Is the number of "great" grandparents in any generation a function of the generation? Why or why not? How do you know?

 This task may also be accessed at

resources.corwin.com/5practices-highschool

As he monitored students' work on the task, Mr. Washington noticed that most students solved the problem in one of the ways he had anticipated—equation (correct and incorrect), graph, picture, or table—as shown in Figure 5.11. Several students who had created a picture had determined that 3 generations ago Ramona had 8 great-grandparents and 4 generations ago Ramona had 16 great-grandparents, but they were having trouble drawing further generations. In an effort to help students move beyond trying to extend the picture, Mr. Washington asked students questions such as "What seems to be happening?" "How does the number of great-grandparents appear to increase as you go back another generation?" "Do you see any patterns?" "Can you organize your finding in some way?"

Figure 5.11 • Strategies used by students in Mr. Washington's class to solve the Family Tree task

Solution A. Incorrect Equation

$$y = 2x$$

At every generation there are 2 times as many great-grandparents as there were in the previous generation.

Solution C. Correct Equation

$$y = 2^x$$

The number of great-grandparents doubles with every generation you go back. So the number of the generation tells you how many 2's get multiplied together.

Solution B. Picture

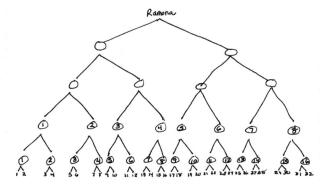

Solution D. Graph

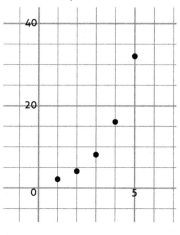

Solution E. Table

Generations Back	# of "Great" Grandparents
3	8
4	16
5	32
6	64
7	128
8	256
9	512
10	1024

Rebekah and Claire were two of the students who had drawn a picture that ended at the fifth generation back (Solution B, Figure 5.11). In response to Mr. Washington's questions, they decided to make a table with the information they had from the picture (i.e., 3 generations back, 8; 4 generations back, 16; 5 generations back, 32). From here they recognized that they were just multiplying the number of great-grandparents in one generation by 2 to get the number of great-grandparents in the next generation. The students then decided that they would show the number of twos that were being multiplied in a separate column so that the pattern they discovered would be clear, as shown in the table in Figure 5.12. Mr. Washington decided to select Rebekah and Claire's more elaborate table to include in the presentations although he had not initially anticipated a table that provided this level of detail. He decided to share it because he thought it would provide a nice bridge between the picture and the correct equation and would clearly make the case that as the input increases by 1 unit, the output changes by a constant factor of 2. Also, it would give him a chance to draw in Rebekah, who struggles and does not always feel she has something to contribute. Explaining the table that she and Claire created would serve to build Rebekah's confidence and provide all students in the class with a clear connection between a pictorial representation (which several other students had) and the equation (which only a few students had produced). So this was a chance to acknowledge Rebekah and engage the whole class in making connections between different representations—one of Mr. Washington's lesson goals.

Figure 5.12 • Rebekah and Claire's solution to the Family Tree task

NUMBER OF GENERATIONS AGO	2'S	NUMBER OF GREAT-GRANDPARENTS
3	$2 \times 2 \times 2$	8
4	$2 \times 2 \times 2 \times 2$	16
5	$2 \times 2 \times 2 \times 2 \times 2$	32
6	$2 \times 2 \times 2 \times 2 \times 2 \times 2$	64
7	$2 \times 2 \times 2 \times 2 \times 2 \times 2 \times 2$	128
8	$2 \times 2 \times 2 \times 2 \times 2 \times 2 \times 2 \times 2$	256
9	$2 \times 2 \times 2 \times 2 \times 2 \times 2 \times 2 \times 2 \times 2$	512
10	$2 \times 2 \times 2 \times 2 \times 2 \times 2 \times 2 \times 2 \times 2 \times 2$	1,024

The point here is that each and every student—students who struggle as well as those who excel—needs the opportunity to participate in whole class discussions in substantive ways so that they can be seen by others as mathematically capable and students can see themselves as doers of mathematics. To support students in developing positive mathematics identities, you as a teacher have a great deal of power in how you might think about *positioning* students. Providing students with opportunities to share their mathematical thinking and respond to the questions and comments of their peers in a whole class discussion can position students in three different ways. First, it positions students as mathematically capable with respect to other students, by providing them with opportunities to elaborate on their thinking and discuss their thinking publicly with others. Second, it positions them as mathematically capable relative to you, as the teacher. This positioning sends important messages to students about how you view them, as someone who represents mathematical authority in the classroom. Finally, it positions them relative to the discipline of mathematics as a person who can engage in mathematical work, explain mathematical thinking, and make a contribution to the field of mathematics. This is particularly important for high school students who are at a key moment in determining college and career pathways.

There may be times when you need to alter your initial plan as Mr. Washington did in order to ensure wider participation. Jansen, Cooper, Vascellaro, and Wandless (2016) describe a strategy for engaging more students in discussion called *rough-draft talk*. At the heart of this strategy is creating a culture of risk taking and inviting students to share initial ideas—rough-draft presentations—before returning to their groups to revise their thinking toward final draft solutions. Rough-talk presentations serve to get a range of ideas on the table to stimulate thinking and reduce the threat of being wrong. According to Jansen and her colleagues (2016),

> If rough-draft talk is valued, brainstormed ideas are welcomed. More students are likely to take risks rather than freeze during challenging tasks. Valuing a wider range of contributions invites greater involvement, in contrast to the same students who participate frequently or not at all. (p. 304)

Deciding What Work to Share When the Majority of Students Were Not Able to Solve the Task and Your Initial Goal No Longer Seems Obtainable

Your lessons may not always go as planned, despite your best efforts. This may result from the task being too challenging for students, students lacking essential prior knowledge, or because students have pursued solution paths that were not productive. In such cases, continuing with your lesson as planned may ensure that you *cover* the material, but if students are struggling with aspects of the task, it is not clear that they will learn what was intended if you simply forge ahead. At times such as this, you need to readjust your lesson goals to meet students where they are.

This was the situation that Gladis Kennedy faced in a lesson on the Hospital Locator task (see Figure 5.13). As a result of engaging in the lesson, Ms. Kennedy wanted her geometry students to understand that geometry could be practically useful. Toward that end, she wanted students to be able to pull together their knowledge of geometric constructions that they had been developing over the last few weeks to investigate and solve a real-world problem. In so doing they would need to draw on and integrate the following understandings:

- A point equidistant from the vertices of a triangle is where the perpendicular bisectors of the triangle's side meet.
- The point where the perpendicular bisectors of the side of a triangle meet is the center of the circumcircle of a triangle.

In addition, Ms. Kennedy wanted students to realize that the center of the circumcircle of a triangle (circumcenter) is equidistant from the three vertices, and so the common distance is the radius of a circle that passes through the vertices. This understanding would allow them to prove that their proposed location for the hospital was in fact equidistant from each of the three cities.

Figure 5.13 • The Hospital Locator task Ms. Kennedy selected for her students

Hospital Locator

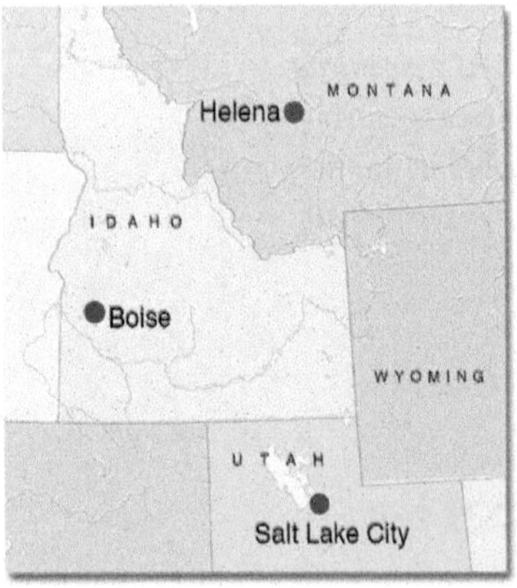

Boise, ID; Helena, MT; and Salt Lake City, UT are three large cities in the northwestern part of the United States. Although each city has a local hospital for minor needs and emergencies, an advanced medical facility is needed for transplants, research, and so forth. Imagine the potential of a high-powered, high-tech, extremely modern medical center that could be shared by the three cities and their surrounding communities!

You have been hired to determine the best location for this facility.

Source: Reprinted with permission from National Council of Teachers of Mathematics (2008). Hospital Locator. Retrieved from http://illuminations.nctm.org.

online resources This task can also be accessed at **resources.corwin.com/5practices-highschool**

Students had previously worked on the Building a New Playground task (Institute for Learning, 2013; also see Boston et al., 2017) in which they were given two points on a coordinate grid, representing the locations of schools A and B, and asked to determine the location of a playground that was equidistant from both schools. While working on this task, students hypothesized, and then proved, that all of the possible locations for the playground were located on the perpendicular bisector of line segment $\overline{AB}$. Hence, the Hospital Locator task was not the students' first exposure to a real-world situation that required application of their geometric knowledge and skills or their first opportunity to consider the utility of constructing a perpendicular bisector.

Ms. Kennedy set the context for the task by explaining that there were no obvious choices for the hospital since there were no major towns between the cities. She told students not to worry about the terrain or whether or not there were currently roads or interstates that were adjacent to the location. She provided each group with a compass, straight edge, ruler, protractor, a copy of the task, an enlarged version of the map showing the relative location of the three cities, and a blank transparency.

As Ms. Kennedy monitored the classroom activity, she noted that all of the groups had created a triangle using the three cities as vertices and appeared to realize that the point they were looking for was somewhere in the interior of the triangle. From that point, however, students pursued several different approaches. Several groups used their rulers to try to find a point that was equidistant from the vertices. Ms. Kennedy challenged them to consider whether there was a way to find the location that would be more exact than measuring. Group 2 (Bryan, Abbey, Alice, and Duncan) was using their compass to find a circle that contained the three vertices of the triangle, without first finding the center of the circle. Ms. Kennedy asked the group to consider what they needed to know to draw a circle that contained specific points.

Group 6 (Jamie, Phoebe, Rylie, and Piper) constructed the perpendicular bisectors of each side of the triangle and determined that the point where the three perpendicular bisectors intersected would be the best location for the hospital. When pressed to explain how they could be sure that this point was equidistant from the three vertices, the students indicated that they had measured the distance with the ruler. Ms. Kennedy pressed the group to prove that the point they found was the best location without measuring and left them to pursue this line of inquiry.

While Ms. Kennedy felt that students were making progress, it was clear to her that with only 10 minutes left she was not going to accomplish exactly what she had planned. She decided to have Group 2 share their efforts to try to find a circle that contained the three points. She asked them to discuss why they thought this approach would be helpful and why it turned out to be difficult. Then she planned to have Group 6 share their construction of the perpendicular bisectors and explain why they thought this approach would be helpful and what they were currently struggling with.

Ms. Kennedy thought that sharing the work of Groups 2 and 6 would generate discussion about these two approaches and, ultimately, stimulate students to consider how bisectors and circles could be helpful. She planned to have students continue to work on this for homework. With this revised agenda for the discussion, Ms. Kennedy felt that she would ultimately reach her goal, but not in one class period as she had initially planned. The next day she planned to give the groups a few minutes to share any additional thoughts they might have on the problem and then resume the discussion.

If the majority of students are struggling with some aspect of the task, moving forward as planned will leave too many students behind. By determining what students are struggling with and how to help them move beyond the struggle, the class will be better positioned to make progress on the initial lesson goals. The student work selected and sequenced needs to help students gain clarity on the aspects of the task with which they struggled.

Moving Forward When a Key Strategy Is Not Produced by Students

When you engage in the practice of anticipating, you consider the correct and incorrect strategies that students are likely to use in solving a task and how you would respond to the work students produced. This is also the time when you consider which of the strategies that you anticipate students using will be most useful in accomplishing the goals for the lesson. Selecting and sequencing for the whole class discussion is intended to build a storyline that moves students towards those goals. What happens then, if during teaching, you discover that no students used a strategy that you consider essential to the mathematical storyline of the lesson. What can you do?

In preparing his lesson based on the Toothpick Hexagons task, Mr. Harmon identified the following goals:

1. Patterns can be described and generalized by finding the underlying structure of the pattern and relating two variables that are changing at the same time.

2. Patterns that grow by a constant rate are linear.

3. There are different but equivalent ways of describing and representing the same pattern.

4. Connections can be made between different representational forms—tables, graphs, equations, words, and pictures.

In order to accomplish Goal 3, students would need the opportunity to consider several different symbolic generalizations that could be compared and identified as equivalent. Specifically, Mr. Harmon wanted students to "move between different descriptions of the same pattern, leading hopefully to a recognition of equivalent equations, the idea that this pattern can be represented in more than one way."

Mr. Harmon anticipated four strategies that he felt students were likely to produce (shown in Figure 3.9). He felt that students were most likely to produce two of the equations he anticipated, $y = 5x + 1$ and $y = 6 + 5(x - 1)$, and he wanted students to share those during the whole class discussion. In monitoring student work, Mr. Harmon found that eight students had $y = 5x + 1$ and eight had $y = 6 + 5(x - 1)$, and two students had no equation and a verbal description that was unclear. He decided to "start the discussion with the more common approaches that I see. Showing kids right off the bat that they're right will be reassuring."

Mr. Harmon selected Zashon to present $y = 6 + 5(x - 1)$ first and Brandon to present $y = 5x + 1$ second. The teacher explained that he selected Zashon because

> [s]he could accurately explain what she saw in the pattern, but she had difficulty coming to a generalization because she had misrepresented the rate of change in her equation. And so that group had worked with her a lot, and I felt confident that she would be able to explain it.

He selected Brandon next because he had visited that group and heard a strong explanation connecting the formula to the visual.

To accomplish Goal 3, Mr. Harmon felt it was important to share at least one additional solution. He was prepared to do this. As he indicated,

> I have some solutions from another class ready to go. So hopefully, we can be able to highlight those in a way that students will be able to immediately access where the observed pattern came from, and then be able to connect it to the other work that they've seen. I'll just have a solution that I will put up [on] the board. Ideally, I'd like to see a student be able to verbalize how that came to be.

The student work he selected to share following the first two presentations is shown below:

$$\begin{array}{r} 9 \\ \times 4 \\ \hline 36 + 10 = 46 \end{array}$$

I did the number of hexagons times 4.
Then the number of hexagons plus 1.
Then added it all.

In reflecting on the lesson, Mr. Harmon explained his rationale behind sharing this work as follows:

The third piece of work was taken from another class and describes the total number of toothpicks in a different way. Specifically, as you move from one hexagon to the next, there was consistently four toothpicks [shown in orange in the figure below], the top two and the bottom two toothpicks (4x), and then one more than the number of hexagons (x + 1) to represent the vertical toothpicks in the arrangement [shown in blue]. And I liked that because she didn't have an equation that was detailed there. It was strictly just the numbers she had multiplied and then added to come up with a number of toothpicks for nine hexagons. And so that gave an opportunity to try and get the class to elicit the equation that can be used to model that.

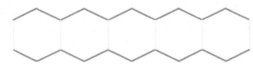

Mr. Harmon knew that a diverse set of solutions were critical to achieving his goals for the lesson. Rather than leaving production of those solutions to chance, he had work from a student in another class ready for his class to consider and discuss in the service of his goals. By preparing critical solutions in advance, or having access to key solutions from a previous year or a different class period, you will be prepared to introduce a solution that your students did not produce in class that day into the sequence of solution strategies presented. The new strategy provides the opportunity for students to consider whether the solution works, whether it will always work, and how it compares to the solutions previously discussed. Asking students to make sense of another student's reasoning is challenging and important work and will give you additional insight into what students truly understand.

Determining How to Sequence Incorrect and/or Incomplete Solutions

You may be most comfortable having students share only work that is both complete and correct so that all students will see accurate solutions. Selecting incorrect or incomplete solutions, however, can provide valuable learning opportunities as students investigate what is going on and why it does or does not make sense (Boaler, 2016). For example, Ms. Moran's decision to start with the recursive solution, which did not lead to a closed-form generalization, might have been seen as sharing a solution that was incomplete. Yet it provided an important entry point upon which to build more sophisticated mathematical ideas. Finding a

correct answer is one thing, but determining why an answer is not correct requires a different level of understanding.

In this section we will explore two examples, one where the teacher begins the discussion with incorrect solutions (Mr. Lemon) and one where the teacher begins the discussion with incomplete solutions (Mr. Moore).

 ## PAUSE AND CONSIDER

Both teachers discussed here, Mr. Moore and Mr. Lemon, planned to use incomplete and incorrect solutions (respectively) in their whole class discussions. What role do incorrect and incomplete solutions play in your instruction? Can you think of a situation you have recently encountered where an incorrect or incomplete solution might have served as a learning opportunity for students?

Travis Lemon was just starting a unit on similarity and right triangle trigonometry in his integrated Secondary Mathematics II class. He planned to begin the unit with the Photocopy Faux Pas task (shown in Figure 5.14), which was intended to develop students' understanding of dilations and would be formalized in subsequent tasks. As a result of engaging in the lesson, Mr. Lemon wants his students to understand the following:

1. In a dilation, lines are taken to lines, and line segments to line segments of proportional length in the ratio given by the scale factor.

2. To describe a mathematical dilation, we need to specify a center of dilation and a scale factor. The center of dilation is a fixed point in the plane about which all points are expanded or contracted. It is the only invariant point under a dilation.

3. Dilations create similar figures—the image and preimage are the same shape, but different sizes (unless the scale factor is 1, then the image and preimage are congruent).

Figure 5.14 • The Photocopy Faux Pas task used by Mr. Lemon

Burnell has a new job at a copy center helping people use the photocopy machines. Burnell thinks he knows everything about making photocopies, and so he didn't complete his assignment to read the training manual.

Mr. and Mrs. Donahue are making a scrapbook for Mr. Donahue's grandfather's 75th birthday party, and they want to enlarge a sketch of their grandfather which was drawn when he was in World War II. They have purchased some very expensive scrapbook paper, and they would like this image to be centered on the page. Because they are unfamiliar with the process of enlarging an image, they have come to Burnell for help.

"We would like to make a copy of this image that is twice as big, and centered in the middle of this very expensive scrapbook paper," Mrs. Donahue says. "Can you help us with that?" "Certainly," says Burnell. "Glad to be of service."

Burnell taped the original image in the middle of a white piece of paper, placed it on the glass of the photocopy machine, inserted the expensive scrapbook paper into the paper tray, and set the enlargement feature at 200%. In a moment, this image was produced.

"You've ruined our expensive paper," cried Mrs. Donahue. "Much of the image is off the paper instead of being centered." "And this image is more than twice as big," Mr. Donahue complained. "One-fourth of grandpa's picture is taking up as much space as the original."

In the diagram below, both the original image—which Burnell taped in the middle of a sheet of paper—and the copy of the image have been reproduced in the same figure.

1. Explain how the photocopy machine produced the partial copy of the original image.

2. Using a "rubber band stretcher," finish the rest of the enlarged sketch.

3. Where should Burnell have placed the original image if he wanted the final image to be centered on the paper?

4. Mr. Donahue complained that the copy was four times bigger than the original. What do you think? Did Burnell double the image or quadruple it? What evidence would you use to support your claim?

5. Transforming a figure by shrinking or enlarging it in this way is a called a *dilation*. Based on your thinking about how the photocopy was produced, list all of the things you need to pay attention to when dilating an image.

Source: © 2013 Mathematics Vision Project, in partnership with the Utah State Office of Education. Mathematics Vision Project, Secondary Mathematics II Module 6, 2017.

 This task may also be accessed at **resources.corwin.com/5practices-highschool**

To solve the task, students needed to determine that the center of dilation is located in the top left-hand corner of the page and that in order to have the enlarged picture centered on the paper, the original picture would need to be centered in the first quadrant of the paper. Mr. Lemon anticipated that students might place the picture in the top left-hand corner of the page, since this placement of the picture would keep the enlargement on the paper and could be seen as compensating for Burnell's enlargement having moved off the bottom of the paper.

The enlarged picture, however, would still be in the top left-hand corner of the paper because the distance from the center of dilation to the corner of the picture was 0. When the copier increases the picture by 200 percent, everything is increased 200 percent, including the distance from the center of dilation to the corner of the picture.

Mr. Lemon began the lesson by reviewing the task scenario with students, ensuring that students understood what Burnell had done and why the outcome was problematic. He explained that for the first question, they would need to explain how the photocopy machine produced the partial image: "How did it take this and turn it into just this little section down here? What happened?" He then explained that they would need to use a rubber band stretcher to complete the enlarged image (question 2) and demonstrated how to use it. (See https://www.instructables.com/id/Enlarging-with-Rubber-Bands if you are not familiar with the process.) Finally, Mr. Lemon explained that students would first work individually so they could quietly organize their thoughts, then they would share their ideas with a partner, and finally they would all come together and have a whole class discussion.

As Mr. Lemon monitored students as they worked on the task, he noticed that more than half the class thought that the picture should be placed in the top left-hand corner of the paper (Solution A, Figure 5.15). A few students correctly placed the photo, centering the picture in the top left quadrant of the paper (Solutions B and C, Figure 5.15). A few students drew a line from the upper left-hand corner of the paper to the upper left-hand corner of the original picture and the upper left corner of the enlarged picture (Solutions C, D, and E, Figure 5.15). The student's drawing in Solution C, however, was not accurate. The center of the student's picture is shown as being on a line that corresponds with the top left corners of the paper, the original picture, and the enlargement, which is not correct. This is due to the fact that the student has made a sketch of where the picture would be and it is not drawn to scale. Some students noted that the segment drawn from the corner of the paper to the enlarged picture was twice as long as the segment drawn from the corner of the paper to the original picture (Solution D, Figure 5.15). A few other students explicitly showed how the length and width of the enlarged picture had doubled and the area of the enlarged picture had quadrupled (Solution E, Figure 5.15). As he began to make decisions about which work to select, the teacher asked specific students if he could take a picture of their work so he could load it onto the electronic whiteboard. This way students' work would be easy to display and students would be able to easily add annotations to their work as they explained it to the class.

Figure 5.15 • The solutions Mr. Lemon observed while monitoring

SOLUTION	DRAWING	STUDENT'S IDEAS
A		**Josh:** *"I first put it so it was a little bit off the page, but then I realized that wasn't right. So I put it in the upper left-hand corner."* *"But now I don't think it would be centered. It would just be in the left-hand corner but bigger."*
B		**Denise:** *"Cut the page in half and then in half again and you center the picture in the middle of the top left quadrant."* *"You have to have a border around the picture if you want it in the center of the page."*
C		**Matthew:** *"The center is one-fourth: 25% to the right and 25% down."*
D		**Jackie:** *"The line from the top left corner to the top left corner of the enlarged image is double the length from the top left corner to the top left corner of the original image. So the top left corner of the original image is the mid-point."*
E		**Ben:** *"The length and width of the picture doubled and the area quadrupled."*

By the time Mr. Lemon completed monitoring students work, he had a good handle on what students had done and the ideas he could draw out based on their thinking. He decided to sequence the solutions in the order shown in Figure 5.15 (A-B-C-D-E) and to invite Josh, Denise, Matthew, Jackie, and Ben to discuss their thinking about the task.

Although Josh's thinking (Solution A) about the placement of the picture was not correct, many students had the same incorrect idea and Mr. Lemon therefore felt that it was a good place to build from. He also knew that there were students with different claims regarding the correct placement of the picture and that bringing these perspectives together could lead to a rich discussion. He intentionally picked Josh to share this incorrect solution because Josh was a strong student and Mr. Lemon thought it would be helpful for him to model the classroom norm that all students need the opportunity to revise their thinking. Mr. Lemon also knew Josh well enough to know that positioning him in this way would not bother him.

The discussion of Josh's solution would engage students in a discussion of whether or not placing the photo in the top left-hand corner would achieve the intended result and if not, where it should be placed. The next presenters—Denise (Solution B) and Matthew (Solution C)—could then offer their ideas about where the photo should be placed and why it made sense to put it there.

Next, Jackie's observation (Solution D) about the length of the line segments drawn from the top left-hand corner of the page would lead to a discussion of the center of dilation and the fact that all of the corresponding points on the two images fell on line segments that emanated from the same point. Finally, Ben (Solution E) would share what he noticed about the relationship between the original and enlarged pictures—that the linear measures of the enlarged picture were twice the size of the original picture and that the area of the enlarged picture was four times bigger that the original. This would lead to a discussion of scale factor—if the scale factor for length is k (in this case, 2), then the scale factor for area would be k^2 (in this case, 4).

This set of solutions, sequenced in this way, would allow all students to enter the conversation and build their understanding of the key ideas of the lesson as they moved through the five different presentations—each of which highlight one critical aspect of the situation. Hence, the whole class discussion would be an opportunity to pull together the ideas offered by different students into an integrated whole and, most likely, for individual students to make connections and learn something that they had not previously figured out.

Mr. Lemon took the process of selecting and sequencing seriously. He knew that it was important to ensure that the mathematical ideas he wanted students to grapple with were made public and equally important to building students' identities as mathematical doers and thinkers. He explained,

> I have come to realize that the selecting and sequencing process not only supports the development of the mathematics but it also supports the development of the mathematical identity for the students. It is so important for students to have opportunities to see their peers share and struggle and to hear the thinking of others and to have an opportunity to present their own thinking.

All incorrect solutions, however, are not worth sharing (Lischka, Gerstenschlager, Stephens, Strayer & Barlow, 2016). If the errors are simply computational in nature, are the result of a misunderstanding of the problem, or are made only by one or two students, you may want to address these individually rather than during the whole group discussion. When several students have made the same error, as we saw in Mr. Lemon's class, then it makes sense to share the incorrect solution and use it as a basis for moving forward.

Sharing solutions that are incomplete can also support students in building from their initial mathematical ideas to larger and more complex mathematical arguments. This is particularly important in high school mathematics. Understanding key elements of algebra, functions, mathematical modeling, and geometry depends on being able to assemble mathematical ideas that have been shown to be true into broader, more generalized mathematical arguments (Arbaugh, Smith, Boyle, Stylianides, & Steele, 2019). Developing mathematical argumentation through reasoning and proving is akin to building the skills to write an evidence-based persuasive piece of writing, or collecting and testing data that test a scientific hypothesis.

In Mr. Moore's Floodlight Shadows lesson, an important goal was for students to understand how to build a proof that the two triangles were similar in order to find the length of the shadows. As we saw in Chapter 3, that proof could take a number of different forms and made use of a number of key lines of thinking put together. For Mr. Moore, showcasing aspects of that reasoning to build toward a complete proof was an important part of his lesson.

As the time approached for Mr. Moore's class to transition into a whole class discussion, he had noticed a few things from his monitoring. First, he had noticed that most—but not all—of the groups in the class had created a diagram in which they could see a pair of triangles that were similar, and that could be useful for finding the length of the shadows from the floodlights. For the groups that had identified triangles, many had stated that they were similar but were in various stages of creating a general argument to support that claim. Only a handful of groups were at or near completion of the general argument. As Mr. Moore completed his monitoring of student work, he decided to select a series of incomplete solutions that would build on each other in order to provide a justification of similarity. Mr. Moore described the solutions he was looking for just before calling the whole class together:

> There are a small number of groups who have struggled just to make a diagram and are just getting to the notion of similarity. So maybe I'll start first with a group that has a wonderful diagram but hasn't really been able to piece together how they have similarity. Then I'll be looking for a group that has identified similar triangles but hasn't been able to find the length of the shadows. Maybe that's where I get the group in with the picture that applied similarity using the two right triangles and made use of scale factor to write their equations for finding the length of the shadow.

Because there were still a small number of groups struggling to see the triangles and several more groups working to justify similarity, starting with a fully articulated argument for similarity and using that argument to solve for the shadow's length may not have been accessible to all of his students. Mr. Moore wanted to ensure that all students had the opportunity to meet some aspects of the goals he had for the lesson. As such, beginning with identifying the triangles, then moving to justifying similarity, and finally to finding the length of the shadow provided all students in the class an entry point to the whole class discussion. In addition, it provided opportunities for continued learning during that whole class discussion.

Incorrect and incomplete work can be used to enhance a discussion and to press students to make sense of someone else's reasoning. This may not be something you need to do in every discussion, but do not avoid something just because it is wrong! Leah Alcala (not a pseudonym) developed a routine for engaging students in analyzing mistakes. She calls it "My Favorite No." At the heart of this routine is giving students a problem to work on, collecting student responses to the problem, reviewing the solutions, identifying the most interesting wrong answers, and selecting a wrong answer for the class to discuss. The incorrect response selected for discussion shows *some good mathematics* but also some error and is not linked to a particular student. The entire class is then engaged in careful analysis of what is correct, what is incorrect, and why. While Ms. Alcala uses this routine as a warm-up activity prior to the lesson for the day, it could be used as a formative assessment activity at any point in a lesson or as a more general technique for sharing incorrect solutions. (See https://www.teachingchannel.org/videos/class-warm-up-routine for more details on "My Favorite No.")

Conclusion

As we have discussed in this chapter, it is through the process of selecting and sequencing that you determine what solutions will be shared and the order in which they will be shared. This is important because the solutions that are shared publicly provide the grist for the discussion that is to follow. Hence, the identified solutions *must* have the potential to highlight the mathematical ideas that are targeted in the lesson. The sequence in which solutions are shared must provide students with access to the discussion and achieve a coherent storyline for students to follow. The first solution presented should be one that all students can make sense of regardless of what they themselves have produced, and as additional presenters share their work, there should be a clear sense of a developing story where one solution builds on the next.

The key to successful selecting and sequencing is careful consideration of what you are trying to accomplish in the lesson. The work of Ms. Moran provides an illustration of a teacher who reflected on what she was trying to accomplish in light of the work students had produced and made a thoughtful determination of what she would feature during the discussion. Her work highlighted how the data she had collected as she monitored students' work on the task served as a resource for decision making when it was time to select and sequence.

While selecting and sequencing are not without their challenges, as we discussed in Part Two of the chapter, these are challenges you can overcome. The illustrations from the classrooms of Ms. Mulligan, Mr. Harmon, Ms. Hansen, Mr. Washington, Mr. Moore, and Mr. Lemon provide some concrete ideas regarding how to select and sequence solutions in order to limit the number of solutions shared, keep the mathematical ideas central, and ensure that different voices are heard.

The situation in which Ms. Kennedy found herself is a critical one to consider. Lessons do not always go as planned, and it is important to be sure that you are teaching adolescents, not teaching a lesson. What students do during the lesson may cause you to revise your plan. In such cases, you will need to think about how the work students produced can help you achieve your revised goals.

Selecting and Sequencing Student Solutions—Summary

Video Clip 5.1
To hear and see more about selecting and sequencing, watch Video Clip 5.1.

Videos may also be accessed at
resources.corwin.com/5practices-highschool

In the next chapter, we explore the practice of connecting. Here, we will return to Ms. Moran's lesson and consider what it takes to engage in this practice and the challenges it presents.

SELECTING AND SEQUENCING

It is now time to reflect on the lesson you taught following Chapter 4, but this time through the lens of selecting and sequencing.

1. What solutions did you select for presentation during the whole group discussion?

   • Did the selected solutions help you address the mathematical ideas that you had targeted in the lesson? Are there other solutions that might have been more useful in meeting your goal?

   • How many solutions did you have students present? Did all of these contribute to better understanding of the mathematics to be learned? Did you conclude the discussion in the allotted time?

   • Which students were selected as presenters? Did you include any students who are not frequent presenters? Could you have?

2. How did you sequence the solutions?

   • Did the series of presentations add up to something? Was the storyline coherent?

   • Did you include any incomplete or incorrect solutions? Where in the sequence did they fit?

3. Based on your reading of this chapter and a deeper understanding of the process of selecting and sequencing, would you do anything differently if you were going to teach this lesson again?

4. What lessons have you learned that you will draw on in the next lesson you plan and teach?

"With connecting, students get to see multiple access points to a problem and multiple ways of representing a problem. And being able to connect those together gives students more tools in their toolbox to use from this point forward."

—MATTHEW HARMON, HIGH SCHOOL MATHEMATICS TEACHER

CHAPTER 6

Connecting Student Solutions

Having selected and sequenced student solutions with the goals of the lesson in mind, you are now ready to conduct a whole class discussion and engage in the last of the five practices, connecting student solutions. While you designed the discussion so that students play a central role as they share their strategies with their peers, you also play an essential role in the discussion. For students to truly learn what is intended, you need to help students see the connections between the solutions that are shared and the goals of the lesson. To do this requires careful facilitation of the discussion on your part.

Smith and Stein (2018) describe connecting in the following way:

> [Connecting involves asking] questions [that] must go beyond merely clarifying and probing what individual students did and how. Instead, they must focus on mathematical meaning and relationships and make links between mathematical ideas and representations. (p. 70)

Facilitating meaningful discussions involves helping students to share their thinking in a way that is understandable to others. You may need to help them recognize where to stand, how loudly to speak, and the importance of explaining both their process and their reasoning using language that is accessible to the class (Boaler & Humphreys, 2005; Kazemi & Hintz, 2014).

Students who are not presenting may also need your help to understand their roles as they engage in active listening and prepare to ask questions of their peers (Hufferd-Ackles, Fuson, & Sherin, 2015). For example, you may need to model initially how to ask a question, how to disagree, and how to share an alternate idea. Working with students to establish explicit norms for participation can help all students better understand what is expected of them during classroom discussions (Horn, 2012).

The practice of connecting goes even further. Connecting involves helping students relate strategies or ideas to one or more of the lesson goals and see the relationships between different solutions. Your task here is to consider the solution strategies you have selected and the kinds of connections that will be important for students to make. Some of this work will need to take place on the fly, during instruction, as you see how students describe their strategies, and what questions arise from peers. Still, it can be helpful to consider, before the discussion, what connections you anticipate will be critical for students to make and the questions you can ask to help students make these connections.

In this chapter, we first describe key aspects of connecting and illustrate what this practice looks like in a high school classroom. We then discuss what aspects of connecting are typically challenging for teachers and provide an opportunity for you to explore connecting in your own teaching practice.

Part One: Unpacking the Practice: Connecting Student Solutions

Connecting student solutions involves relating the ideas that students present to the class, both to the goals of the lesson and to each other. Here we explore each of these components by looking inside Ms. Moran's classroom. Figure 6.1 highlights the components of this practice along with key questions to guide the process of connecting.

Figure 6.1 • Key questions that support the practice of connecting

WHAT IT TAKES	KEY QUESTIONS
Connecting student work to the goals of the lesson	What questions about the student work will make the mathematics being targeted in the lesson visible?
Connecting different solutions to each other	What questions will help students make connections between the different solution strategies presented?

Connecting Student Work to the Goals of the Lesson

In selecting solution strategies to have students share in class, you purposefully choose student work that contains important mathematical ideas that advance the goals of the lesson. As the discussion unfolds in your classroom, you will want to keep those ideas in mind. While it is possible that students will make these connections in their presentations, this will not always be the case. You want to be prepared to ask questions about the students' work that will make the important mathematics in the lesson visible for the class. In this way, connecting involves creating bridges from what students share to the mathematically significant ideas underlying the lesson (Leatham, Peterson, Stockero, & Van Zoest, 2015). Without seeing these connections, students may walk away from the lesson without clarity about what it was they were supposed to learn.

How can you do this? For each solution shared, you want to keep in mind the key mathematical takeaways for the class. Many times, this will have less to do with *what* a student did and more to do with *why* a student used a particular approach given the task at hand. You may need to draw out these ideas from students by asking them to share why they chose a particular solution path and to explain the reasoning that guided their work.

You will also want to highlight explicit connections between the student work and the goals of the lessons. "How does this approach help us answer the question we are working on?" "Where does this idea fit with what we are trying to figure out?" Students may be applying mathematical ideas that have important connections to the lesson goals and yet be unaware of these connections. Your objective is to help make these connections visible to the presenter and to the class. Boaler and Brodie (2004) describe the importance of using such questions because they target the key concepts in a lesson for students.

Once such ideas have been made public, it is often helpful to give everyone a chance to digest these connections. Using a *turn-and-talk* strategy (Kazemi & Hintz, 2014) can provide needed time for students to consider new information with a partner and reflect on how an idea might fit (or not) with their own approach.

What does engaging students in making connections look like in practice? Let us return to our investigation of Ms. Moran's classroom. At the beginning of the discussion, Ms. Moran invites Elijah, Nyleah, Lauren, and John to present their strategy for using recursion to explore the staircases. As we discussed in Chapter 5, Ms. Moran decided to start here because this group created both a table and a visual model to reflect recursion. In their presentation, the students highlighted that the staircases grow by "more and more each stage" (Goal 1). The class also focused on the two-dimensional growth of the staircases (Goal 2). Nyleah explained that "the length and the width are growing" and other students in class added to this idea. Adreana stated that "you're squaring it" and Collin suggested "that would get the value for the whole square" but the staircase is "a partial square." In addition, the class discussed the idea that this approach provides a consistent way to find the area of any staircase given the area of the previous staircase, but "it doesn't work if you just have the stage number" (first part of Goal 3). With these ideas in mind, Ms. Moran believes the class is now ready to explore more explicit approaches to characterizing the staircase function.

In Analyzing the Work of Teaching 6.1, you will have an opportunity to view the next part of the class discussion and explore how Ms. Moran helps her students make connections between the solutions that are presented and her goals for the lesson. We encourage you to view the video clips and consider the questions posed before you read our analyses. Note that Erin, who has been a member of this group, had been called out of class just before the discussion began so she does not participate in her group's presentation.

Analyzing the Work of Teaching 6.1

Connecting Student Work to the Goals of the Lesson—Part One

Video Clip 6.1

As you watch Video Clip 6.1, consider Aidan, Micki, and Emily's presentation of their solution and the comments made by Ms. Moran and other students in the class. Recall that Ms. Moran selected this group's work in order to address Goals 3 and 4 of the lesson. Here is what the students write on the board during their presentation:

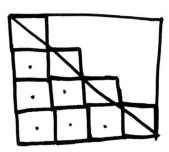

Stage 4

- What questions does Ms. Moran ask to connect Aidan, Micki, and Emily's presentation to Goals 3 and 4 of the lesson?

- How do students' responses address these goals?

Goal 3: Quadratic growth can be expressed in both recursive and explicit forms.

Goal 4: Quadratic growth can be modeled in a variety of ways—with a diagram in which width and height increase linearly, with a table where the second difference is constant, with a graph where the shape of a function is a parabola, and with an equation of degree 2.

 Videos may also be accessed at
resources.corwin.com/5practices-highschool

Connecting Student Work to the Goals of Lesson, Part One—Analysis

In this video clip, Emily refers to the image of Staircase 4 to explain her group's method of drawing a diagonal line and counting the resulting squares and triangles (see Analyzing the Work of Teaching 4.6 for more information on this group's method). Aidan and Micki then write the equation they found to represent this model and explain it as "length times width divided by 2 plus $\frac{1}{2} x$," with the x being "the unsolved stage." What is it about this approach that Ms. Moran wanted to make public?

To gain insight into Ms. Moran's objective, we can look closely at the questions she asks in response to this group's explanation. First, Ms. Moran asks the group to clarify the variables in their equation. Emily responds, "x equals [the] stage number and y is going to be the number of squares." Ms. Moran repeats, "x is your stage number" and asks, "And your length and width?" In doing so, it seems that Ms. Moran's goal is to highlight for the class the different terms in Emily, Aidan, and Micki's equation. Araia soon comments that "your length times width" could be replaced with "x squared." Aidan confirms this point and explains that the stage number, the length, and the width are the same, "so we could just do x squared." Aidan then rewrites the equation as $y = x^2(\div 2) + \frac{1}{2}x$.

This shift in the equation from "length times width" to x^2 is essential to achieving Goal 3, writing an explicit equation that allows one to determine the number of squares in a staircase directly from the stage number. Ms. Moran then asks students to turn and talk and test the equation for various stages. Here she intends for students to use the equation and see for themselves that it "works for the other stages as well."

Ms. Moran also makes progress on addressing Goal 4. In addition to Elijah, Nyleah, Lauren, and John's previous illustration of increasing growth in a table, here Aidan and his group generate an equation of degree 2, as a way of representing two-dimensional growth. Following Aidan, Micki, and Emily's presentation, Ms. Moran asks Mae and Isabel to explain their approach. In Analyzing the Work of Teaching 6.2, you will take a close look at how Ms. Moran connects Mae and Isabel's solution to the goals of the lesson.

Analyzing the Work of Teaching 6.2

Connecting Student Work to the Goals of the Lesson–Part Two

Video Clip 6.2

As you watch Video Clip 6.2, consider Mae and Isabel's explanation of how they solved the Staircase task. The students' writing on the board is reproduced on the following page.

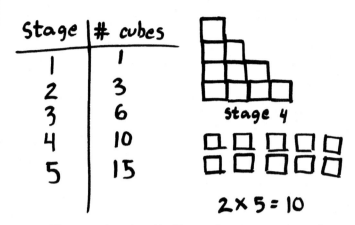

- What questions does Ms. Moran ask to connect Mae and Isabel's presentation to Goals 3 and 4 of the lesson?

- How do students' responses address these goals?

Goal 3: Quadratic growth can be expressed in both recursive and explicit forms.

Goal 4: Quadratic growth can be modeled in a variety of ways— with a diagram in which width and height increase linearly, with a table where the second difference is constant, with a graph where the shape of a function is a parabola, and with an equation of degree 2.

 Videos may also be accessed at
resources.corwin.com/5practices-highschool

Connecting Student Work to the Goals of Lesson, Part Two—Analysis

In this video clip, Ms. Moran begins by asking Mae and Isabel to explain their solution to the Staircase task. As Mae explains the process, Ms. Moran asks several clarifying questions, including "What shape did you rearrange it into?" and "What pattern did you notice once you got your tiles into that shape?" After Mae draws a 2×5 rectangle to reflect having rearranged the tiles in Staircase 4, Ms. Moran asks two additional questions: How did Mae and Isabel "connect the 2 [in 2×5] to the 4" in Staircase 4? and How did they "relate 5 to that stage number?" These questions are intended to help make Mae and Isabel's solution accessible to the class and to help draw together the specific example Mae and Isabel showed with Staircase 4 to their more generalized equation, $y = (n \div 2)(n+1)$. As she does this, Ms. Moran is explicitly connecting Mae and Isabel's work to Goal 3 of the lesson.

As before, Ms. Moran's questions also serve to address Goal 4 and to connect Mae and Isabel's approach to another way of illustrating the two-dimensional growth of the staircase, this time by rearranging the tiles into a familiar shape. At the end of the video clip, Ms. Moran asks Mae and Isabel to graph their equation, bringing in yet another representation for visualizing the relationship between the stage number and the area of the staircase.

Connecting Different Solutions to Each Other

In addition to connecting students' solutions to the goals of the lesson, it is important to connect students' solutions to each other. Different strategies can open up new opportunities for problem solving and increase students' learning (Schukajlow & Krug, 2014). Doing so can also help build connections for students among mathematics ideas rather than adding to a sense of mathematics as a set of disconnected facts.

You might find it important to help students investigate how various solution methods lead to the same answer, and you may help students examine whether some methods are more efficient than others. This can provide students with valuable information should they be ready to use a more sophisticated strategy in the future (Murata & Fuson, 2006). Alternatively, you might find yourself in a situation where it is necessary to investigate why different approaches lead to different answers and how to explain those differences.

Students also need the opportunity to investigate the relationship between different representations. Many rich high school tasks can be solved using multiple representations (refer back to Figure 3.12 for a discussion of different ways to represent a mathematical idea). Students should develop *representational fluency*—that is, students should have the ability to move among different representations efficiently and understand how key features in one representation appear in another representation (Suh, Johnston, Jamieson, & Mills, 2008). In addition, when exploring functions, for example, students should understand how particular representations highlight certain aspects of a function (Moore-Russo & Golzy, 2005). For example, in a lesson on the Cycle Shop task, Clairice Robinson (Chapter 4) wanted her students to understand that a system of equations can be solved using different representations (i.e., tables, graphs, equations, pictures) and that connections can be made between different representational forms, including the problem context.

Another connection that is valuable for students to consider is the relationship between more concrete and more abstract solutions. The ability to generalize from a set of specific cases to any case is a powerful mathematical idea and one that is essential in high school mathematics.

For example, in the Family Tree task, Marco Washington (Chapter 5) indicated that he planned to have students share three different solutions to the task—the picture, the expanded table, and the equation. By starting with the picture, the context would be clear and accessible to all students. The table, which includes more specific cases, made the pattern more visible. Finally, the equation—the most abstract—could be connected to both the table and the picture. (Mr. Washington's lesson on the Family Tree task is explored further in Part Two in this chapter.)

In Analyzing the Work of Teaching 6.3, you will return to Ms. Moran's class and look further into the ways that the teacher highlights connections among the students' solutions. At this point, Isabel has typed $y = (x \div 2)(x + 1)$ into Desmos on the computer that is projected on the board.

Analyzing the Work of Teaching 6.3

Connecting Different Solutions to Each Other

Video Clip 6.3

As you watch Video Clip 6.3, listen to Ms. Moran's comments and questions to the class about Mae and Isabel's solution.

$$\left(\frac{x}{2}\right)(x+1) = y$$

$$\frac{1}{2}x^2 + \frac{1}{2}x = y$$

- What connections does Ms. Moran encourage students to make between Mae and Isabel's solution and other approaches students have taken?

- How do students respond?

 Videos may also be accessed at
resources.corwin.com/5practices-highschool

Connecting Different Solutions to Each Other—Analysis

In the video, Ms. Moran asks the class what they notice about the graph of Mae and Isabel's equation. Students respond, "It's a parabola." Ms. Moran then presses, "Why do you think it's a parabola?" Here students make several important connections—equations represented by a parabola have an x^2 in them, this is equivalent to having "two of the same numbers," and, in this case, those two numbers are the length and the width of the staircase. With this in mind, Ms. Moran moves the class to an exploration of the relationship between Aidan, Emily, and Micki's equation and Mae and Isabel's equation. She points out that Aidan, Emily, and Micki have an x^2 in their equation and asks if the class could also "get an x^2" in Mae and Isabel's equation and whether the two equations are equivalent. Near the end of the video, John comes to the board, rewrites $\frac{x}{2}$ as $\frac{1}{2}x$, and then uses the distributive property to show that the equations are the same.

In discussing the lesson, Ms. Moran said that it was important to her to "get to that x^2 term" and to have students connect the two solutions and "see their equivalence." She also had in mind two issues that she planned to discuss with students the next day: "I want to bring back the idea that the two equations are equivalent" and use that "as a jumping-off point to looking at the domain of the function." Ms. Moran explained that she hoped to explore with students that in the context of the staircase problem, the domain was the natural numbers and thus was represented by only part of the parabola that Mae and Isabel displayed for the class. "I want them to look at the figures and think about the stage numbers we were using and compare [them] to the graph," she said. Thus, in addition to connecting the different equations that students shared, Ms. Moran planned to connect different representations that the students presented as well.

Cori Moran's Attention to Key Questions: Connecting

In facilitating the class discussion of the Staircase task, Ms. Moran encouraged students to draw connections between the work that was being discussed and the goals that she had established for the lesson. While Ms. Moran had chosen specific student solutions because they related to the lesson goals, during the discussion, Ms. Moran asked questions in order to ensure that those connections were visible for students.

Ms. Moran also made an effort to highlight for the class the ways that different solutions were related and in particular that it was important to connect features of the problem across different representations. Connecting students' solutions to the goals of the lesson and to each other is critical in order to fully realize the benefits of the five practices.

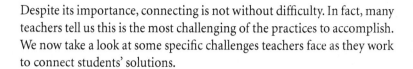

Despite its importance, connecting is not without difficulty. In fact, many teachers tell us this is the most challenging of the practices to accomplish. We now take a look at some specific challenges teachers face as they work to connect students' solutions.

Part Two: Challenges Teachers Face: Connecting Student Responses

The whole group discussion that takes place around the work students share is an opportunity for students to continue to solidify their learning. It is during the discussion that you need to ensure that the key mathematical ideas that you have targeted during the lesson are made public and accessible to the students in your class. The key to a successful discussion is building on the ideas put forth by students without telling students what it is you want them to know. This is not easy. The pressures of time and accountability weigh heavily on teachers, and the temptation to summarize the lesson for students is strong. In this section, we focus on four specific challenges associated with this practice, shown in Figure 6.2, that we have identified from our work with teachers.

Figure 6.2 • Challenges associated with the practice of connecting

CHALLENGE	DESCRIPTION
Keeping the entire class engaged and accountable during individual presentations	Often, the sharing of solutions turns into a *show and tell* or a dialogue between the teacher and the presenter. The rest of the class needs to be held accountable for understanding and making sense of the solutions that are presented.
Ensuring key mathematical ideas are made public and remain the focus	It is possible to have students share and discuss a lot of interesting solutions and never get to the point of the lesson. It is critical that the key mathematical ideas that are being targeted in the lesson are explicitly discussed.
Making sure that you do not take over the discussion and do the explaining	As students are presenting their solutions, the teacher needs to ask questions that engage the presenters and the rest of the class in explaining and making sense of the solutions. There is a temptation for the teacher to take over and tell the students what they need to know. When this happens, opportunities for learning are diminished. Remember whoever is doing the talking is doing the thinking!
Running out of time	Teachers may not have enough time to conduct the whole class discussion the way they had planned it. In such cases it is important to come up with a *Plan B* that provides some closure to the lesson but does not turn into telling.

Keeping the Entire Class Engaged and Accountable During Individual Presentations

It is easy for the student presentations that take place at the end of a lesson to turn into a series of show and tells, where each presenter explains what he or she did and the rest of the class is silent. Having some students sit passively, while other students explain, however, is not sufficient to ensure learning. The teacher needs to make certain that the entire class is engaged in and accountable for what is being presented. According to Michaels, O'Conner, Hall, and Resnick (2013),

> When classroom talk is accountable to the learning community, students listen to one another, not just obediently keeping quiet until it is their turn to take the floor, but attending carefully so that they can use and build on one another's ideas. Students and teachers paraphrase and expand upon one another's contributions. If speakers aren't sure they understood what someone else said, they make an effort to clarify. They disagree respectfully, challenging a claim, not the person who made it. Students move the argument forward, sometimes with the teacher's help, sometimes on their own. (pp. 2–3)

So what exactly can you do to hold students accountable? In Figure 6.3, we have identified a set of moves that teachers can make to hold students accountable for attending to the discussion.

Figure 6.3 • Talk moves intended to hold students accountable for participation in a discussion

TEACHER MOVES	PURPOSE	EXAMPLES	SOURCE
Adding on: Prompting students for further participation	To invite additional contributions to the discussion in order to engage more students or to gain a deeper understanding of an idea	• Would someone like to add on to what she just said? • Can you say more about how you figured that out?	Chapin, O'Connor, & Anderson (2009, pp. 13–16)
Reasoning: Asking students to compare their own reasoning to someone else's reasoning	To allow students to engage with and make sense of their peer's ways of thinking that may be different from their own	• Do you agree or disagree? Why? • How is what he said the same as or different from how you thought about it?	

TEACHER MOVES	PURPOSE	EXAMPLES	SOURCE
Repeating: Having a student repeat what another student has said in her own words	To give students another version of a contribution and to ensure that students are engaged in listening to their peers	• Can someone repeat what he just said in their own words?	
Revoicing: Repeating what a student has said and then checking with the student to make sure you have accurately captured their idea	To clarify what a student has said or to amplify an important idea	• So, you are saying… • So, here is what I heard you say…	
Waiting: Giving students time to think about the question that has been posed before asking for a response	To ensure that all students have an opportunity to think about the question posed and to provide a student who has been called on time to gather his or her thoughts	• Take a minute to think about this. • I am going to wait until I see more hands. • Take your time… we will wait.	
Revise: Allowing students to revise their initial thinking based on new insights	To make it clear to students that changing one's mind based on new information is how learning occurs and that this is valued	• Would anyone like to revise his or her thinking? • Has anyone's thinking changed? Why?	Kazemi & Hintz (2014, p. 21)
Turn and talk: Allowing time for students to discuss an idea that has been presented with a partner or small group	To give students time to think about a question that has been posed rather than be expected to answer immediately and to clarify and share ideas with a small number of peers before doing so publicly	• Take two minutes and turn and talk to your table group about…	
Challenging: Redirecting a question raised back to students or using students' contributions for further investigation	To turn the responsibility for reasoning and sense-making back to students and develop shared understandings in the classroom	• That's a good question. What do you think about what she just said?	Michaels, O'Conner, Hall, & Resnick (2013, p. 22)

(Continued)

Figure 6.3 • (Continued)

TEACHER MOVES	PURPOSE	EXAMPLES	SOURCE
Marking: Noting a valuable contribution that was made to the discussion	To highlight a contribution that is directly relevant to what the teacher is trying to accomplish in the lesson	• Did everyone hear what she just said? She… • That's an important point.	
Recapping: Summarizing key points made in the discussion by several students	To make public in a concise and coherent way what can be concluded at a particular point	• So in looking across the presentations, here is what I am hearing… • Here is what we have discovered…	
Inviting: Asking a student to contribute in the discussion	To make diverse points of view available for public discussion	• _____, would you share what you and your group came up with? • _____, you have a puzzled look on your face. What are you thinking? • _____, your strategy was not the same as this one. What did you do differently?	Herbel-Eisenmann, Cirillo, Steele, Otten, & Johnson (2017, pp. liv–lvii)
Probing: Following up on what an individual student has explained or produced	To make a student's thinking process more transparent to others, to elicit additional justification for why he took a particular action	• Can you explain how you got…? • How do you know that? • Why does that work?	

[See Appendix D for a summary of each of the identified sources. Although we have associated particular authors with specific moves, you will find that many of the moves are addressed in each of the resources.]

In Analyzing the Work of Teaching 6.4, we return to Marco Washington's class during the whole class discussion of solutions to the Family Tree task (shown in Figure 5.11). As we indicated in Chapter 5, Mr. Washington wants his students to understand the following:

1. An exponential relationship of the form $f(x) = ab^x$ has a rate of change that varies by a constant multiplicative factor; as the

function's input values increase by 1 the output value changes by a constant factor.

2. Linear functions increase by a constant amount (additive) and exponential functions increase by a constant factor (multiplicative).

3. An exponential function can be represented in different ways and connections can be made among the representations.

In the portion of the discussion you will be analyzing, Mr. Washington is focusing explicitly on Goals 1 and 2.

Analyzing the Work of Teaching 6.4

Holding Students Accountable

As you read the vignette, consider the following questions:

1. What does Mr. Washington do to help his students make sense of the ideas that are being presented? What talk moves (see Figure 6.3) does he use?

2. What evidence is there that students *are* making sense of the presented ideas?

Family Tree Vignette

1   *The whole group discussion began with Ricardo's presentation of the picture (shown below) that*
2   *he and his partner had created.*

3

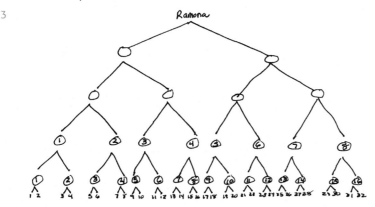

4   *The discussion of the picture surfaced the idea that every time you go back a generation, you*
5   *have twice as many people as the generation before—Ramona had 2 parents born 1 generation*
6   *back, 4 grandparents born 2 generations back, 8 great-grandparents born 3 generations back,*
7   *16 great-great-grandparents born 4 generations back, and 32 great-great-great-grandparents born*
8   *5 generations back. Ricardo explained, "You could keep going but I couldn't draw anymore.*

9 I think that in the sixth generation back, 64 great-great-great-great-grandparents would
10 have been born." At this point, Mr. Washington asked Rebekah if she agreed with Ricardo. She said,
11 "That's what we got too!" At this point, Mr. Washington invited Rebekah to come up and share
12 the table that she and Claire had created.
13
14 Rebekah: We started with a picture like Ricardo's but we gave up too. When
15 Mr.Washington came over, we were trying to decide what to do next.
16 He asked us, "Can you organize your findings in some way?" "Do you see any
17 patterns?" So we decided to make this table.
18

NUMBER OF GENERATIONS AGO	2s	NUMBER OF GREAT-GRANDPARENTS
3	2 × 2 × 2	8
4	2 × 2 × 2 × 2	16
5	2 × 2 × 2 × 2 × 2	32
6	2 × 2 × 2 × 2 × 2 × 2	64
7	2 × 2 × 2 × 2 × 2 × 2 × 2	128
8	2 × 2 × 2 × 2 × 2 × 2 × 2 × 2	256
9	2 × 2 × 2 × 2 × 2 × 2 × 2 × 2 × 2	512
10	2 × 2 × 2 × 2 × 2 × 2 × 2 × 2 × 2 × 2	1,024

19 Mr. W.: So can you tell us about your table? It looks different from the other
20 tables I saw.
21 Rebekah: Well, our first table only had two columns—the number of generations ago
22 and the number of great-grandparents—and we only went to 5 generations
23 back. Then we noticed a pattern—you keep multiplying the number of
24 "great" grandparents born in one generation by 2 to get the number of
25 "great" grandparents born in the next generation back. So 8 × 2 = 16, 16 ×
26 2 = 32, 32 × 2 = 64, and so on. So we went up to 10 generations back.
27 So then we decided to keep track of how many 2's were being multiplied,
28 so we put in a middle column.
29 Mr. W.: Does anyone have any questions for Rebekah? (Two students raise their
30 hands. Mr. Washington calls out, "David then Sofia," indicating that they can
31 ask their questions in that order.)
32 David: Why did you start with 3 generations back instead of starting at 0 or 1?
33 Rebekah: Well, Ramona didn't have "great" grandparents born until 3 generations
34 back like we saw in the picture, so we just decided to start there. Any of
35 the numbers before that wouldn't be "great" grandparents. (David gives a
36 thumbs up indicating he understands.)
37 Sofia: I am not sure I understand what the middle column represents.
38 Mr. W.: Can someone explain in their own words how Rebekah thought about the
39 middle column? Damien?
40 Damien: Rebekah said it was the number of 2's that were multiplied. So for the
41 3 generations back, there were 8 great-grandparents born—so 2 × 2 × 2 = 8.
42 For 4 generations back, there were 16 great-grandparents born—so 2 × 2 ×
43 2 × 2 = 16. It keeps going like that.

44	Mr. W.:	Could someone connect what Rebekah and Damien are saying to Ricardo's
45		picture? *(Two hands go up.)* I am going to wait until I see a few more
46		hands. *(After 10 seconds there are a few more hands in the air. Mr. W. calls on a*
47		*student he hasn't heard from recently.)* Elise?
48	Elise:	So if we go back to Ricardo's picture and look at any generation, each of the
49		people born in one generation had 2 parents born in the previous
50		generation. *(Elise makes a notation on Ricardo's picture as shown below after*
51		*asking Ricardo's permission to write on his work.)* So that means that the
52		number of "greats" has to double every time you go back a generation. And
53		doubling is the same as multiplying by 2.
54		

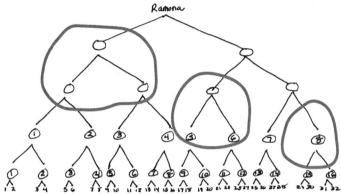

55	Mr. W.:	So what I am hearing so far is that for every generation back, there are
56		2 times more people born than the previous generation. And that the
57		number of 2's you multiply together is related to the number of generations
58		you go back. So let's continue the discussion with Ozzie and Tanya's
59		equation. Ozzie, can you come and explain what you and Tanya figured out?
60	Ozzie:	We decided that the equation would be $y = 2^x$, where x is the number of
61		generations back and y is the "great" grandparents that were born x
62		generations back. So for 3 generations ago, it would be $y = 2^3$, which
63		would be $y = 2 \times 2 \times 2$ or $y = 8$. So you get the same thing that we saw in
64		Ricardo's picture and in Rebekah's table.
65	Mr. W.:	So can someone tell us what 2^3 means? Keisha?
66	Keisha:	It means 2 to the third power. So the 3 tells you how many 2's to multiply.
67		So like Ozzie said, it's $2 \times 2 \times 2$.
68	Mr. W.:	So Keisha is saying that 3 tells you how many 2's to multiply. Devon, you
69		look puzzled.
70	Devon:	I agree with Keisha about what 2^3 means, but we thought the equation
71		should be $y = 2x$.
72	Mr. W.:	So we have two different ideas there about an equation. Devon thinks it
73		would be $y = 2x$ and Ozzie thinks it would be $y = 2^x$. Take a few minutes
74		to turn and talk to your partner about which equation you think accurately
75		depicts this situation and why.
76	Mr. W.:	*(As Mr. W. monitors the discussion among partners, he notices that Kalia and*
77		*her partner agree with Devon.)* Kalia, tell us why you think it should be $y = 2x$.
78	Kalia:	$2x$ means two times more. And in this case, for each generation back, 2 times
79		more "greats" are born.
80	Mr. W.:	Does everyone agree with Kalia? *(Lots of students showing a thumbs down.)*

81		Miray, why do you disagree?
82	Miray:	Well I tried $y = 2x$ and it gives you the right answer if x is 1 or 2. But if you
83		use $x = 3$, then $2 \times 3 = 6$, which is not what we saw in the picture or in the
84		table. Three generations ago, 8 of Ramona's "great" grandparents were born.
85	Ali:	In $y = 2x$, x is that number of generations back. So all you are doing is
86		multiplying the generation by 2, not the number of "great" grandparents
87		from the previous generation. Rebekah's table shows it best—the middle
88		column tells you that the number of "great" grandparents born in one
89		generation is two times as many as were born in the previous generation.
90		So with each generation, you need to multiply by one more 2.
91	Gabriel:	$y = 2x$ is linear, so every time x increases by 1, y increases by 2. So basically,
92		you are just adding 2 every time. This function doesn't work that way. Like
93		we saw in Rebekah's table, every time x increases by 1, you are multiplying
94		by another 2 like Ali said. So in $y = 2x$ you keep adding 2 and in $y = 2^x$ you
95		keep multiplying by 2. So it has to be $y = 2^x$.
96	Mr. W.:	Gabriel is making an important point. He is saying that $y = 2x$ and $y = 2^x$ have
97		different rates of change—one is additive and the other is multiplicative.
98		Take a few minutes to turn and talk with your partner and decide whether
99		you agree with Gabriel and if so why.

100 *The class ultimately concludes that Gabriel is right and $y = 2^x$ has to be correct in this situation*
101 *since the increase in the number of "great" grandparents born is multiplicative, not additive.*
102 *The class concludes with a discussion of the general form of an exponential function. For*
103 *homework Mr. Washington asks students to graph the function and to be prepared to talk*
104 *about how the picture, table, equation, and graph are connected.*

Holding Students Accountable—Analysis

Mr. Washington wanted his students to understand that the Family Tree scenario would be modeled by an exponential function because the value of the function (number of "great" grandparents born) increased by a constant factor for each successive value of x (each generation back). Relatedly, he wanted students to recognize the difference between the rate of change in a linear versus exponential function. Rather than simply telling students what he wanted them to know, the teacher orchestrated a discussion around the work students produced so that students could figure things out for themselves.

Throughout the discussion, Mr. Washington used nine different talk moves (see Figure 6.4) to engage students and hold them accountable for making sense of the ideas being discussed. He promoted broad participation in the discussion, made different points of view available, and ensured that important ideas were made public and elaborated on by different students.

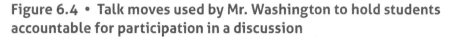

Figure 6.4 • Talk moves used by Mr. Washington to hold students accountable for participation in a discussion

TALK MOVE	WHAT THE TEACHER SAID [LINE NUMBER(S)]
Probing	• So what can you tell us about your table? [19] • Miray, why do you disagree? [81]
Inviting	• Does anyone have any questions for Rebekah? [29] • Could someone connect what Rebekah and Damien are saying to Ricardo's picture? [44–45] • Ozzie, can you come and explain what you and Tanya figured out? [59] • Devon, you look puzzled. [68–69] • Kalia, tell us why you think it should be $y = 2x$. [77]
Repeating	• Can someone explain in their own words how Rebekah thought about middle column? [38–39]
Waiting	• I am going to wait until I see a few more hands. [45–46]
Recapping	• So what I am hearing so far is that for every generation back, there are 2 times more people born than the previous generation. And that the number of 2's you multiply together is related to the number of generations you go back. [55–58]
Reasoning	• So can someone tell us what 2^3 means? [65] • So we have two different ideas there about an equation. Devon thinks it would be $y = 2x$ and Ozzie thinks it would be $y = 2^x$. Take a few minutes to turn and talk to your partner about which equation you think accurately depicts this situation and why. [72–75] • Does everyone agree with Kalia? [80] • Gabriel is making an important point. He is saying that $y = 2x$ and $y = 2^x$ have different rates of change—one is additive and the other is multiplicative. Take a few minutes to turn and talk with your partner and decide whether you agree with Gabriel and if so why. [96–99]
Revoicing	• So Keisha is saying that 3 tells you how many 2s to multiply. [68]
Turn and Talk	• Take a few minutes to turn and talk to your partner about which equation you think accurately depicts this situation and why. [73–75] • Take a few minutes to turn and talk with your partner and decide whether you agree with Gabriel and if so why. [98–99]
Marking	• Gabriel is making an important point. He is saying that $y = 2x$ and $y = 2^x$ have different rates of change—one is additive and the other is multiplicative. [96–97]

Take, for example, the portion of the discussion that began with the introduction of the equation $y = 2^x$ (lines 58–59) and the series of talk moves Mr. Washington made. Mr. Washington *invited* Ozzie to share his equation ($y = 2^x$) with the class, knowing that other students, like Devon, thought the equation should be $y = 2x$. Since understanding that the Family Tree scenario was modeled by an exponential function that increased by a constant factor (and therefore was not linear) was at the heart of what Mr. Washington wanted students to learn, he positioned the two equations as the poles of a debate, encouraging students to compare their *reasoning* with the reasoning of their peers and to *turn and talk* about which equation they thought was correct (lines 72–75). By asking students to turn and talk, Mr. Washington slowed down the pace of the discussion and provided students with the opportunity to engage in thinking and reasoning while providing himself with time to listen in on the conversations and gain insight into what students were thinking. As a result, Mr. Washington was able to identify another student (Kaila) who thought that $y = 2x$ was the correct equation and *invite* her to explain her thinking (line 77). Mr. Washington then asked the class "Does everyone agree with Kalia" (line 80), again asking them to engage in *reasoning*. Kalia's position led to a series of explanations by Miray, Ali, and Gabriel that made clear the differences between the two equations.

What is important to consider in this segment of the discussion is not just the teacher's use of a particular move or the number of moves. It is about the purposeful use of moves, individually and in combination, that serve to get more students involved in and making sense of the discussion and ensure that they have something important to talk about. Mr. Washington's pattern of *inviting* specific students to share their ideas because of the discussion those ideas are likely to stimulate and then giving students time (*turn and talk*) to *reason* about the ideas and take a position were key to the lesson.

But were students making sense of the ideas that were presented? Over the course of the portion of the discussion shown in the excerpt, 13 different students (of the 25 in the class) made contributions to the whole group discussion. Three different representations were shared—picture, table, and equation—that provided students with grounding for discussing what was happening to the number of "great" grandparents born every time they went back one generation. Several students referred explicitly to specific representations when providing their arguments. For example, Elise referred to Ricardo's picture (lines 48–53) when explaining that the number of "greats" has to double when they go back another generation and Miray, Ali, and Gabriel all referred to Rebekah's table when arguing that $y = 2x$ was not the correct equation.

The "debate" that Mr. Washington instigated (lines 72–75) served to bring different ideas about the relationship between the number of "great" grandparents born in a generation and the number of generations back, which culminated with Gabriel contrasting the rate of change of the two equations that were being discussed. The active involvement of several students in this discussion and the progression of ideas as the discussion continued provide evidence that students were indeed trying to make sense of the Family Tree scenario. Although it is impossible to say whether each of the students in the class came away with the targeted understanding, it is clear that ideas were made public and articulated by several students over the course of the discussion. While not all of the students in the class participated in the discussion, they all had access to the ideas being discussed. Hatano and Inagaki (1991) argue that silent participants can learn from discussions:

> Silent members may be actively participating. They can learn much by observing the ongoing discussion or debate carefully. This is often characterized as a vicarious process, but it is more than that. In a sense, these students are all trying to find an agent, someone who really speaks for them. A good agent or vocal participant can articulate what a silent member has been trying without success to say. (p. 346)

In looking at the discussion that took place in Mr. Washington's class, we see a teacher who strategically used talk moves to actively engage students in making sense of the ideas he had targeted in the lesson and we hear students who were coming to understand key features of exponential functions. The critical point here is that the entire class is being held accountable for expressing their ideas clearly and for listening closely to and thinking deeply about the mathematics being discussed. A review of students' work on the homework assignment—to graph the function and to be prepared to talk about how the picture, table, equation, and graph are connected—will give Mr. Washington an opportunity to see how individual students are making sense of exponential functions.

Ensuring That Key Mathematical Ideas Are Made Public and Remain the Focus

Productive discussions are ones that clearly and explicitly target the mathematical ideas that you want students to learn as a result of engaging in the lesson. Having selected students to present their solutions—even solutions of the highest quality—is not sufficient to ensure that students will learn what is intended. Students need assistance in drawing connections among methods and in tying specific solutions to key mathematical concepts (Smith & Stein, 2018).

Consider, for example, a lesson featuring the Cycle Shop task shown in Figure 5.5. As we discussed in Chapter 5, one set of goals for a lesson built around the Cycle Shop task would be for students to understand the following:

1. Equations can be created that represent real-world constraints.

2. There is a point of intersection between two (unique nonparallel) linear equations that represents where the two

equations have the same x- and y-values; this point is the solution to the system since it satisfies both equations.

3. A system of equations can be solved using different representations (i.e., tables, graphs, equations, pictures) and connections can be made between different representational forms, including the problem context.

Imagine that during the lesson students produced the solutions shown in Figure 5.6. Although all of the solutions shown (except Solution H) are correct, getting the correct answer is not equivalent to understanding the targeted ideas. In fact, no combination of these solutions is going to make the lesson goals transparent on their own. For example, although a student can write an equation and solve it either algebraically (Solution F in Figure 5.6) or use it to produce a graph (Solution B in Figure 5.6), this does not imply that they understand what the solution or the point of intersection represents or how different representations are related to each other. By asking questions about the equations, the graphs, and the algebraic solution (such as those shown in Figure 6.5), students can reflect on their work and make connections that may not have been clear to them. The point is that student solutions do not make the mathematics to be learned transparent. You need to identify the solutions that have the potential to address the lesson goals, and then you must ask specific questions of students that will help them make connections to the concepts you have targeted. A visit to the whole class discussions in Mr. Moore and Mr. Harmon's classes illuminates the ways in which teachers can showcase key mathematical ideas that students generate through the use of specific talk moves.

> **TEACHING TAKEAWAY**
>
> Correct solutions alone are not enough. Teachers must ask questions in order to help students make connections to the targeted mathematical ideas.

Figure 6.5 • Questions to ask about different representations

REPRESENTATION	QUESTIONS
Equations	• What does each equation mean? • What do x and y represent?
Graph	• Which equation matches with which graph? What does each line represent in the context of the situation? • Do all the points on your graph have meaning in the context of the problem? • What does the point (11, 13) represent?
Algebraic solution	• Why can you set the two equations equal to each other? • How does that relate to what is happening if you looked at a graph of the equations?

As we noted in Chapter 5, Mr. Moore's students struggled with aspects of the Floodlight Shadows task, including identifying triangles, proving similarity, or finding the length of the shadows. Since Mr. Moore wanted to ensure that all students had the opportunity to meet some aspects of the goals he had for the lesson, he decided to invite students to present their work on components of the task, thus building the storyline from identifying triangles, to proving similarity, to finding the length of shadows using knowledge of similar triangles. These three aspects of students' work had the potential to bring forward important mathematical ideas related to Mr. Moore's goals.

Toward that end, he first selected Franci to share her diagram, which identified two triangles that might be similar but did not feature a clear justification of the similarity (Figure 6.6 A). Next, he selected Lexi's work to establish similarity between two of the triangles (Figure 6.6 B). Finally, he selected Jerry's work (Figure 6.6 C), which built on the similarity argument and used a scale factor to calculate the length of the shadow.

Figure 6.6 • Student work on the Floodlight Shadows task

A. Franci's Work

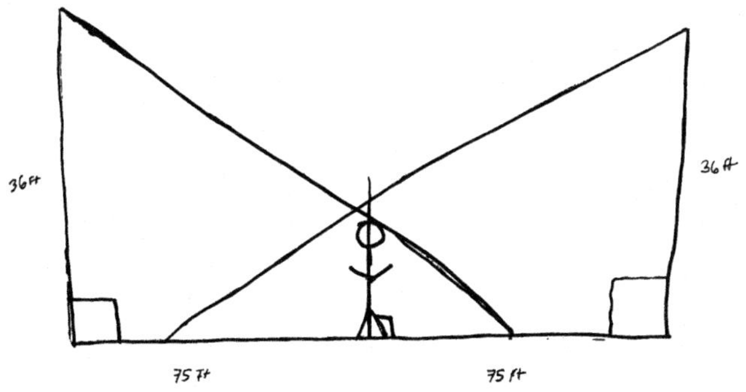

B. Lexi's Work

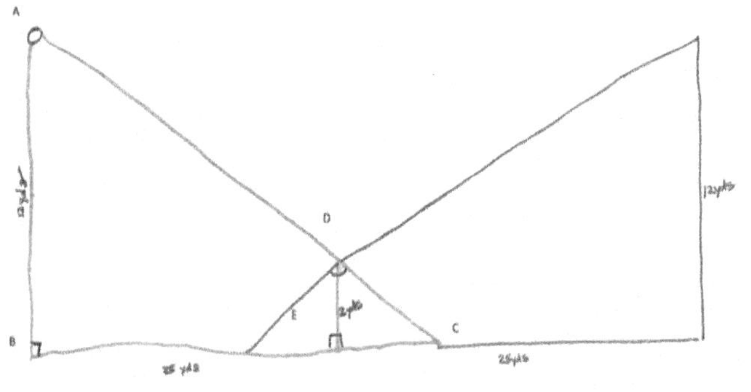

(Continued)

Figure 6.6 • (*Continued*)

C. Jerry's Work

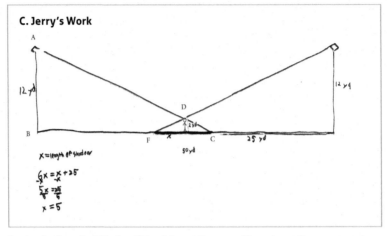

$x = $ length of shadow

$$\frac{6}{x}x = \frac{x}{x} + 25$$
$$\frac{5x}{5} = \frac{25}{5}$$
$$x = 5$$

In Analyzing the Work of Teaching 6.5, you will analyze the presentations made by Franci, Lexi, and Jerry and determine which ideas were made public and how.

▶ **Analyzing the Work of Teaching 6.5**

Making Key Ideas Public—Part One

Video Clip 6.4

In Video Clip 6.4, Franci, Lexi, and Jerry present their work (see Figure 6.6) on the Floodlight Shadows task.

As you watch the clip, consider the following questions:

1. What key mathematical ideas related to Mr. Moore's goals are evident in each of the three student presentations?

2. What talk moves did Mr. Moore make that highlighted the key mathematical ideas?

3. What other talk moves might you want to make as a teacher to highlight the key mathematical ideas?

Recall that Mr. Moore's goals were as follows:

1. Creating mathematical models of geometric situations is helpful in identifying key features that can be used to make mathematical arguments.

2. Similar triangles are related in two ways: their corresponding angles are congruent, and the lengths of their corresponding sides are related by a common scale factor.

3. Justifying that two triangles are similar means making arguments about the ways in which corresponding angles are congruent, and corresponding sides are scaled using ideas such as corresponding parts of triangles and scale factor.

 Videos may also be accessed at
resources.corwin.com/5practices-highschool

Making Key Ideas Public, Part One—Analysis

Each of the three student presentations contributed to making Mr. Moore's mathematical goals public. Looking at the diagrams produced by each of the three students (see Figure 6.6) shows both similarities and differences. All three students' diagrams show a sketch with four right triangles, two pairs of which could be justified as similar. The three sketches have varying levels of accuracy with respect to the proportions between the light towers and the field, with each successive diagram—moving from Franci, to Lexi, to Jerry—featuring more accuracy. In the analysis that follows, we track the key mathematical ideas related to Mr. Moore's goals in each student's presentation.

Franci's diagram and explanation model the situation, including the length of the field, height of the lights, position of Eliot, and the shadow the lights cast on the field, capturing the key elements of the context. Her explanation establishes key ideas related to Goal 1 by noting how the diagram made apparent the sets of similar triangles. She also hints at aspects of Goal 2, in noting that the right angles of the two triangles might help justify similarity.

The talk moves Mr. Moore uses following Franci's explanation pick up on this aspect of Goal 2. He *probes* students on what makes triangles similar and *invites* Noah to contribute his thinking on the question. When Noah establishes that all three angles need to be congruent, Mr. Moore *marks* this idea and raises the question of whether we yet know that the triangles are similar. Franci's work is somewhat incomplete, but it was a solution that everyone could relate to, and it sets up Lexi's explanation, which Mr. Moore transitions into at this point.

Lexi's diagram also models the situation and meets Goal 1, with slightly more accurate proportions visible in her diagram. Lexi's explanation further unpacks aspects of Goal 2 as she points to specific angles and begins to provide mathematical justification for why they are congruent:

> This triangle and this triangle are similar, because they have the same angles. ... This angle [ABC in Figure 6.7] and this angle [DEC Figure 6.7] is 90°, and then like the reflexive property, this angle [ACB/DCE Figure 6.7] is the same for this triangle and that triangle because it like falls on the same line ...

Lexi uses a "magical number" of 30° as an assumed value for the measure of the shared angle in order to find the third angle using the fact that the sum of the measures of the angles in both triangles must be 180°. She says,

> And knowing that, like all triangles add up to 180°, what our group did was that we like gave this angle a magical number. So we said that that's 90°, and that's 30°. So that adds up to 120°. So that means that this and this have to be like the missing piece, which would be like 60° in our case.

Thus, she was able to justify similarity by showing that the three angles of one triangle were congruent to three angles of the other triangle (Goal 3).

Figure 6.7 • Lexi's diagram with additional labels

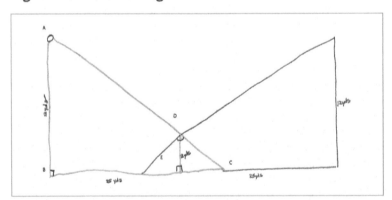

Mr. Moore makes a number of important talk moves following Lexi's presentation. He engages in *recapping* by first asking Lexi to walk through each pair of angles again, one at a time. In this way, he is also *marking* the comparison of the pairs of angles as an important activity in justifying that the two triangles are similar. This again makes public key mathematical ideas related to Goals 2 and 3. Both Mr. Moore and Lexi engage in some key *adding on* as they review the three pairs of angles, which is particularly notable in the explanation of the reflexive property. Mr. Moore *probes* for the idea that the sum of the measures of the angles in the two triangles is 180°, an idea that was implicit in Lexi's initial explanation. He *invites* the class to pose questions to Lexi (although none are offered), and sets up for Jerry to share his explanation next.

Jerry's argument, although lacking in precision, builds on the notion of similarity and introduces the idea of scale factor as a way of finding the measures of the sides of the triangles. Jerry says,

> *And we know that the height of the small triangle [DEC in Figure 6.8] is 2 yards, and the large triangle [ABC in Figure 6.8] is 12 yards. And if we take 2 divided by 12, that's 6 so we know… that [each side of] the small triangle multiplied by a scale factor of 6 would give you the [corresponding side of the] large triangle.*

This explanation brings forward aspects of Goals 2 and 3 that had not yet been addressed in the explanations thus far. Jerry's explanation identifies the scale factor and uses it to identify how corresponding sides are scaled and ultimately to find the length of the shadow:

> *We could set the two bases [BC and EC in Figure 6.8] to be equal each other. So [we] have 6x x + 25, which I wrote down here. Then I subtract x from both sides, which gave me 5x = 25, and divide by 5 so which gave me x = 5. So we know that each of those shadows [is] 5 yards long. So [the] total length of the shadows is 10 yards.*

Jerry's dialogue shows how he is using the scale factor to determine a missing side measurement and using that fact to derive the length of the shadow.

Figure 6.8 • Jerry's diagram with additional labels

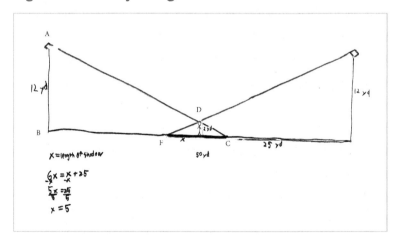

Mr. Moore immediately *marks* the idea of scale factor following Jerry's explanation, and does so by *inviting* students to identify the new math idea that was present in Jerry's explanation. When Franci names the scale factor, the teacher probes the class about what the scale factor means, and Kwami offers an explanation. While not shown on the video, Mr. Moore finishes the exchange by going back and *marking* the important contribution from Lexi's explanation, establishing the congruent angles and similarity, which allowed Jerry's use of the scale factor to be contextualized. This move also draws together aspects of all three goals into a coherent mathematical storyline.

At this point, Mr. Moore was running out of class time. With additional time and opportunity, what other talk moves might a teacher have made to keep the focus on the key mathematical ideas? Lexi's use of the "magic number" for her angle does not get unpacked and could be further probed and explored. Do we know that the angle she identified as 30° is 30°? More broadly, does it matter what the specific measure of that angle is to move her argument forward? Mr. Moore could have also used repeating more often, to have students use their own words to explain what was said. This would have been valuable for Lexi and Jerry's presentations, particularly for the aspects of those presentations that relied significantly on the visual (e.g., talking about "this angle" and "this angle"). With additional time, there may have been more opportunities to have students turn and talk to one another to ensure that all students were taking away the important mathematical ideas from the discussion.

Even though his students had not gotten as far with the problem as he had hoped, Mr. Moore found an effective way to select and sequence explanations that featured important mathematical ideas and to connect those explanations in ways that created a coherent, meaningful mathematical storyline. Mr. Moore's talk moves made effective use of student contributions and kept the intellectual ownership of those ideas with the students rather than appropriating them himself as the teacher.

What occurred in Mr. Harmon's class provides a context for further exploring the ways in which teacher moves can bring students' key mathematical ideas forward. As we first discussed in Chapter 3, as a result of engaging in the Toothpick Hexagons task, Mr. Harmon wanted his students to understand the following:

1. Patterns can be described and generalized by finding the underlying structure of the pattern and relating two variables that are changing at the same time.

2. Patterns that grow by a constant rate are linear.

3. There are different but equivalent ways of describing and representing the same pattern.

4. Connections can be made between different representational forms—tables, graphs, equations, words, and pictures.

In Analyzing the Work of Teaching 6.6, you will analyze a portion of the discussion that took place at the end of class and determine which ideas were made public and how.

Analyzing the Work of Teaching 6.6

Making Key Ideas Public—Part Two

Video Clip 6.5

In Video Clip 6.5, three different solutions are shared.

- First, Zashon shares her equation, $y = 6 + 5(x - 1)$.

- Next, Brandon shares his equation, $y = 5x + 1$.

- Finally, Mr. Harmon shares a solution produced by a student in another class (shown below).

> I did the number of hexagons times 4.
> Then the number of hexagons plus 1. $\frac{x4}{9}$
> Then added it all. $36 + 10 = 46$

As you watch the clip, consider the following questions:

1. What mathematical ideas are being targeted in each of these presentations?

2. What does Mr. Harmon do to highlight the mathematics he wants students to learn?

 Videos may also be accessed at
resources.corwin.com/5practices-highschool

Making Key Ideas Public, Part Two—Analysis

As we discussed in Chapter 5, Mr. Harmon decided to begin the discussion with the more common approaches used by students in the class, since "showing kids right off the bat that they're right will be reassuring." Toward that end, he *invites* Zashon and then Brandon to share their equations with the class.

Zashon shares her equation, $y = 6 + 5(x - 1)$, and explains,

> *The y equals the total number of toothpicks, and the 6 equals the six sides that you start for every hexagon, plus 5 is the five toothpicks you add for each side, because you already use the sixth side for the first one. And then x is the amount of hexagons you have.*

She struggles to articulate what $x - 1$ represented, saying, "And then for every hexagon that you add, you minus 1 cause the side is used for the first."

Mr. Harmon attempts to bring some clarity to Zashon's explanation by asking a few *probing* questions about what the different components of her equation represent. He first asks, "Why did you have to minus 1 in there?" When this did not result in a clearer explanation, he asks, "Where does the 5 come into play?" Zashon responds, "The 5 comes from the five toothpicks added for every hexagon." With this information in hand, Mr. Harmon asks Zashon to use her equation to find the number of toothpicks in a row of 9 hexagons (part b). Zashon correctly substitutes 9 for x in the equation and determined that 8 would be multiplied by 5. At this point, Mr. Harmon *invites* the class to consider "Where does the 8 come from?" Grace responds, "You already have 1 hexagon. You're only adding 8 more and not 9 more," thus clarifying that 8 (or $x - 1$) represents the number of hexagons that are each built with 5 toothpicks.

Next Brandon explains that he got 46 (the answer to part b of the task) by "doing 9 times 5 plus 1, because you have 9 hexagons, and each one has 5 sides, except the one that has an extra 1 toothpick on it. So you have to add that extra 1 on as the like the starting value." Mr. Harmon seeks clarification by *probing*, "You said you have 9 hexagons, and each one has 5 sides?" Brandon explains, "No, each one has 5 except one, which has an extra six side and basically I'm adding that extra 1 to account for that extra side."

At this point Mr. Harmon *probes* further in order to understand exactly where this "extra side" that Brandon is talking about might be located. Brandon points to the hexagon sides and counts 5 sides for each, moving left to right in the row; for the last hexagon, he indicates that you need to add 1 to account for this extra side. Mr. Harmon then indicates that you could also think of the +1 as the starting number and building the hexagons out from that point, using 5 toothpicks for each. It is likely that Mr. Harmon's explanation resonated with some students, including Alexander, Jordyn, and Neveah who we observed in Analyzing the Work of Teaching 4.4 and who clearly saw 1 toothpick as the starting point for building a row of hexagons from toothpicks.

Finally, Mr. Harmon shares the work produced by a student in another class. As we discussed in Chapter 5, he selected this particular piece of work because, although it had a written description and a calculation, it did not have an equation and therefore would provide the class an opportunity to determine an equation that would model the description. Mr. Harmon introduced students to this activity by telling them,

> *I'm going to pose a problem here to you and see if you follow what this person did. I'm not quite sure if this is correct. I mean, they came up with the same answer, but I'm not sure if their work is accurate.*

In so doing, the teacher challenged students to take on and make sense of someone else's *reasoning* and to connect the description to the diagram of hexagons and to write an equation that would model the students' description.

The presentations by Zashon and Brandon made salient that different equations can be written (Goal 1) that describe and represent the same pattern (Goal 3) and that connections can be made between equations and pictures (in this case, a row of hexagons) (Goal 4). By engaging students in making sense of a third piece of work that did not express the thinking of any of the students in the class, they were given the opportunity to make sense of a written description, connect it to the diagram, and write an equation to model it. Perhaps most importantly, this was an opportunity for everyone to learn something new in the whole class discussion. Unfortunately, class ended before students could fully engage in this activity.

What did Mr. Harmon do to highlight the mathematics to be learned? First and foremost, he identified student solutions to be shared (and in two cases, the students who produced them) that had the potential to highlight the ideas that were at the heart of the lesson. He set the tone for the whole class discussion by telling students, "We're going to have a discussion about some possible methods and ask you to see if there something different that someone else did that might help improve your understanding." This set the expectation that students needed to listen to the presenters and consider how a solution produced by someone else might be different from the one they came up with.

Throughout the discussion, Mr. Harmon used a subset of the talk moves we introduced earlier in this chapter to ensure that key ideas were made public and that students' explanations were clear. Since the three presentations featured in the video occurred within the last 10 minutes of class, each was a bit rushed. Given more time, Mr. Harmon might have invited more students to weigh in on the ideas being discussed in order to ensure that students had a firm grasp of the ideas. But the discussion did surface some of the key ideas he was targeting, thus laying the groundwork for future lessons where the full set of ideas identified in the goals could be explored in more depth. (Mr. Harmon's reflection on the lesson and thoughts about what he might do in future lessons is discussed further in the "Running Out of Time" challenge).

The key takeaway from the discussion in Mr. Harmon's class is that he did not leave it to chance that the ideas he wanted students to grapple with would surface. By carefully selecting the work that would be presented and using several of the talk moves described in Figure 6.3, he was able to draw students' attention to specific aspects of the work.

Making Sure That You Do Not Take Over the Discussion and Do the Explaining

As a teacher, you know what it is you want students to learn from a lesson, and you may at times feel that the most expedient way to communicate this to students is to simply tell them what you want them to know. It is not clear, however, what students learn and retain when they simply listen to the teacher explain. Steven Reinhart (2000), an experienced teacher, said it best:

> When I was in front of the class demonstrating and explaining, I was learning a great deal, but many of my students were not! Eventually, I concluded that if my students were to ever really learn mathematics, they would have to do the explaining, and I, the listening. My definition of a good teacher has since changed from "one who explains things so well that students understand" to "one who gets students to explain things so well that they can be understood." (p. 478)

 PAUSE AND CONSIDER

Think of a time when you found yourself doing all the explaining at the end of a lesson. What do you think students learned when this occurred? How do you know? What might you have done differently that would have provided more insight into what students understood about the ideas you were targeting?

Let us return to Ms. Kennedy's class that we explored in Chapter 5 where students were working on the Hospital Locator task, shown in Figure 6.9. Her goal for this lesson was for students to realize that the center of the circumcircle of a triangle is equidistant from the three vertices, and the optimal hospital location was the center of the circle whose radii pass through the vertices. Recall that Ms. Kennedy's students had not made

as much progress as she had intended toward the end of the lesson, and she made a decision to revise her goal. Specifically, she asked one group to discuss in turn how they attempted to find a circle that contained the three points and why that approach was helpful, and she asked a second group to discuss their approach of constructing perpendicular bisectors.

Figure 6.9 • The Hospital Locator task used in Ms. Kennedy's class

Hospital Locator

Boise, ID; Helena, MT; and Salt Lake City, UT are three large cities in the northwestern part of the United States. Although each city has a local hospital for minor needs and emergencies, an advanced medical facility is needed for transplants, research, and so forth. Imagine the potential of a high-powered, high-tech, extremely modern medical center that could be shared by the three cities and their surrounding communities!

You have been hired to determine the best location for this facility.

Source: Reprinted with permission from National Council of Teachers of Mathematics (2008). Hospital Locator. Retrieved from http://illuminations.nctm.org. All rights reserved.

 This task can also be accessed at **resources.corwin.com/5practices-highschool**

Ms. Kennedy made a determination that pursuing these two student explanations would help set her up to meet her goal in her next lesson. This meant that she would spend at least part of the next day with her class continuing the work, which had not been an initial part of her plan. Consider the implication of an alternative approach to this situation, in which Ms. Kennedy spends the last 10 minutes of the class period walking students through the solution to the task. What would this approach have afforded? On the surface, one might argue that it would have allowed Ms. Kennedy to accomplish her goals for the lesson and expose students to the geometry concepts she had intended for them to explore within a single class period. While it may be true that students would have been able to listen to the solution and ask a handful of questions about it, it would not be entirely clear what Ms. Kennedy's students learned, and the teacher would not have any evidence in the form of student work or talk that would help her assess whether her students had met the goals of the lesson.

Sometimes when we as teachers make a decision to take over the thinking and explain the mathematics, we are making that choice with the best of intentions. We are trying to expose our students to important mathematical ideas and move efficiently through a set of curricular goals. But there are two important implications to this choice. First, it robs students of the opportunity to struggle productively with important mathematical ideas and to gain a meaningful conceptual understanding of the mathematics through their own work and talk. Second, it deprives us as teachers of important formative assessment information about how our own students are thinking about the mathematics. Without those two pieces, it is impossible to say whether the students have truly had an opportunity to learn the important mathematics that we had targeted.

The pressures of the clock can be particularly acute in high school, with class periods as short as 42 minutes per day. Additionally, high school teachers often feel a strong commitment to prepare students well for their mathematical futures in high school, college, or career. These good-hearted intentions and time constraints can often lead teachers to take over explaining the mathematics. Novice and experienced teachers alike continually fight this battle, as Mr. Moore described:

> I think every single teacher on the face of the earth struggles with not telling, right? Saying to myself, "Be careful with your leading," and feeling sure I will fall into the pit of saying too much as I always do. You want to point things out, you want to put fingers on students' papers. I do my absolute best to never take a pencil from somebody, [and] draw on their drawing, but it's always tempting. It's super tempting to say, "Oh, let me just add a little line to your picture here. Now do you see the triangle? Of course you do, because I drew it there!" [Try] to be conscious of it as much as possible. If you try to make it a point every day, it becomes routine.

In the case of Ms. Kennedy, she could have just stopped after the two groups had presented their explanations and introduced the idea of the circumscribed circle that led to the solution. This would have been much faster and less *messy* than the discussion that took place. Instead, because Ms. Kennedy viewed classroom discussions as critical to student learning, she resisted the urge to step in and take over the discussion. Reinhart (2000) echoes this sentiment:

> Good discussions take time; at first, I was uncomfortable in taking so much time to discuss a single question or problem. The urge to simply tell my students and move on for the sake of expedience was considerable. Eventually, I began to see the value in what I now refer to as a "less is more" philosophy. I now believe that all students learn more when I pose a high-quality problem and give them the necessary time to investigate, process their thoughts, and reflect on and defend their findings. (p. 480)

Running Out of Time

As Reinhart states in the quote above, good discussions take time. So can you facilitate a good discussion when you may only have 45 minutes for the entire class? Here are a few suggestions that might help. First, you can extend the lesson over two days. For example, you might plan to do a lesson featuring the Compy Attack! task (see Figure 2.10) as a two-day lesson. On day one, you could introduce students to the task by engaging them in Act 1 activities (i.e., notice and wonder about the video clip, determine the information and tools you need to make a decision) and then have students work in groups to determine the height of a typical compy (Act 2). At the end of the first day, you could collect the work students produce. You could then review the work prior to day two and determine which responses you wanted to have shared, who would share them, and in what order they would be presented. Then on day two, you could conduct the whole class discussion. This approach has several advantages. It gives you time to review the work and make thoughtful decisions regarding selecting and sequencing. It also gives you time to conduct the discussion without feeling rushed. This, however, is a solution that needs to be used judiciously since every lesson cannot take two days!

Another thing to consider is limiting the time students have to work on a task in groups. Some of the teachers with whom we have worked have set timers so that groups know exactly how much time they have and how much is remaining at any point. This will hold students accountable for moving along in their work and keep you aware of how much time has passed. You can always extend the time if students have not made sufficient progress.

It is also important to keep in mind that when monitoring student work, your goal is to help students make progress on the task, not to ensure that each and every student has a correct answer before beginning the discussion. Rather the goal is to make sure that students are positioned so that they can make sense of the discussion. As Cartier and her colleagues (Cartier, Smith, Stein, & Ross, 2013) noted,

> The teacher's goal when intervening in a small group is not to make sure that, by the end of the work session, all students have produced a complete and correct response. Rather it is to support students' fledgling efforts to make sense of the task before them and to make sure that students are working in a productive direction. Later in the lesson, students will have the opportunity to compare their work with what other students have produced and to participate in a class-wide discussion that clarifies the thinking behind and the features of a good explanation for whatever task on which they are working. (p. 88)

Mr. Moore's class provides a good example of not waiting until everyone has the correct answer or has completed the task to begin the discussion. Not all of Mr. Moore's students came to the whole class discussion having found the length of the shadows using what they knew about similar triangles. Beginning the discussion with Franci's diagram provided a starting point for all students to engage with the discussion and slowly build their understanding, first by looking at the triangles that Franci identified with right angles that she *thought* were similar, then considering what it means to be similar and how to prove it (Lexi), and concluding with a discussion of the relationship between similar triangles and how that relationship can be used to find the length of the shadow (Jerry). By carefully determining a starting point for the discussion that all students have access to and then carefully building students' understanding through subsequent presentations, students can move beyond where they may have entered the discussion and actually take away new mathematical learning from the discussion.

TEACHING TAKEAWAY

All students do not have to have a correct answer or need to have completed the entire task in order to participate in and benefit from the whole class discussion.

Even if you don't wait for every student to have a correct and complete solution to the task before beginning the whole class discussion, you may still run out of time. This is what happened to Mr. Harmon whose class period was only 43 minutes. In reflecting on the lesson, Mr. Harmon indicated, "I felt like the conclusion was a little bit rushed. The work samples were rushed too. I'm definitely planning on wrapping up these ideas tomorrow. I definitely want to hit this learning target a little bit more solidly."

So what should Mr. Harmon do as a follow-up to this lesson? If we review his goals for the lesson in light of what he was able to accomplish during the lesson, we see that while he made some progress on Goals 1, 3, and 4, there are several ideas that were not explicitly addressed. Specifically, although students had produced linear equations, there was no explicit discussion of linearity (Goal 2). While connections were made between the picture of a row of hexagons and the equations, connections between other representations such as tables and graphs had not yet been made (Goal 4). Finally, while the students discussed different equations that represented the same pattern, they did not explicitly address equivalence (Goal 3).

One way to start the follow-up discussion would be to return to the three solutions that were examined during class—$y = 5x + 1$, $y = 6 + 5(x - 1)$, and $y = 4x + x + 1$—and provide students with a set of questions that would focus them on the specific ideas you want to target. These questions could first be discussed in a small group and then with the whole class. Here are some examples:

- Can these three equations all be correct? Why or why not? (equivalence)

- What would each equation look like when graphed? How do you know? (linearity)

- What do the points on the graph represent? (connection between graph and context)

- How are the graph and the equation connected? (connection between graph and equation)

Alternatively, Mr. Harmon might review the work that students had produced and select one or more pieces of work that would stimulate discussion of the target ideas. Since most students did not get to part g of the task, where they were asked to create a graph and make observations about it, answers to this question could be the catalyst for discussion. For example, Alexander, Jordyn, and Nevaeh (who were featured in Analyzing the Work of Teaching 4.4) initially thought that the equations $y = 5x + 1$ and $y = 6 + 5(x - 1)$ would result in two different lines with different y-intercepts, as shown in Figure 6.10. While they seemed to realize that this was not correct, as indicated by the x's on the dots, the work could generate an interesting discussion about equivalence as well as the domain of the function.

Figure 6.10 • Nevaeh's graph for the Toothpick Hexagons task

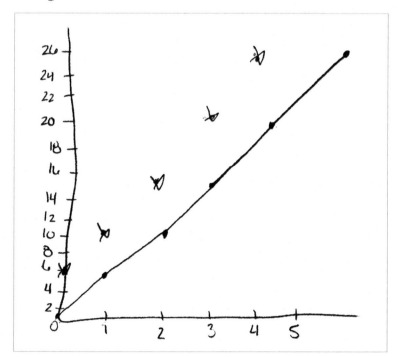

Alayna's response to part g, shown in Figure 6.11, could also be the stimulus for exploring the relationship between the table and graph, what it means to be linear, which equation is shown on the graph, and why it is linear.

Figure 6.11 • Alayna's graph for the Toothpick Hexagons task

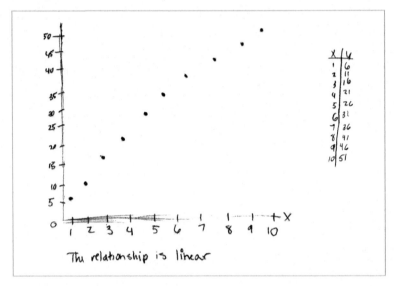

The key point here is that if you did not have time to fully address the ideas that you had targeted during a lesson, you need to revisit the targeted ideas in subsequent lessons. This could be done by introducing a similar task that would surface the target ideas, reflecting on the work completed the previous day, or analyzing student work that would provoke discussion.

Conclusion

The practices that we have discussed in the previous chapters—setting goals, selecting tasks, anticipating, monitoring, selecting, and sequencing—are intended to prepare you to orchestrate a productive discussion. The discussion is the culmination of all your work in carefully planning the lesson and in closely attending to what students do and say as they work on a task. It is in the discussion that connections are made and the mathematical ideas that you target in the lesson are made public.

The work of students, when purposefully and carefully selected and sequenced, becomes the central basis for the classroom discussion. The discussions orchestrated by Cori Moran, Matthew Harmon, and Michael Moore illustrated this point. Each teacher positioned students as authors of mathematical ideas and allowed them to explain what they did and why. Through careful questioning the teachers were able to help students elaborate and clarify their explanations and to engage the entire class in making sense of the presenter's work. In this way, all students were held accountable for making sense of the presenter's work and the mathematical ideas that were at the heart of the lesson.

As we noted, orchestrating a discussion can be challenging. Perhaps the biggest obstacle to overcome is yourself—resisting the temptation to tell students what you want them to know and take over the thinking. As noted in *Principles and Standards for School Mathematics* (NCTM, 2000) two decades ago, "teachers must decide… how to support students without taking over the process of thinking for them and thus eliminating the challenge" (p. 19). The challenges we have identified highlight some of the pitfalls you may encounter as you engage students in whole class discussion. We hope that the ways in which Mr. Moore, Mr. Harmon, and Mr. Washington handled these challenges will help you as you continue to orchestrate discussions in your own classroom.

Connecting Student Responses— Summary

Video Clip 6.6

To hear and see more about connecting student responses, watch Video Clip 6.6.

 Videos may also be accessed at
resources.corwin.com/5practices-highschool

In the next chapter, we address questions about why you should consider using the five practices model and how you can get started in making these practices a component of your instructional toolkit.

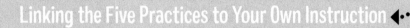

CONNECTING

It is now time to reflect on the lesson you taught following Chapter 4, but this time through the lens of connecting student responses.

1. What connections were made between student responses and the lesson goals?

2. What connections were made between different student responses?

3. To what extent were the mathematical ideas that were targeted in the lesson made public?

4. What did you do to ensure that all students in the class were participating in and accountable for making sense of the ideas being presented?

5. Based on your reading of this chapter and a deeper understanding of the process of connecting, would you do anything differently if you were going to teach this lesson again?

6. What have you learned from this chapter that you will draw on in the next lesson you plan and teach?

" The five practices get me to just be much more thoughtful and plan about what I intend to do. "

—MATTHEW HARMON, HIGH SCHOOL MATHEMATICS TEACHER

" It's really important to plan, plan, plan! It's a lot of work but it will really pay off in the end. "

—CORI MORAN, HIGH SCHOOL MATHEMATICS TEACHER

" I think whenever you have a framework, like the five practices, it really helps give you that lens of what you're trying to get out of your class period. The goal of the time we have together is to foster a productive discussion that advances everybody's understanding. "

—MICHAEL MOORE, HIGH SCHOOL MATHEMATICS TEACHER

CHAPTER 7
Looking Back and Looking Ahead

In Chapters 2 to 6, we explored each of the five practices for orchestrating productive mathematics discussions, identifying the components of each practice and the related challenges. The lessons taught by Matthew Harmon, Michael Moore, and Cori Moran brought the five practices to life and provided a rich context for analyzing teaching and learning in real urban classrooms.

At this point, you may be feeling overwhelmed. You may be starting to wonder if you can really do this and if it is really worth the effort. If so, you are not alone. What we are asking you to do takes a considerable amount of time to *get good at*, and it may require rethinking current practices. The three Milwaukee area teachers had similar feelings. They offer the following advice:

> *When you're dealing with a rich task that is going to be a challenge for your students, you need to really anticipate what their level is coming in, where they're going to hit roadblocks, and to have questions ready to ask. Your students are going to feel so much more successful in the task and their understanding is going to be on display and moving in a positive direction.*
>
> —*Matthew Harmon*

It's hard to do this type of discourse. And working with the five practices is going to be challenging at first, but it does pay off. The more you practice it and the more the students get used to it, the more it'll just become something that's natural. In the end, it is worth that initial investment.

—Michael Moore

Try it! You're going to feel uncomfortable at first but it just gets better and better as you work with these practices. I think that the most important part of it is that you really can see what students can do when they're given that opportunity to engage with high-level tasks.

—Cori Moran

In the remainder of this chapter, we address three questions: Why should you consider using the five practices model? How can you get started in making these practices a component of your instructional toolkit? How often should you engage your students in discussions around high-level tasks? Answers to these questions may relieve some of your anxiety and provide a pathway for moving forward with the five practices.

Why Use the Five Practices Model

Discussions around high-level mathematical tasks, such as those discussed in Chapters 2 to 6, are the primary means through which students develop an understanding of mathematics. Research shows that learning outcomes are the greatest when students have consistent opportunities to engage with high-level tasks (Boaler & Staples, 2008; Stein & Lane, 1996; Stigler & Hiebert, 2004). High school is a particularly critical time for students to engage in high-level tasks that strengthen conceptual understanding, as the mathematical thinking and reasoning skills that they have the opportunity to develop will carry them forward in their college and career trajectories. As this book has illustrated, high-level tasks can be found for any content in the high school curriculum, from algebra to statistics and geometry to calculus.

High-level tasks, however, are the most difficult to implement in ways that maintain the demands of the task (Stein, Grover, & Henningsen, 1996). When the cognitive demands of a task are not maintained during a lesson, opportunities for students' thinking and problem solving are lost, and students are often left to apply a rule or procedure with limited effort. (For example, see "Exploring Exponential Relationships: The Cases of Vanessa Culver and Steven Taylor" in Boston et al. [2017] or "The Cases of Charlie Sanders and Gina Burrows" in Arbaugh et al. [2019].)

The five practices model is intended to help teachers maintain the cognitive demands of a high-level task during a lesson by focusing on thoughtful and thorough planning prior to the lesson. By limiting the number of decisions that you need to make during the lesson, you are better prepared to support students by asking questions rather than telling them what to do. As Smith and Stein (2018) note:

> Simply put, the five practices can equip teachers in supporting students' work on challenging tasks without lowering the demands of the task. In particular, by anticipating what students are likely to do when solving the task (including not being able to get started) and the questions that can be asked to assess and advance their understanding, the teacher is in a much better position to provide scaffolds that support students' engagement and learning without taking over the thinking for them. (p. 131)

Each of our three featured teachers was successful in maintaining the demands of the high-level task they selected, and we would argue, this was due in large measure to their use of the five practices. Each of the teachers had a clear goal for what the lesson should accomplish, selected a high-level task that was aligned with the goal, and anticipated what students would do and how to respond. As a result, the teachers were prepared to interact with students in ways that supported students' work on the tasks, without doing too much of the thinking for them, and kept them moving toward the goal. For example, when Ms. Moran interacted with Aidan, Micki, Emily, and Erin as they worked on the Staircase task (Analyzing the Work of Teaching 4.2), the students were initially unsure of how to account for the small triangles above the diagonal. Ms. Moran could have simply showed them that the number of small triangles above the diagonal was equal to the stage number, so they only needed to add the area of the small triangles to one-half the area of the larger square enclosing the staircase but instead, she asked them questions: "What shape would you have? How can you relate the figure to the figure number?" In doing so, Ms. Moran allowed the students to explore the geometry of the staircases in their own way and to investigate together how they might account for the different triangles they created by adding the diagonal. While telling students how to find the area of the staircase would have been more expedient, it is not clear that an explanation over which students had no ownership would have contributed to their understanding. Through her actions, Ms. Moran was able to maintain the demands of the task and maximize students' opportunity to make sense of the situation and come to a new understanding through their own efforts.

In addition to promoting learning, discussions around high-level tasks can also promote access and equity. According to the National Council of Teachers of Mathematics (2014), providing access and equity requires teaching that "ensures that all students have opportunities to engage successfully in the mathematics classroom and learn challenging mathematics" (p. 68). Using high-level tasks that have multiple entry points, allow for the use of different representations, and can be solved in different ways is the first step in giving each and every student access to meaningful mathematics. According to Boaler and Staples (2008), "When there are many ways to be successful, many more students are successful" (p. 16).

· · · · · · · · · · · · · · · · ·
TEACHING TAKEAWAY

Using the five practices model helps teachers enact high-level tasks without lowering the demands of the task.

Engaging students in discussions featuring their work on a high-level task is the next step in achieving access and equity. Discussions provide the opportunity to honor student thinking, position students as authors of mathematical ideas, and acknowledge contributions to understanding the task and its solution. Sorto and Bower (2017) describe the ways in which discourse can advance access and equity:

> Productive discourse provides opportunities for students to contribute and to understand, through discussion, mathematical concepts and strategies. Students also are offered access to the problem and its understanding while being supported by fellow students. As the teacher creates an environment of safe intellectual contributions, there is a sense of high expectations and accountability for everyone in the classroom. Students' participation and reasoning is always validated to the extent that it contributes to the approach to successfully solving the problem. (p. 68)

Take, for example, the discussions that took place in the classrooms of Matthew Harmon, Michael Moore, and Cori Moran. Each teacher identified a set of students to share their work with the class. In so doing, the teachers were honoring the thinking of these students and positioning them as authors of important mathematical work. Through the discussion of these targeted solutions, each and every student had access to challenging mathematics and had the opportunity to extend their understanding of the problem.

Discussions around high-level tasks can also support the development of students' identities as mathematical doers. Aguirre, Mayfield-Ingram, and Martin (2013) define *mathematical identities* as "the dispositions and deeply held beliefs that students develop about their ability to participate and perform effectively in mathematical contexts and to use mathematics in powerful ways across the contexts of their lives" (p. 14).

So how do you help students develop positive mathematical identities? Aguirre and colleagues (2013) identify a set of equity-based teaching practices that help build students' positive identities. At the heart of these practices is engaging students in high-cognitive-demand tasks that offer multiple entry points, supporting students in justifying their solutions, promoting persistence, and positioning students as sources of expertise.

Our three featured teachers made an effort to select students to share their work who had not had an opportunity to do so recently or who often struggle in class, thus giving them an opportunity to be seen by their peers as capable mathematics doers. For example, Mr. Harmon selected Zashon to present her work on the Toothpick Hexagons task because she had initially struggled to come up with a generalization but through her interactions with her group members, she was able to generalize the pattern and explain the equation. Presenting her work to the whole class—an equation that nearly half the class had created—gave

Zashon the opportunity to demonstrate competence and gave the entire class access to the discussion.

In looking across all three classrooms, we see the teachers—Ms. Moran, Mr. Harmon, and Mr. Moore—positioning students as sources of expertise. While not all students presented, several students in each class had the opportunity to share their solutions. In addition, many other students had the opportunity to have their voices heard during the discussion.

We would argue that the five practices lessons developed and enacted by Cori Moran, Matthew Harmon, and Michael Moore supported students' learning of meaningful mathematics, provided access and equity for each and every student, and in so doing, helped students develop identities as competent and capable of doing mathematics.

TEACHING TAKEAWAY

Using the five practices model helps teachers develop students' positive identities.

Getting Started With the Five Practices

Whether you are a newcomer to the five practices or someone who was using them prior to reading this book, practice and reflection will help you either begin or continue your journey to orchestrating productive mathematics discussions in your classroom. The key to making progress on this challenging work is to collaborate with and learn from other teachers. The Milwaukee Master Teacher Partnership, in which Matthew Harmon, Michael Moore, and Cori Moran participated, provided such an opportunity for sustained teacher learning and collaboration. As we described in Chapter 1, teachers across schools and districts worked together regularly to engage in inquiry about their classroom practice and to share both successes and challenges. Michelle Musumeci, a teacher with whom we have worked, sums up the benefit of seeking opportunities to engage with other teachers:

> It's important to participate in any professional development that you can, or talk with other teachers about it, because I think that really helps you reflect and see what went well, what didn't go well, and it's always a learning process.

In the sections that follow, we provide some guidance on how to get started with or continue your work on the five practices.

Plan Lessons Collaboratively

Plan lessons with colleagues. While planning with teachers in your school or district may be optimal since you are working in the same context, given the technologies now available, your collaborators could live in another city, state, or country!

The three lessons that we featured in this book—Toothpick Hexagons, Floodlight Shadows, and Staircase—were planned collaboratively using the lesson-planning template shown in Appendix E and the monitoring chart shown in Appendix B. Working on the lessons in collaboration with colleagues provides teachers with access to a broader set of ideas regarding what can be learned from engaging in a task, the ways in which students could respond to the task, questions that will assess and advance student learning, and the solutions that will be most useful in ensuring that the mathematical ideas that are targeted in the lesson are made public. Such detailed collaborative lesson planning shares many of the characteristics of lesson study, a professional development approach that originated in Japan (Lewis, Perry, & Hurd, 2004).

The lesson-planning template supports the discussion by providing a set of questions that focus on key aspects of the lesson. While many lesson-planning tools focus on what the teacher is going to do during the lesson, the lesson-planning template shifts the focus to what students are going to do and how the teacher is going to support them. As Smith, Bill, and Hughes (2008) explain, "The goal is to move beyond the structural components often associated with lesson planning to a deeper consideration of how to advance students' mathematical understanding during the lesson" (p. 137).

TEACHING TAKEAWAY

The lesson-planning template shifts the focus to what students are doing and how the teacher will support them.

While the five practices model addresses many of the key aspects of planning (shown in gray shading on the lesson-planning template in Appendix E), there are other aspects of planning that should also be considered, such as the prior knowledge that students will draw on in solving the task; the tools, resources, and materials that will be provided to students; how the task will be launched; what homework will be assigned that will extend the learning; and what you will take as evidence that students understand the ideas you have targeted. These additional questions help ensure that students have what they need to engage with the task and that the teacher is clear on what will count as evidence of learning. (See Boston et al. [2017] and Smith and Stein [2018] for examples of lesson plans created with the lesson-planning template.)

If taking on the entire lesson-planning template initially seems overwhelming, you can begin by focusing on the subset of the practices. While the five practices when taken together are greater than the sum of their parts—there is synergy in doing all of the practices—you could begin by focusing on setting goals, selecting tasks, and anticipating responses and questions. Engaging in these three practices as a first step will prepare you to support students by giving you clarity regarding what you are trying to accomplish, a task that will give students something challenging to work on, and questions to help students make progress. Once you are comfortable with the practices that can be done in advance, you can begin to add others to your repertoire.

Observe and Debrief Lessons

Engage in observations and analysis of teaching with one or more colleagues. The point of the observation is not to see if you can find evidence that the teacher used the five practices but rather to see if you can find evidence that students learned mathematics. The following questions could structure your observation and debriefing of the lesson:

- What are students doing and saying? Who are students talking with?
- Who is asking questions? What questions are being asked?
- Who is offering explanations? What counts as an explanation?
- What evidence is there of learning?

In a live observation of a five practices lesson, each observer could be given a copy of the completed monitoring tool to use to collect data on what students are doing and saying during the lesson. The annotated monitoring charts produced by observers can then be used to support an evidence-based discussion on what students were doing and saying during the lesson and the extent to which students appeared to learn what was intended.

Reflect on Your Lesson

Reflect on your lesson in close proximity to the completion of your lesson. At the end of each lesson, it is important for you to ask yourself whether you accomplished what you set out to do and what you take as evidence that students learned (or are in the process of learning) what was intended. While it is easy to feel satisfied with a lesson if there were no major disruptions and students were engaged with the task, this does not necessarily imply that students learned what was intended. It is important to press yourself to find evidence to support your beliefs about what occurred. A video recording of the class discussion, student work from the lesson, your completed monitoring chart, and/or an exit ticket given at the end of class are a few sources of data that can inform your reflection of student learning.

If you cannot find evidence that students learned what was intended, you need to decide your next steps. Reflection is only worth doing if you are willing to do something different as a result of what you learned. This may mean doing something different the next day, and/or it might mean changing some aspect of your instruction.

In his reflection following the lesson, Mr. Moore noted that he was able to create a strong mathematical storyline in the lesson:

> With Franci and her group, we had a great start in terms of identifying where there could be similar triangles in the picture. Lexi then provided us with that ability to justify that we know we have similar triangles, and then Jerry took us to the end of the problem.

But as he reflected on what *all* students might have had the opportunity to learn during class, Mr. Moore wondered if there were additional moves he could have made to amplify a wider range of student voices.

> *When Lexi shared, I maybe missed an opportunity there. I had Lexi talk us through the three angle pairs. I really wish I'd had other students in the class explain where those three congruent pairs were and how they were thinking about them. I think I missed an opportunity there to see what other students understand about these three pairs of congruent angles. I made a note to myself to remember to engage a wider array of students during our whole class discussion. I'm going to start tomorrow's lesson getting them talking about similarity and angles in order to gain more insight on their understanding. This will help me as we move on to dilations.*

Orchestrating productive mathematical discussions is complex, and it is easy to focus primarily on the students presenting. Mr. Moore's candid assessment of his lesson helps us remember that our focus as teachers always must be multifaceted—on our mathematical storyline and how it relates to the learning goals, on formative assessment moves that provide information about all students' understandings, and on the ways in which we position our students as mathematical knowers and doers.

Video Clubs

Start a video club at your school. Video clubs are opportunities for groups of teachers to come together to view and discuss videos of one another's teaching. These clubs could meet before or after school, during a designated shared planning period, or during a meeting of a professional learning community.

The purpose of video clubs is to help teachers learn to notice and make sense of significant events that occur in their classrooms and the classrooms of their colleagues (Sherin & Linsenmeier, 2011). Learning to notice through the use of video helps teachers learn where to focus their attention in the moment as events unfold in their classrooms. According to Sherin and Dyer (2017),

> *Working with video can help shift how teachers make sense of what they notice. The reasons underlying student thinking are often complex and not easily observable on first glance. Video provides space for teachers to consider intricacies of student thinking in ways that are not always possible during the moment of instruction.* (pp. 51, 53)

However, simply looking at any video, without guidance, does not guarantee that teachers will attend to aspects of instruction that matter most. Sherin and Linsenmeier (2011) provide a set of guidelines for using video, which support the development of teachers' professional vision (i.e., the ability to make sense of significant classroom events):

- Attend to the evidence: Focus on what did take place, not on what might have been.

- Attend to the details: Focus on specific aspects of classroom events (e.g., student thinking).

- Attend to what's typical: Focus on examples of everyday practice, not on exemplars. (p. 41)

It is also critical to capture video that will provide interesting fodder for discussion. If you and your colleagues are working on the five practices, you may find it particularly helpful to focus on capturing what happens during monitoring when the teacher interacts with students as they work on a task or on students' presentations when the teacher helps students make connections between strategies and to the mathematical ideas targeted in the lesson.

Sherin and Dyer (2017) provide suggestions on how to best capture video in your own classroom. These guidelines can help you consider where and when to video record so that you capture interesting interactions, where to place the video recorder, the value of annotation tools, and the lens through which your colleagues will view your video.

Using video recordings in this way can make it possible to *get inside* classrooms that would otherwise be impossible to visit, to collaborate with teachers near and far, to expand your professional networks, and to further develop your ability to notice and attend to classroom events.

Organize a Book Study

Organize a book study with colleagues either face-to-face or virtually around this book. Set up a regular meeting (weekly, biweekly, monthly) during which time you and your colleagues near or far can work through the chapters in this book together, discussing the Pause and Consider questions, the Analyzing the Work of Teaching activities, and the Linking the Five Practices to Your Own Instruction assignments. Through discussion of each chapter you can share your insights and reactions, personal experiences, and challenges and determine next steps.

Explore Additional Resources

Explore resources outside of this book that may give you additional tools to enact the practices. For example, in Chapter 6, we identify several resources that provide additional insights for holding students accountable during whole class discussions. In addition, throughout the book we have identified references that will provide more insight on particular topics.

PAUSE AND CONSIDER

What will you do to get started? Who will be your collaborators?

Frequency and Timing of Use of the Five Practices Model

Two questions you may be asking at this point are "How often do I need to engage my students in a discussion using the five practices to support my work?" and "Is this something I should be doing every day?" While you do not have to engage students in discussions around challenging tasks every day, we do know from research that students need regular opportunities to engage in high-level thinking and reasoning—hence, once a unit, once a month, or once a quarter is not sufficient.

We recommend that you work toward engaging students in a whole class discussion around a *doing-mathematics* task once a week. To start, it is often productive to partner with one or more colleagues (face-to-face or virtually) and collaboratively plan lessons, even taking turns leading the planning effort. By collaborating with others, you will share the responsibility for creating lesson plans and at the same time benefit from a broader set of ideas about a specific lesson. Over time, you will compile a set of lesson plans that you can continue to refine and use in subsequent years. As your library of lessons grows, you can continue to add to it, increasing the number of lessons and relatedly the frequency with which you engage students in such discussions.

In addition to frequency, it is important to decide when working on a doing-mathematics task will be most beneficial to students. If you give such a task after you have taught a procedure that could be used to solve the task, you are likely to see many students doing what has been taught. When this occurs, there is limited opportunity for students to think and reason, and you will learn little about what students understand about mathematics. By contrast, by engaging students in solving a doing-mathematics task before they have learned specific procedures, they will have the opportunity to actually learn through their engagement in the task. In the process, you will learn how students are making sense of the situation and what it is they understand.

So what happens on days when you are not engaging students in a whole class discussion around a doing-mathematics task? Students will also need time to engage in other activities such as making sense of procedures and developing procedural fluency (for examples of what this might look like, see Boston et al., 2017). While such activities may not require the same level of planning or discussion, we encourage you to look for ways to elicit and support student thinking regardless of the level and kind of activity in which you engage your students.

Conclusion

Making the five practices a central component of your instructional toolkit will not happen overnight. It is a personal journey that will take time and effort. As with any journey, taking someone along with you can enhance the experience by providing a sounding board when you need one as well as having someone with whom to share the joys and tribulations.

We encourage you to keep a journal throughout your journey, documenting the challenges you have faced, noting how you are dealing with them, and describing your personal victories. There may be times when you want to tweet about something you have discovered, write a blog about a victory or challenge, or post a request for assistance through an established network. Extending your professional network can provide you with additional insights and support.

Keep documentation from your completed lessons! This includes lesson plans, completed monitoring charts, photos or scanned images of student work, and exit tickets. These artifacts will provide evidence to support your reflection on the lesson immediately following the lesson, but they will also be useful when you are ready to teach the lesson again. You can begin your planning of a previously taught lesson by reviewing what occurred in previous implementations of the lesson—what went well, what did not, what should change, and what should remain the same. Rather than start planning from scratch each time, you can build on your prior work and gradually improve your lessons (and your teaching) over time. Through this cycle of planning, teaching, reflecting, and revising, you will build a storehouse of good lessons to which you can continue to add.

The best advice we can give you is *do not give up*! As a teacher commented,

> *Investing time and effort into learning/implementing the five practices is far from easy and has taken me a while (and I still have a long way to go) but is well worth the investment. Using them has*

created "magical moments" where students are engaged and truly learning from one another, discovering mathematics, and gaining insight into the mathematical process of discovery, connections, revision, etc. It truly shifts the responsibility and workload onto the students, allowing the teacher to become a facilitator and empower students to take responsibility for their learning. In [this] day and age, the five practices become an incredibly powerful tool to push students toward problem solving and critical thinking. (Smith & Stein, 2018, p. 131)

Resources

National Council of Teachers of Mathematics:

> **Activities with Rigor and Coherence (ARCs):** Sequences of lessons (K–12) that address a specific mathematical topic and support the implementation of the eight effective mathematics teaching practices (NCTM, 2014) and the five practices for orchestrating productive discussions (Smith & Stein, 2018).
>
> http://www.nctm.org/ARCs
>
> **Illuminations:** Lessons and activities (K–12) that are aligned with NCTM's *Principles and Standards for School Mathematics* (2000) and the National Governors Association Center for Best Practices & Council of Chief State School Officers' *Common Core State Standards for School Mathematics* (2010).
>
> http://illuminations.nctm.org
>
> **Problems of the Week:** Tasks per grade band (K–2, 3–5, 6–8) and content strand (algebra, geometry, trigonometry, and calculus) plus solution strategies, rubrics, and teaching suggestions.
>
> http://www.nctm.org/Classroom-Resources/CRCC/Math-Forum-Problems-of -the-Week-Resources
>
> **Reasoning and Sense Making Task Library:** High school tasks that engage students in reasoning and sense-making that are linked directly to *Focus in High School: Reasoning and Sense Making* (NCTM, 2009), along with suggestions for facilitating student work on the task and insights into how students might think about the task.
>
> http://www.nctm.org/rsmtasks

Inside Mathematics: A K–12 resource for educators that includes video lessons, problems of the month, performance assessment tasks, and a range of resources.

> http://www.insidemathematics.org

Mathalicious: Real-world lessons, aligned to Common Core State Standards, designed to build proficiency in mathematical practices and build conceptual understanding; some lessons are free but access to all resources requires membership and a fee.

> http://www.mathalicious.com

Mathematics Assessment Project: Formative assessment lessons and summative assessment tasks (including scoring rubrics and student work samples) from Grades 6–12.

> http://map.mathshell.org/materials/index.php

Robert Kaplinsky's Lessons: Lessons for K–8, Algebra 1, Algebra 2, and geometry built around visual images and general questions that are intended to engage students in further exploration.

> http://robertkaplinsky.com/lessons

Dan Meyer's Three-Act Lessons: Lessons for Grades 6–12 that follow a particular structure—show students an image or video that depicts an interesting situation; engage students in asking questions about and identifying information in the image or video; and create models to answer the questions.

http://blog.mrmeyer.com/2011/the-three-acts-of-a-mathematical-story

Illustrative Mathematics: A collection of rich tasks correlated to the Common Core State Standards for Mathematics for Grades K–12, and an open-source coherent curriculum with support for five practices planning and teaching built in.

Tasks: https://tasks.illustrativemathematics.org/content-standards

Curriculum: https://curriculum.illustrativemathematics.org/HS/teachers/index.html

YouCubed: A collection of tasks and lesson plans that focus on developing productive mathematical mindsets with students. The YouCubed collection includes a Week of Inspirational Math, which can be used as norm-setting activities for the first week of mathematics class.

https://www.youcubed.org

Mathematics Vision Project: An open-source high school mathematics curriculum that offers both an integrated mathematics curriculum and a traditional mathematics curriculum. The curriculum utilizes a task-based problem-solving approach to develop conceptual understanding and procedural fluency.

https://www.mathematicsvisionproject.org/curriculum.html

MathMontana: An open-source integrated high school mathematics curriculum that is technology dependent. The curriculum features explorations in a variety of contexts that support students' thinking and reasoning.

https://mathmontana.org

APPENDIX B Monitoring Chart

Strategy	Assessing Questions	Advancing Questions	Who and What	Order

APPENDIX C Ms. Moran's Monitoring Chart

Solution Strategy	Assessing Questions	Advancing Questions	Who and What	Order
Students Cannot Get Started	• What have you noticed so far? • How many tiles were needed for Stage 1? For Stage 2? • What is the task asking you to figure out?	• Can you try building the staircase for Stage 5? How would you get started? • What do you notice about how the staircases grow at each stage?		
Solution A. Identify the Recursive Pattern Student uses a table or visual inspection of staircases to determine that the number of squares in a stage is the number of squares in the previous stage plus the stage number.	• What have you noticed so far? • How would you describe how the staircases grow? • If you had Staircase 3, what would you do to find the number of squares in Staircase 4? • How would you describe the number of squares at Stage 5? At Stage 10?	• What if you did Stage 50? Or Stage 100? Would you want to use that pattern? • Is there a way to use the tiles to help you visualize what's happening with the pattern? *Goes up by extra number each stage: Araia, Kyle, Esme, Adreana (1st visit)* *2nd visit: Seeing "missing" part of square as previous stage*	*Create table for Stages 1–9. Add stage number each time* *–Maya, Taylor, Collin (1st visit)* *– Also Aidan, Micki, Emily, Erin (1st visit)* *Goes up by stage number each time: Elijah, Nyleah, Lauren, Josh (1st visit)*	**Start here: back at recursive. Bring out growth 2D and not constant. 1st presentation (Araia group)*
Solution B. Double the Staircase to Create a Rectangle Student creates the $n \times (n+1)$ rectangle by putting two copies of the same staircase together. Student finds the area of the original staircase by taking $\frac{1}{2}$ of the area of the resulting rectangle. Area of staircase in Stage $n = \frac{n(n+1)}{2}$	• What have you noticed so far? • What shape are you creating? Why? • Can you describe how this works for Stage 3? For Stage 4?	• How can you relate the stage number to the shape you've created? • (If equation) How does this equation relate to the staircase? • (If no equation) Using what you noticed, what would the equation be for the nth stage?	*Araia, Kyle, Esme, Adreana (2nd visit)* *Start: make square out of current and previous stage* *Then make rectangle with two copies of current stage* *3rd visit: $y = \frac{x^2}{2} + \frac{1}{2}x$? (not connected to rectangle model)*	

230

Solution Strategy	Assessing Questions	Advancing Questions	Who and What	Order
Solution C. Divide the Staircase Into Triangles Student draws a diagonal through the staircase to create one large triangle and several smaller triangles. Student uses $A = \frac{1}{2}(bh)$ to determine the area of a large triangle. Since base and height are the same as the stage number, $A = \frac{1}{2}n^2$. Student determines that the area of each small triangle is $\frac{1}{2}$ and that the number of small triangles is the same as the stage number. This means that the combined area of the small triangles is $\frac{1}{2}n$. Total area $= \frac{1}{2}n^2 + \frac{1}{2}n$	• What have you noticed so far? • What shape are you creating? Why? • How did you figure out the number of squares in the large triangle? In the smaller triangles? • How does this work for Stage 3? For Stage 4?	• How can you relate the stage number to the different triangles? How is the size of the large triangle related to the stage number? How are the small triangles related to the stage number? • (If equation) How does this equation relate to the staircase? • (If no equation) Using what you noticed, what would the equation be for the nth stage?	*Aidan, Micki, Emily, Erin* (1st visit): draw diagonal, triangles above and below 2nd visit: using triangles to find area "count 'whole' ones); then $\frac{1}{2}\triangle s$ above diagonal and below $y = \frac{l \cdot w}{2} + \frac{l \cdot x}{2}$ (3 variables, $l \cdot w \cdot x$)	*2nd presentation (Aidan et al.)* Focus on geometric solution, then explore variables with whole class
Solution D. Rearrange the Staircase Into a Rectangle Student rearranges the squares in a staircase to create a rectangle. Student determines the area of the original staircase by calculating the area of the resulting rectangle. Student uses a slightly different approach for even-number stages and for odd-number stages. Area $= \frac{1}{2}n(n+1)$	• What have you noticed so far? • What shape are you creating? Why? • How does this shape relate to the stage number of the staircase? • Can you do the same process with another stage?	• Would your process work better for Stage 3 or Stage 4? Why? • (If equation) How does this equation relate to the staircase? • (If no equation) Using what you noticed, what would the equation be for the nth stage?	*Mae & Isabel*: table/square tiles, Stage 10 is 5×11, explain in words $\frac{1}{2}n \times (n+1)$, no equation. 2nd visit: $(n \div 2)(n+1) = y$	3rd: Mae and Isabel method Look across equations ***Also show graph with Desmos

Solution Strategy	Assessing Questions	Advancing Questions	Who and What	Order
Solution E. Suggest Growth Is Exponential Student recognizes that the difference in the number of squares in each stage is not constant and that the growth is not linear. Because the amount each staircase grows keeps getting bigger, the student decides that the growth must be exponential.	• Why do you think the pattern is exponential? • How would you describe the growth in the staircases? • What does it mean for a function to be exponential?	• $y = 3^x$ is an exponential function. How does the growth in $y = 3^x$ relate to the growth you identified in the staircase pattern?		
Other *Looking at equations with x^2* *Graphing!*	*Guess/check $x^2 + 1$, $x^2 + 2$ ... (Maya, Taylor, Collin)* *2nd visit: height $\times$ base* *Mae and Isabel: graph with Desmos $(n+2)(n+1) = y$*	*Maya group: $x^2 - x + 1$ (works for stages 1, 2 not 3)* *Maya group: sketch graph from table*	*Elijah group (2nd visit): length/width growing* *$x^2 \leftarrow$ subtract something*	

Chapin, S. H., O'Connor, C., & Anderson, N. C. (2009). *Classroom discussions: Using math talk to help students learn* (2nd ed.). Sausalito, CA: Math Solutions.

In this book, the authors describe five talk moves that they have found effective in supporting students' mathematical thinking and learning: revoicing, asking students to restate someone else's reasoning, asking students to apply their own reasoning to someone else's reasoning, prompting students for further participation, and using wait time. (See Smith & Stein, 2018 for an illustration of these moves in the context of a lesson.)

Herbel-Eisenmann, B., Cirillo, M., Steele, M. D., Otten, S., & Johnson, K. R. (2017). *Mathematics discourse in secondary classrooms: A practice-based resource for professional learning.* Sausalito, CA: Math Solutions.

This resource includes a set of discourse moves and tools that provide support for teachers to begin to change discourse practices in their classrooms. The videos and cases provide powerful images of discussion-based learning in middle and high school classrooms.

Kazemi, E., & Hintz, A. (2014). *Intentional talk: How to structure and lead productive mathematical discussions.* Portsmouth, NH: Stenhouse.

In this book, the authors provide a set of principles and a collection of tools that will help you in facilitating productive classroom discussions. The classroom vignettes provide images of productive talk in elementary classrooms.

Michaels, S., O'Conner, M. C., Hall, M. W., & Resnick, L. B. (2013). *Accountable Talk™ sourcebook: For classroom conversations that work.* Pittsburgh, PA: Institute for Learning, University of Pittsburgh.

This resource provides an overview of the three components of accountable talk—accountability to the community, accountability to rigorous thinking, and accountability to accurate knowledge—and a set of talk moves associated with each component. (Free download available at http://iflpartner.pitt.edu/index.php/educator_resources/accountable_talk)

Learning Goals (Residue)	Evidence
What understandings will students take away from this lesson?	What will students say, do, or produce that will provide evidence of their understandings?

Task	Instructional Support—Tools, Resources, Materials
What is the main activity that students will be working on in this lesson?	What tools or resources will be made available to give students entry to—and help them reason through—the activity?

Prior Knowledge	Task Launch
What prior knowledge and experience will students draw on in their work on this task? **Essential Questions** What are the essential questions that I want students to be able to answer over the course of the lesson?	How will you introduce and set up the task to ensure that students understand the task and can begin productive work, without diminishing the cognitive demand of the task?

Anticipated Solutions and Instructional Supports

What are the various ways that students might complete the activity? Be sure to include incorrect, correct, and incomplete solutions.

What questions might you ask students that will support their exploration of the activity and *bridge* between *what they did* and *what you want them to learn*? These questions should *assess* what a student currently knows and *advance* him or her toward the goals of the lesson. Be sure to consider questions that you will ask students who cannot get started as well as students who finish quickly.

Use the monitoring chart to provide the details related to Anticipated Solutions and Instructional Support.

Sharing and Discussing the Task

Selecting and Sequencing	Connecting Responses
Which solutions do you want students to share during the lesson? In what order? Why?	What specific questions will you ask so that students • make sense of the mathematical ideas that you want them to learn? • make connections among the different strategies/solutions that are presented?

Homework/Assessment

What will you ask students to do that will allow you to determine what they learned and what they understand?

Connections to the five practices are noted by the gray shading.

This template is taken from Smith, Steele, and Raith (2017, pp. 219–221) and was adapted from Smith, Bill, and Hughes (2008).

Source: Reprinted with permission from Smith, Steele, and Raith (2017), *Taking action: Implementing effective mathematics teaching practices in Grades 6–8*, copyright 2017, by the National Council of Teachers of Mathematics. All rights reserved.

 Download this Lesson-Planning Template from **resources.corwin.com/5practices-highschool**

References

Aguirre, J., Herbel-Eisenmann, B., Celedon-Pattichis, S., Civil, M., Wilkerson, T., Stephan, M., Pape, S., & Clements, D. H. (2017). Equity within mathematics education research as a political act: Moving from choice to intentional collective professional responsibility. *Journal for Research in Mathematics Education, 48*(2), 124–147.

Aguirre, J., Mayfield-Ingram, K., & Martin, D. (2013). *The impact of identity in K–8 mathematics: Rethinking equity-based practices.* Reston, VA: National Council of Teachers of Mathematics.

Arbaugh, F., Smith, M. S., Boyle, J. D., Stylianides, G. J., & Steele, M. D. (2019). *We reason and we prove: Putting critical skills at the heart of your mathematics teaching.* Thousand Oaks, CA: Corwin.

Ball, D. L., Lubienski, S. T., & Mewborn, D. S. (2001). Research on teaching mathematics: The unsolved problem of teachers' mathematical knowledge. *Handbook of Research on Teaching, 4*, 433–456.

Boaler, J. (2016). *Mathematical mindsets: Unleashing students' potential through creative math, inspiring messages, and innovative teaching.* San Francisco, CA: Jossey-Bass.

Boaler, J., & Brodie, K. (2004). The importance, nature, and impact of teacher questions. In D. E. McDougall & J. A. Ross (Eds.), *Proceedings of the twenty-sixth annual meeting of the North American Chapter of the International Group for the Psychology of Mathematics Education* (Vol. 2, pp. 774–790). Toronto: Ontario Institute for Studies in Education at the University of Toronto.

Boaler, J., & Humphreys, C. (2005). *Connecting mathematical ideas: Middle school video cases to support teaching and learning.* Portsmouth, NH: Heinemann.

Boaler, J., & Staples, M. (2008). Creating mathematical futures through an equitable teaching approach: The case of Railside School. *Teachers College Record, 110*(3), 608–645.

Boston, M., Dillon, F., Smith, M. S., & Miller, S. (2017). *Taking action: Implementing effective mathematics teaching practices in Grades 9–12.* Reston, VA: National Council of Teachers of Mathematics.

Boston, M. D., & Wilhelm, A. G. (2015). Middle school mathematics instruction in instructionally focused urban districts. *Urban Education, 52*(7), 829–861.

Boyle, J. D., & Kaiser, S. B. (2017). Collaborative planning as a process. *Mathematics Teaching in the Middle School, 22*(7), 407–411.

Brookings Institution. (2018). Black-white segregation edges downward since 2000, census shows. Retrieved from https://www.brookings.edu/blog/the-avenue/2018/12/17/black-white-segregation-edges-downward-since-2000-census-shows/

Cartier, J. L., Smith, M. S., Stein, M. K., & Ross, D. K. (2013). *Practices for orchestrating productive science discussions.* Reston, VA: National Council of Teachers of Mathematics.

Chapin, S. H., O'Connor, M. C., & Anderson, N. C. (2009). *Classroom discussions: Using math talk to help students learn, Grades K–6.* Sausalito, CA: Math Solutions.

Danielson, C., & Meyer, D. (2016). Increased participation and conversation using networked devices. *Mathematics Teacher, 110*(4), 258–264.

Franke, M. L., Webb, N. M., Chan, A. G., Ing, M., Freund, D., & Battey, D. (2009). Teacher questioning to elicit students' mathematical thinking in elementary school classrooms. *Journal of Teacher Education, 60*(4), 380–392.

Hatano, G., & Inagaki. K. (1991). Sharing cognition through collective comprehension activity. In L. B. Resnick, J. M. Levine, & S. D. Teasley (Eds.), *Perspectives on socially shared cognition* (pp. 331–48). Washington, DC: American Psychological Association.

Herbel-Eisenmann, B., Cirillo, M., Steele, M. D., Otten, S., & Johnson, K. R. (2017). *Mathematics discourse in secondary classrooms: A practice-based resource for professional learning.* Sausalito, CA: Math Solutions.

Herbel-Eisenmann, B., & Shah, N. (2019). Detecting and reducing bias in questioning patterns. *Mathematics Teaching in the Middle School, 24*(5), 282–289.

Hiebert, J., Carpenter, T. P., Fennema, E., Fuson, K. C., Wearne, D., Murray, H., Olivier, A., & Human, P. (1997). *Making sense: Teaching and learning mathematics with understanding.* Portsmouth, NH: Heinemann.

Hiebert, J., Gallimore, R., & Stigler, J. W. (2003). The new heroes of teaching. *Education Week, 23*(10), 42, 56.

Hiebert, J., Morris, A. K., Berk, D., & Jansen, A. (2007). Preparing teachers to learn from teaching. *Journal of Teacher Education, 58*(1), 47–61.

Holliday, B., Cuevas, G. J., Marks, D., Casey, R. M., Moore-Harris, B., Carter, J. A., Day, R., Hayek, L. M. (2005). *Algebra 1.* New York: Glencoe.

Horn, I. S. (2012). *Strength in numbers: Collaborative learning in secondary mathematics.* Reston, VA: National Council of Teachers of Mathematics.

Hufferd-Ackles, K., Fuson, K. C., & Sherin, M. G. (2015). The math-talk learning community: Looking back and looking ahead. In E. A. Silver & P. A. Kenney (Eds.), *Lessons learned from research: Volume 1, useful and useable research related to core mathematical practices* (pp. 125–134). Reston, VA: National Council of Teachers of Mathematics.

Hung, M. (2015). Talking circles promote equitable discourse. *Mathematics Teacher, 109*(4), 256–260.

Hunt, J., & Stein, M. K. (forthcoming). Constructing goals for student learning through conversation. *Mathematics Teacher: Learning and Teaching PreK–12.*

Imm, K. L., Stylianou, D. A., & Chae, N. (2008). Student representations at the center: Promoting classroom equity. *Mathematics Teaching in the Middle School, 13*(8), 458–463.

Institute for Learning. (2013). *Geometry set of related lessons: Investigating coordinate geometry and its use to solve problems.* Pittsburgh, PA: Institute for Learning, University of Pittsburgh.

Institute for Learning. (2017). *Algebra II lesson set: Building polynomial functions.* Pittsburgh, PA: Institute for Learning, University of Pittsburgh.

Jackson, K. J., Shahan, E. C., Gibbons, L. K., & Cobb, P. A. (2012). Launching complex tasks. *Mathematics Teaching in the Middle School, 18*(1), 24–29.

Jacobs, V. R., & Philipp, R. A. (2010). Supporting children's problem solving. *Teaching Children Mathematics, 17*(2), 98–105.

Jansen, A., Cooper, B., Vascellaro, S., & Wandless, P. (2016). Rough-draft talk in mathematics classrooms. *Mathematics Teaching in the Middle School, 22*(5), 304–307.

Jilk, L. M. (2016). Supporting teacher noticing of students' mathematical strengths. *Mathematics Teacher Educator, 4*(2), 188–199.

Kazemi, E., Gibbons, L. K., Lomax, K., & Franke, M. L. (2016). Listening to and learning from student thinking. *Teaching Children Mathematics, 23*(3), 182–190.

Kazemi, E., & Hintz, A. (2014). *Intentional talk: How to structure and lead productive mathematical discussions.* Portsmouth, NH: Stenhouse.

Lambert, R., & Stylianou, D. A. (2013). Posing cognitively demanding tasks to all students. *Mathematics Teaching in the Middle School, 18*(8), 500–506.

Lampert, M., & Graziani, F. (2009). Instructional activities as a tool for teachers' and teacher educators' learning. *The Elementary School Journal, 109*(5), 491–509.

Lannin, J. K. (2004). Using explicit and recursive reasoning. *Mathematics Teacher, 98*(4), 216–223.

Leatham, K. R., Peterson, B. E., Stockero, S. L., & Van Zoest, L. R. (2015). Conceptualizing mathematically significant pedagogical opportunities to build on student thinking. *Journal for Research in Mathematics Education, 46*(1), 88–124.

Lewis, C., Perry, R., & Hurd, J. (2004). A deeper look at lesson study. *Educational Leadership, 61*(5), 18.

Lischka, A. E., Gerstenschlager, N. E., Stephens, D. C., Barlow, A. T., & Strayer, J. F. (2018). Making room for inspecting mistakes. *Mathematics Teacher, 111*(6), 432–439.

Louie, N. L. (2017). The culture of exclusion in mathematics education and its persistence in equity-oriented teaching. *Journal for Research in Mathematics Education, 48*(5), 488–519.

Martin, D. B., Gholson, M. L., & Leonard, J. (2010). Mathematics as gatekeeper: Power and privilege in the production of knowledge. *Journal of Urban Mathematics Education, 3*(2), 12–24.

McGee, E. O. (2013). Threatened and placed at risk: High achieving African American males in urban high schools. *The Urban Review, 45*(4), 448–471.

Michaels, S., O'Conner, M. C., Hall, M. W., & Resnick, L. B. (2013). *Accountable Talk™ sourcebook: For classroom conversations that work.* Pittsburgh, PA: Institute for Learning, University of Pittsburgh.

Mills, V. L. (2014). Mathematical goals: The alpha and omega of effective practice. *NCSM Summer Newsletter, 44*(4), 2–3.

Moore-Russo, D., & Golzy, J. B. (2005). Helping students connect functions and their representations. *Mathematics Teacher, 99*(3), 156–160.

Murata, A., & Fuson, K. (2006). Teaching as assisting individual constructive paths within an interdependent class learning zone: Japanese first graders learning to add using 10. *Journal for Research in Mathematics Education, 37*(5), 421–456.

Nasir, N. S., McKinney de Royston, M., O'Connor, K., & Wischnia, S. (2017). Knowing about racial stereotypes versus believing them. *Urban Education, 52*(4), 491–524.

National Council of Teachers of Mathematics. (2000). *Principles and standards for school mathematics.* Reston, VA: National Council of Teachers of Mathematics.

National Council of Teachers of Mathematics. (2008). Hospital locator. NCTM Illuminations. https://www.nctm.org/Classroom-Resources/Illuminations/Lessons/Hospital-Locator/

National Council of Teachers of Mathematics. (2009). *Focus in high school: Reasoning and sense making.* Reston, VA: National Council of Teachers of Mathematics.

National Council of Teachers of Mathematics. (2014). *Principles to actions: Ensuring mathematical success for all.* Reston, VA: National Council of Teachers of Mathematics.

National Council of Teachers of Mathematics. (2018). *Catalyzing change in high school mathematics.* Reston, VA: National Council of Teachers of Mathematics.

National Governors Association Center for Best Practices & Council of Chief State School Officers. (2010). *Common core state standards for mathematics.* Washington, DC: Author.

Oakes, J. (2008). Keeping track: Structuring equality and inequality in an era of accountability. *Teachers College Record, 110*(3), 700–712.

Polya, G. (2014). *How to solve it: A new aspect of mathematical method.* Princeton, NJ: Princeton University Press.

Reinhart, S. C. (2000). Never say anything a kid can say. *Mathematics Teaching in the Middle School, 5*(8), 478–483.

Reinholz, D. L., & Shah, N. (2018). Equity analytics: A methodological approach for quantifying participation patterns in mathematics classroom discourse. *Journal for Research in Mathematics Education, 49*(2), 140–177.

Rhoads, K., & Alvarez, J. A. M. (2017). Data modeling using finite differences. *Mathematics Teacher, 110*(9), 709–713.

Santagata, R., & Bray, W. (2016). Professional development processes that promote teacher change: The case of a video-based program focused on leveraging students' mathematical errors. *Professional Development in Education, 42*(4), 547–568.

Schukajlow, S., & Krug, A. (2014). Do multiple solutions matter? Prompting multiple solutions, interest, competence, and autonomy. *Journal for Research in Mathematics Education, 45*(4), 497–533.

Senk, S. L., & Thompson, D. R. (Eds.). (2003). *Standards-based school mathematics curricula: What are they? What do students learn?* Mahwah, NJ: Lawrence Erlbaum Associates.

Shah, N. (2017). Race, ideology, and academic ability: A relational analysis of racial narratives in mathematics. *Teachers College Record, 119*(7), 1–42.

Sherin, M. G., & Dyer, E. B. (2017). Teacher self-captured video: Learning to see. *Phi Delta Kappan, 98*(7), 49–54.

Sherin, M. G., & Linsenmeier, K. A. (2011). Pause, rewind, reflect: Video clubs throw open the classroom doors. *The Learning Professional, 32*(5), 38.

Sherin, M. G., & van Es, E. A. (2009). Effects of video club participation on teachers' professional vision. *Journal of Teacher Education, 60*(1), 20–37.

Smith, M. S. (2001). *Practice-based professional development for teachers of mathematics.* Reston, VA: National Council of Teachers of Mathematics.

Smith, M. S., Bill, V., & Hughes, E. (2008). Thinking through a lesson protocol: A key for successfully implementing high-level tasks. *Mathematics Teaching in the Middle School, 14*(3), 132–138.

Smith, M. S., Bill, V., & Sherin, M. G. (2020). *The 5 practices in practice: Successfully orchestrating mathematics discussions in your elementary school classroom.* Thousand Oakes, CA: Corwin.

Smith, M. S., & Sherin, M. G. (2019). *The 5 practices in practice: Successfully orchestrating mathematics discussions in your middle school classroom.* Thousand Oakes, CA: Corwin.

Smith, M. S., Steele, M. D., & Raith, M. L. (2017). *Taking action: Implementing effective mathematics teaching practices in Grades 6–8.* Reston, VA: National Council of Teachers of Mathematics.

Smith, M. S., & Stein, M. K. (1998). Selecting and creating mathematical tasks: From research to practice. *Mathematics Teaching in the Middle School, 3*(5), 344–350.

Smith, M. S., & Stein, M. K. (2011). *5 practices for orchestrating productive mathematics discussions.* Reston. VA: National Council of Teachers of Mathematics.

Smith, M. S., & Stein, M. K. (2018). *5 practices for orchestrating productive mathematics discussions* (2nd ed.). Reston, VA: National Council of Teachers of Mathematics.

Sorto, M. A., & Bower, R. S. G. (2017). Quality of instruction in linguistically diverse classrooms: It matters! In A. Fernandes, S. Crespo, & M. Civil (Eds.), *Access and equity: Promoting high-quality mathematics in Grades 6–8* (pp. 27–40). Reston, VA: National Council of Teachers of Mathematics.

Steele, M. D., & Smith, M. S. (2018). The mathematical tasks framework and formative assessment. In E. A. Silver and V. L. Mills (Eds.). *A fresh look at formative assessment in mathematics teaching* (pp. 103–125). Reston, VA: National Council of Teachers of Mathematics.

Stein, M. K., Grover, B. W., & Henningsen, M. (1996). Building student capacity for mathematical thinking and reasoning: An analysis of mathematical tasks used in reform classrooms. *American Educational Research Journal, 33*(2), 455–488.

Stein, M. K., & Lane, S. (1996). Instructional tasks and the development of student capacity to think and reason: An analysis of the relationship between teaching and learning in a reform mathematics project. *Educational Research and Evaluation, 2*(1), 50–80.

Stigler, J. W., & Hiebert, J. (2004). Improving mathematics teaching. *Educational Leadership, 61*(5), 12–17.

Suh, J. M., Johnston, C., Jamieson, S., & Mills, M. (2008). Promoting decimal number sense and representational fluency. *Mathematics Teaching in the Middle School, 14*(1), 44–50.

Warshauer, H. K. (2015). Productive struggle in middle school mathematics classrooms. *Journal of Mathematics Teacher Education, 17*(4), 375–399.

White, D. Y., Fernandes, A., & Civil, M. (Eds.). (2018). *Access and equity: Promoting high-quality mathematics in Grades 9–12.* Reston, VA: National Council of Teachers of Mathematics.

Zbiek, R., & Shimizu, J. (2005). Multiple solutions: More paths to an end or more opportunities to learn mathematics. *Mathematics Teacher, 99*(4), 279–287.

Index

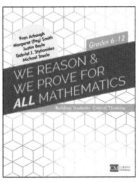
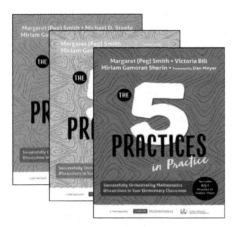

ALL students should have the opportunity to be successful in mathematics!

Trusted experts in mathematics education offer clear and practical guidance to help students move from surface to deep mathematical understanding, from procedural to conceptual learning, and from rote memorization to true comprehension. Through books, videos, consulting, and online tools, we offer a truly blended learning experience that helps you demystify mathematics for students.

JOHN HATTIE, DOUGLAS FISHER, NANCY FREY, LINDA M. GOJAK, SARA DELANO MOORE, WILLIAM MELLMAN

The what, when, and how of teaching practices that evidence shows work best for student learning in mathematics.
Grades K–12

JOHN ALMARODE, DOUGLAS FISHER, JOSEPH ASSOF, SARA DELANO MOORE, KATERI THUNDER, JOHN HATTIE, NANCY FREY

In this sequel to the best-selling *Visible Learning for Mathematics*, these grade-banded companions show Visible Learning strategies in action in Grades K–2, 3–5, 6–8, and high school mathematics classrooms.
Grades K–2, 3–5, 6–8, and High School

ROBERT Q. BERRY III, BASIL M. CONWAY IV, BRIAN R. LAWLER, JOHN W. STALEY

Timelier than ever, teaching mathematics through the lens of social justice will connect content to high school students' daily lives and fortify their mathematical understanding.

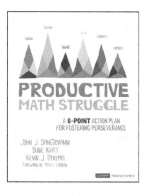

JOHN J. SANGIOVANNI, SUSIE KATT, KEVIN J. DYKEMA

Guiding teachers through six specific actions—valuing, fostering, building, planning, supporting, and reflecting on struggle—this book provides an essential plan for embracing productive perseverance in mathematics.

A SAGE Publishing Company

CORWIN HAS ONE MISSION: to enhance education through intentional professional learning.

We build long-term relationships with our authors, educators, clients, and associations who partner with us to develop and continuously improve the best evidence-based practices that establish and support lifelong learning.

NATIONAL COUNCIL OF
TEACHERS OF MATHEMATICS

The National Council of Teachers of Mathematics supports and advocates for the highest-quality mathematics teaching and learning for each and every student.